SELECTIONS

FROM

THE AMERICAN POETS.

BY

WILLIAM CULLEN BRYANT,

NEW YORK:
HARPER & BROTHERS, PUBLISHERS,
FRANKLIN SQUARE.
1860.

TO THE READER.

This collection, although embracing specimens from the writings of a very great number of American poets, may not yet contain the names of all who deserve admission. Of some authors, however, the best things, in a literary point of view, are of a nature which did not fall within the plan of the compiler. Amatory poems and drinking songs, notwithstanding the skill or the spirit with which they might be written, have been invariably excluded, as not proper for a book designed to be placed in a school or family library, and, therefore, to be read by very young persons. If it had been the sole object of the compiler to present samples of the poetical literature of his country, he would have adopted a less rigid rule in this respect. There are also scattered in our magazines and other periodicals many poems of much merit, some accompanied by the names of their authors, and others, the authorship of which might with due pains be ascertained, which would add to the value and interest of a compilation like this. The necessity of preparing the work for the press within a stipulated time has, however, prevented the compiler from making the necessary researches for the purpose, except in a few instances ; and, even if the time had been sufficient, the size of the volume would not have permitted a much more various selection than has been made. If this volume should meet with a favourable reception from the public, another may be prepared from the materials yet untouched.

New-York, October, 1840.

CONTENTS.

SELECTIONS

FROM

AMERICAN POETS.

PHILIP FRENEAU.

COLUMBUS TO FERDINAND.

Columbus was a considerable number of years engaged in soliciting the court of Spain to fit him out, in order to discover a new continent, which he imagined to exist somewhere in the western parts of the ocean. During his negotiations, he is here supposed to address King Ferdinand in the following stanzas.

ILLUSTRIOUS monarch of Iberia's soil,
Too long I wait permission to depart;
Sick of delays, I beg thy listening ear—
Shine forth the patron and the prince of art.

While yet Columbus breathes the vital air,
Grant his request to pass the western main:
Reserve this glory for thy native soil,
And, what must please thee more, for thy own reign.

Of this huge globe, how small a part we know—
Does heaven their worlds to western suns deny?
How disproportion'd to the mighty deep
The lands that yet in human prospect lie!

Does Cynthia, when to western skies arrived,
Spend her moist beam upon the barren main,
And ne'er illume with midnight splendour, she,
The natives dancing on the lightsome green?

Should the vast circuit of the world contain
Such wastes of ocean and such scanty land?
'Tis reason's voice that bids me think not so;
I think more nobly of the Almighty hand.

Does yon fair lamp trace half the circle round
To light mere waves and monsters of the seas?
No; be there must, beyond the billowy waste,
Islands, and men, and animals, and trees.

An unremitting flame my breast inspires
To seek new lands amid the barren waves,
Where, falling low, the source of day descends,
And the blue sea his evening visage laves.

Hear, in his tragic lay, Cordova's sage:*
"*The time may come, when numerous years are past,*
When ocean will unloose the bands of things,
And an unbounded region rise at last;

And TYPHIS *may disclose the mighty land,*
Far, far away, where none have roved before;
Nor will the world's remotest region be
Gibraltar's rock, or THULE'S *savage shore.*"

Fired at the theme, I languish to depart;
Supply the bark, and bid Columbus sail;
He fears no storms upon the untravell'd deep;
Reason shall steer, and skill disarm the gale.

Nor does he dread to miss the intended course,
Though far from land the reeling galley stray,
And skies above, and gulfy seas below,
Be the sole objects seen for many a day.

* Seneca, the poet, a native of Cordova in Spain:

"*Venient annis secula seris,*
Quibus oceanus vincula rerum
Laxet, et ingens pateat tellus,
Typhisque novos detegat orbes;
Nec sit terris ultima Thule."

Seneca. Med., act III, v. 375.

Think not that Nature has unveiled in vain
The mystic magnet to the mortal eye:
So late have we the guiding needle planned
Only to sail beneath our native sky?

Ere this was known, the ruling power of all
Formed for our use an *ocean in the land*,
Its breadth so small we could not wander long,
Nor long be absent from the neighbouring strand.

Short was the course, and guided by the stars,
But stars no more must point our daring way;
The Bear shall sink, and every guard be drowned,
And great Arcturus scarce escape the sea,

When southward we shall steer. Oh grant my wish,
Supply the bark, and bid Columbus sail;
He dreads no tempests on the untravelled deep;
Reason shall steer, and skill disarm the gale.

THE DYING INDIAN.—*Tomo-Chequi.*

"On yonder lake I spread the sail no more!
Vigour, and youth, and active days are past;
Relentless demons urge me to that shore
On whose black forests all the dead are cast:
Ye solemn train, prepare the funeral song,
For I must go to shades below,
Where all is strange and all is new;
Companion to the airy throng!
    What solitary streams,
    In dull and dreary dreams,
  All melancholy, must I rove along!

To what strange lands must *Chequi* take his way
Groves of the dead departed mortals trace;
No deer along those gloomy forests stray,
No huntsmen there take pleasure in the chase,

But all are empty, unsubstantial shades,
That ramble through those visionary glades;
  No spongy fruits from verdant trees depend,
    But sickly orchards there
    Do fruits as sickly bear,
And apples a consumptive visage shew,
And withered hangs the hurtleberry blue.

Ah me! what mischiefs on the dead attend!
Wandering a stranger to the shores below,
Where shall I brook or real fountain find?
Lazy and sad deluding waters flow:
Such is the picture in my boding mind!
        Fine tales, indeed, they tell
        Of shades and purling rills,
        Where our dead fathers dwell
        Beyond the western hills;
But when did ghost return his state to show,
Or who can promise half the tale is true?

I too must be a fleeting ghost! no more;
None, none but shadows to those mansions go;
I leave my woods, I leave the Huron shore,
        For emptier groves below!
        Ye charming solitudes,
        Ye tall ascending woods,
  Ye glassy lakes and prattling streams,
        Whose aspect still was sweet,
        Whether the sun did greet,
  Or the pale moon embraced you with her beams--
        Adieu to all!
To all that charmed me where I strayed,
The winding stream, the dark, sequestered shade;
        Adieu all triumphs here!
  Adieu the mountain's lofty swell,
  Adieu, thou little verdant hill,
And seas, and stars, and skies—farewell.
        For some remoter sphere!

Perplexed with doubts, and tortured with despair,
Why so dejected at this hopeless sleep?
Nature at last these ruins may repair, [weep;
When fate's long dream is o'er, and she forgets to
Some real world once more may be assign'd,
Some newborn mansion for the immortal mind!
Farewell, sweet lake; farewell, surrounding woods,
To other groves, through midnight glooms, I stray,
Beyond the mountains and beyond the floods,
Beyond the Huron Bay!
Prepare the hollow tomb, and place me low,
My trusty bow and arrows by my side,
The cheerful bottle and the venison store;
For long the journey is that I must go,
Without a partner and without a guide."
He spoke, and bid the attending mourners weep,
Then closed his eyes, and sunk to endless sleep!

THE INDIAN BURYING-GROUND.

In spite of all the learned have said,
I still my old opinion keep;
The posture that *we* give the dead,
Points out the soul's eternal sleep.

Not so the ancients of these lands:
The Indian, when from life released,
Again is seated with his friends,
And shares again the joyous feast.*

His imaged birds and painted bowl,
And venison for a journey dressed,
Bespeak the nature of the soul,
Activity, that knows no rest.

* The North American Indians bury their dead in a sitting posture; decorating the corpse with wampum, the images of birds, quadrupeds, &c.; and, if that of a warrior, with bows, arrows, tomahawks, and other military weapons.

His bow for action ready bent,
And arrows with a head of stone,
Can only mean that life is spent,
And not the old ideas gone.

Thou, stranger, that shalt come this way,
No fraud upon the dead commit;
Observe the swelling turf, and say,
They do not *lie*, but here they *sit*.

Here still a lofty rock remains,
On which the curious eye may trace
(Now wasted half by wearing rains)
The fancies of a ruder race.

Here still an aged elm aspires,
Beneath whose far-projecting shade
(And which the shepherd still admires)
The children of the forest played!

There oft a restless Indian queen
(Pale Shebah, with her braided hair),
And many a barbarous form is seen,
To chide the man that lingers there.

By midnight moons, o'er moistening dews,
In habit for the chase arrayed,
The hunter still the deer pursues,
The hunter and the deer, a shade!

And long shall timorous fancy see
The painted chief and pointed spear,
And Reason's self shall bow the knee
To shadows and delusions here.

STANZAS OCCASIONED BY LORD BELLAMONT'S, LADY HAY'S, AND OTHER SKELETONS BEING DUG UP IN FORT GEORGE (N. Y.), 1790.

To sleep in peace when life is fled,
Where shall our mouldering bones be laid;
What care can shun (I ask with tears)
The shovels of succeeding years!

Some have maintained, when life is gone,
This frame no longer is our own:
Hence doctors to our tombs repair,
And seize death's slumbering victims there.

Alas! what griefs must man endure!
Not even in forts he rests secure:
Time dims the splendours of a crown,
And brings the loftiest rampart down.

The breath, once gone, no art recalls!
Away we haste to vaulted walls:
Some future whim inverts the plain,
And stars behold our bones again.

Those teeth, dear girls—so much your care—
(With which no ivory can compare),
Like these (that once were Lady Hay's),
May serve the belles of future days.

Then take advice from yonder scull;
And, when the flames of life grow dull,
Leave not a tooth in either jaw,
Since dentists steal—and fear no law.

He that would court a sound repose,
To barren hills and deserts goes:
Where busy hands admit no sun,
Where he may doze till all is done.

Yet there, even there, though slily laid,
'Tis folly to defy the spade:
Posterity invades the hill,
And plants our relics where she will.

But oh! forbear the rising sigh!
All care is past with them that die:
Jove gave, when they to fate resign'd,
An opiate of the strongest kind:

Death is a sleep that has no dreams,
In which all time a moment seems;
And skeletons perceive no pain
Till Nature bids them wake again.

Joel Barlow.

THE HASTY PUDDING.

CANTO I.

Ye Alps audacious, through the heavens that rise
To cramp the day and hide me from the skies:
Ye Gallic flags, that o'er their heights unfurl'd,
Bear death to kings and freedom to the world,
I sing not you. A softer theme I choose,
A virgin theme, unconscious of the muse,
But fruitful, rich, well suited to inspire
The purest phrensy of poetic fire.
Despise it not, ye bards to terror steel'd,
Who hurl your thunders round the epic field;
Nor ye who strain your midnight throats to sing
Joys that the vineyard and the stillhouse bring;
Or on some distant fair your notes employ,
And speak of raptures that you ne'er enjoy.
I sing the sweets I know, the charms I feel,
My morning incense, and my evening meal,
The sweets of Hasty Pudding. Come, dear bowl
Glide o'er my palate, and inspire my soul.

The milk beside thee, smoking from the kine,
Its substance mingled, married in with thine,
Shall cool and temper thy superior heat,
And save the pains of blowing while I eat.
  Oh! could the smooth, the emblematic song
Flow like thy genial juices o'er my tongue,
Could those mild morsels in my numbers chime,
And, as they roll in substance, roll in rhyme,
No more thy awkward, unpoetic name
Should shun the muse or prejudice thy fame;
But, rising grateful to the accustom'd ear,
All bards should catch it, and all realms revere!
  Assist me first with pious toil to trace
Through wrecks of time thy lineage and thy race;
Declare what lovely squaw, in days of yore
(Ere great Columbus sought thy native shore),
First gave thee to the world; her works of fame
Have lived indeed, but lived without a name
Some tawny Ceres, goddess of her days,
First learn'd with stones to crack the well-dried [maize,
Through the rough sieve to shake the golden shower,
In boiling water stir the yellow flour:
The yellow flour, bestrew'd and stirr'd with haste,
Swells in the flood and thickens to a paste,
Then puffs and wallops, rises to the brim,
Drinks the dry knobs that on the surface swim;
The knobs at last the busy ladle breaks,
And the whole mass its true consistence takes.
  Could but her sacred name, unknown so long,
Rise, like her labours, to the son of song,
To her, to them, I'd consecrate my lays,
And blow her pudding with the breath of praise.
Not through the rich Peruvian realms alone
The fame of Sol's sweet daughter should be known,
But o'er the world's wide clime should live secure,
Far as his rays extend, as long as they endure.
  Dear Hasty Pudding, what unpromised joy
Expands my heart, to meet thee in Savoy!

Doom'd o'er the world through devious paths to roam,
Each clime my country, and each house my home,
My soul is soothed, my cares have found an end,
I greet my long-lost, unforgotten friend.
For thee through Paris, that corrupted town,
How long in vain I wandered up and down,
Where shameless Bacchus, with his drenching hoard,
Cold from his cave usurps the morning board.
London is lost in smoke and steep'd in tea;
No Yankee there can lisp the name of thee;
The uncouth word, a libel on the town,
Would call a proclamation from the crown.
For climes oblique, that fear the sun's full rays,
Chill'd in their fogs, exclude the generous maize.
A grain whose rich, luxuriant growth requires
Short gentle showers, and bright ethereal fires.
But here, though distant from our native shore,
With mutual glee, we meet and laugh once more.
The same! I know thee by that yellow face,
That strong complexion of true Indian race,
Which time can never change, nor soil impair,
Nor Alpine snows, nor Turkey's morbid air;
For endless years, through every mild domain,
Where grows the maize, there thou art sure to reign.
But man, more fickle, the bold license claims,
In different realms to give thee different names.
Thee the soft nations round the warm Levant
Polanta call; the French, of course, *Polante.*
E'en in thy native regions, how I blush
To hear the Pennsylvanians call thee *Mush!*
On Hudson's banks, while men of Belgic spawn
Insult and eat thee by the name of *Suppawn.*
All spurious appellations, void of truth;
I've better known thee from my earliest youth,
Thy name is *Hasty Pudding!* thus our sires
Were won't to greet thee fuming from their fires;
And while they argued in thy just defence
With logic clear, they thus explained the sense:

"In *haste* the boiling caldron, o'er the blaze,
Receives and cooks the ready powder'd-maize;
In *haste* 'tis served, and then in equal *haste*,
With cooling milk, we make the sweet repast.
No carving to be done, no knive to grate
The tender ear and wound the stony plate,
But the smooth spoon, just fitted to the lip,
And taught with art the yielding mass to dip,
By frequent journeys to the bowl well stored,
Performs the *hasty* honours of the board."
Such is thy name, significant and clear,
A name, a sound to every Yankee dear,
But most to me, whose heart and palate chaste
Preserve my pure hereditary taste.
  There are who strive to stamp with disrepute
The luscious food, because it feeds the brute;
In tropes of high-strain'd wit, while gaudy prigs
Compare thy nursling man to pamper'd pigs;
With sovereign scorn I treat the vulgar jest,
Nor fear to share thy bounties with the beast.
What though the generous cow gives me to quaff
The milk nutritious; am I then a calf?
Or can the genius of the noisy swine,
Though nursed on pudding, thence lay claim to mine?
Sure the sweet song I fashion to thy praise,
Runs more melodious than the notes they raise.
  My song resounding in its grateful glee,
No merit claims: I praise myself in thee.
My father loved thee through his length of days!
For thee his fields were shaded o'er with maize;
From thee what health, what vigour he possess'd,
Ten sturdy freemen from his loins attest;
Thy constellation ruled my natal morn,
And all my bones were made of Indian corn.
Delicious grain! whatever form it take,
To roast or boil, to smother or to bake,
In every dish 'tis welcome still to me,
But most, my *Hasty Pudding*, most in thee.

Let the green succotash with thee contend,
Let beans and corn their sweetest juices blend,
Let butter drench them in its yellow tide,
And a long slice of bacon grace their side;
Not all the plate, how famed soe'er it be,
Can please my palate like a bowl of thee.
Some talk of *Hoe-Cake*, fair Virginia's pride,
Rich *Johnny-Cake* this mouth hath often tried;
Both please me well, their virtues much the same
Alike their fabric, as allied their fame,
Except in dear New-England, where the last
Receives a dash of pumpkin in the paste,
To give it sweetness and improve the taste.
But place them all before me, smoking hot,
The big, round dumpling, rolling from the pot;
The pudding of the bag, whose quivering breast
With suet lined, leads on the Yankee feast;
The *Charlotte* brown, within whose crusty sides
A belly soft the pulpy apple hides;
The yellow bread, whose face like amber glows,
And all of Indian that the bakepan knows,
You tempt me not; my fav'rite greets my eyes,
To that loved bowl my spoon by instinct flies.

CANTO II.

To mix the food by vicious rules of art,
To kill the stomach and to sink the heart,
To make mankind to social virtue sour,
Cram o'er each dish, and be what they devour,
For this the kitchen muse first framed her book,
Commanding sweat to stream from every cook;
Children no more their antic gambols tried,
And friends to physic wonder'd why they died.
Not so the Yankee: his abundant feast,
With simples furnish'd and with plainness dress'd,
A numerous offspring gathers round the board,
And cheers alike the servant and the lord;
Whose well-bought hunger prompts the joyous taste,
And health attends them from the short repast.

While the full pail rewards the milkmaid's toil,
The mother sees the morning caldron boil;
To stir the pudding next demands their care;
To spread the table and the bowls prepare:
To feed the children as their portions cool,
And comb their heads, and send them off to school.
Yet may the simplest dish some rules impart,
For nature scorns not all the aids of art.
E'en *Hasty Pudding*, purest of all food,
May still be bad, indifferent, or good,
As sage experience the short process guides,
Or want of skill, or want of care presides.
Whoe'er would form it on the surest plan,
To rear the child and long sustain the man;
To shield the morals while it mends the size,
And all the powers of every food supplies,
Attend the lesson that the muse shall bring;
Suspend your spoons, and listen while I sing.
But since, oh man! thy life and health demand
Not food alone, but labour from thy hand,
First in the field, beneath the sun's strong rays,
Ask of thy mother earth the needful maize;
She loves the race that courts her yielding soil,
And gives her bounties to the sons of toil.
When now the ox, obedient to thy call,
Repays the loan that fill'd the winter stall,
Pursue his traces o'er the furrow'd plain,
And plant in measured hills the golden grain.
But when the tender germe begins to shoot,
And the green spire declares the sprouting root,
Then guard your nursling from each greedy foe,
The insidious worm, the all-devouring crow.
A little ashes sprinkled round the spire,
Soon steep'd in rain, will bid the worm retire;
The feather'd robber with his hungry maw
Swift flies the field before your man of straw,
A frightful image, such as schoolboys bring,
When met to burn the pope or hang the king.

Thrice in the season, through each verdant row,
Wield the strong ploughshare and the faithful hoe;
The faithful hoe, a double task that takes,
To till the summer corn and roast the winter cakes.
Slow springs the blade, while check'd by chilling rains,
Ere yet the sun the seat of Cancer gains;
But when his fiercest fires emblaze the land,
Then start the juices, then the roots expand;
Then, like a column of Corinthian mould,
The stalk struts upward and the leaves unfold;
The busy branches all the ridges fill,
Entwine their arms and kiss from hill to hill.
Here cease to vex them, all your cares are done.
Leave the last labours to the parent sun;
Beneath his genial smiles, the well-dress'd field,
When autumn calls, a plenteous crop shall yield.
Now the strong foliage bears the standards high
And shoots the tall top-gallants to the sky;
The suckling ears the silken fringes bend,
And pregnant grown, their swelling coats distend;
The loaded stalk, while still the burden grows,
O'erhangs the space that runs between the rows;
High as a hopfield waves the silent grove,
A safe retreat for little thefts of love,
When the pledged roasting-ears invite the maid
To meet her swain beneath the new-form'd shade;
His generous hand unloads the cumbrous hill,
And the green spoils her ready basket fill;
Small compensation for the twofold bliss,
The promised wedding, and the present kiss.
Slight depredations these; but now the moon
Calls from his hollow trees the sly raccoon;
And while by night he bears his prize away,
The bolder squirrel labours through the day.
Both thieves alike, but provident of time,
A virtue rare, that almost hides their crime.
Then let them steal the little stores they can,
And fill their gran'ries from the toils of man;

We've one advantage where they take no part—
With all their wiles, they ne'er have found the art
To boil the *Hasty Pudding;* here we shine
Superior far to tenants of the pine;
This envied boon to man shall still belong,
Unshared by them in substance or in song.
At last the closing season browns the plain,
And ripe October gathers in the grain;
Deep-loaded carts the spacious cornhouse fill,
The sack distended marches to the mill;
The lab'ring mill beneath the burden groans,
And showers the future pudding from the stones;
Till the glad housewife greets the powder'd gold,
And the new crop exterminates the old.

CANTO III.

The days grow short; but though the falling sun
To the glad swain proclaims his day's work done,
Night's pleasing shades his various tasks prolong,
And yield new subject to my various song.
For now, the cornhouse fill'd, the harvest home,
The invited neighbours to the *husking* come;
A frolic scene, where work, and mirth, and play,
Unite their charms to chase the hours away.
Where the huge heap lies centred in the hall,
The lamp suspended from the cheerful wall,
Brown, corn-fed nymphs, and strong, hard-handed beaus,
Alternate ranged, extend in circling rows,
Assume their seats, the solid mass attack;
The dry husks rustle, and the corncobs crack;
The song, the laugh, alternate notes resound,
And the sweet cider trips in silence round.
The laws of husking every wight can tell,
And sure no laws he ever keeps so well:
For each red ear a general kiss he gains,
With each smut ear he smuts the luckless swains;
But when to some sweet maid a prize is cast,
Red as her lips and taper as her waist,

She walks the round and culls one favoured beau,
Who leaps the luscious tribute to bestow.
Various the sport, as are the wits and brains
Of well-pleased lasses and contending swains;
Till the vast mound of corn is swept away,
And he that gets the last ear wins the day.
 Meanwhile the housewife urges all her care,
The well-earn'd feast to hasten and prepare.
The sifted meal already waits her hand,
The milk is strain'd, the bowls in order stand,
The fire flames high; and as a pool (that takes
The headlong stream that o'er the milldam breaks)
Foams, roars, and rages with incessant toils,
So the vex'd caldron rages, roars, and boils.
 First with clean salt she seasons well the food,
Then strews the flour, and thickens all the flood.
Long o'er the simmering fire she lets it stand;
To stir it well demands a stronger hand;
The husband takes his turn: and round and rouna
The ladle flies; at last the toil is crown'd;
When to the board the thronging huskers pour,
And take their seats as at the corn before.
 I leave them to their feast. There still belong
More copious matters to my faithful song.
For rules there are, though ne'er unfolded yet,
Nice rules and wise, how pudding should be ate
 Some with molasses line the luscious treat,
And mix, like bards, the useful with the sweet.
A wholesome dish and well deserving praise,
A great resource in those bleak wintry days,
When the chill'd earth lies buried deep in snow,
And raging Boreas dries the shivering cow.
 Bless'd cow! thy praise shall still my notes em
ploy,
Great source of health, the only source of joy;
Mother of Egypt's god—but sure, for me,
Were I to leave my God, I'd worship thee.
How oft thy teats these precious hands have press'd'
How oft thy bounties prove my only feast!

How oft I've fed thee with my favourite grain!
And roar'd, like thee, to find thy children slain!
Yes, swains who know her various worth to prize,
Ah! house her well from winter's angry skies.
Potatoes, pumpkins, should her sadness cheer,
Corn from your crib, and mashes from your beer;
When spring returns, she'll well acquit the loan,
And nurse at once your infants and her own.
Milk then with pudding I would always choose;
To this in future I confine my muse,
Till she in haste some further hints unfold,
Well for the young, nor useless to the old.
First in your bowl the milk abundant take,
Then drop with care along the silver lake
Your flakes of pudding; these at first will hide
Their little bulk beneath the swelling tide;
But when their growing mass no more can sink,
When the soft island looms above the brink,
Then check your hand; you've got the portion due,
So taught our sires, and what they taught is true.
There is a choice in spoons. Though small appear
The nice distinction, yet to me 'tis clear.
The deep-bowl'd Gallic spoon, contrived to scoop
In ample draughts the thin diluted soup,
Performs not well in those substantial things,
Whose mass adhesive to the metal clings;
Where the strong labial muscles must embrace
The gentle curve, and sweep the hollow space.
With ease to enter and discharge the freight,
A bowl less concave but still more dilate,
Becomes the pudding best. The shape, the size,
A secret rests, unknown to vulgar eyes.
Experienced feeders can alone impart
A rule so much above the lore of art.
These tuneful lips, that thousand spoons have tried,
With just precision could the point decide,
Though not in song; the muse but poorly shines
In cones, and cubes, and geometric lines;

Yet the true form, as near as she can tell,
Is that small section of a goose egg shell,
Which in two equal portions shall divide
The distance from the centre to the side.
  Fear not to slaver; 'tis no deadly sin:
Like the free Frenchman, from your joyous chin
Suspend the ready napkin; or, like me,
Poise with one hand your bowl upon your knee,
Just in the zenith your wise head project,
Your full spoon, rising in a line direct,
Bold as a bucket, heeds no drops that fall,
The wide-mouth'd bowl will surely catch them all

Robert C. Sands.

SLEEP OF PAPANTZIN.

'Twas then, one eve, when o'er the imperial lake
And all its cities, glittering in their pomp,
The lord of glory threw his parting smiles,
In Tlatelolco's palace, in her bower,
Papantzin lay reclined; sister of him
At whose name monarchs trembled. Yielding there
To musings various, o'er her senses crept
Or sleep or kindred death.

                                        It seemed she stood
In an illimitable plain, that stretched
Its desert continuity around,
Upon the o'erwearied sight; in contrast strange
With that rich vale, where only she had dwelt,
Whose everlasting mountains, girdling it,
As in a chalice held a kingdom's wealth;
Their summits freezing, where the eagle tired,
But found no resting-place. Papantzin looked
On endless barrenness, and walked perplexed
Through the dull haze, along the boundless heath,

Like some lone ghost in Mictlan's cheerless gloom
Debarred from light and glory.

Wandering thus,
She came where a great sullen river poured
Its turbid waters with a rushing sound
Of painful moans; as if the inky waves
Were hastening still on their complaining course
To escape the horrid solitudes. Beyond
What seemed a highway ran, with branching paths
Innumerous. This to gain, she sought to plunge
Straight in the troubled stream. For well she knew
To shun with agile limbs the current's force,
Nor feared the noise of waters. She had played
From infancy in her fair native lake,
Amid the gay plumed creatures floating round,
Wheeling or diving, with their changeful hues,
As fearless and as innocent as they.

A vision stayed her purpose. By her side
Stood a bright youth; and startling, as she gazed
On his effulgence, every sense was bound
In pleasing awe and in fond reverence.
For not Tezcatlipoca, as he shone
Upon her priest-led fancy, when from heaven
By filmy thread sustained he came to earth,
In his resplendent mail reflecting all
Its images, with dazzling portraiture,
Was, in his radiance and immortal youth,
A peer to this new god. His stature was
Like that of men; but matched with his, the port
Of kings all dreaded was the crouching mien
Of suppliants at their feet. Serene the light
That floated round him, as the lineaments
It cased with its mild glory. Gravely sweet
The impression of his features, which to scan
Their lofty loveliness forbade: his eyes
She felt, but saw not: only, on his brow—
From over which, encircled by what seemed

A ring of liquid diamond, in pure light
Revolving ever, backward flowed his locks
In buoyant, waving clusters—on his brow
She marked a Cross described; and lowly bent,
She knew not wherefore, to the sacred sign.
From either shoulder mantled o'er his front
Wings dropping feathery silver; and his robe
Snow-white in the still air was motionless,
As that of chiselled god, or the pale shroud
Of some fear-conjured ghost.

Her hand he took,
And led her passive o'er the naked banks
Of that black stream, still murmuring angrily.
But, as he spoke, she heard its moans no more;
His voice seemed sweeter than the hymnings raised
By brave and gentle souls in Paradise,
To celebrate the outgoing of the sun
On his majestic progress over heaven.
"Stay, princess," thus he spoke, "thou mayst not yet
O'erpass these waters. Though thou knowest it not,
Nor Him, God loves thee." So he led her on,
Unfainting, amid hideous sights and sounds;
For now, o'er scattered sculls and grisly bones
They walked; while underneath, before, behind,
Rise dolorous wails and groans protracted long,
Sobs of deep anguish, screams of agony,
And melancholy sighs, and the fierce yell
Of hopeless and intolerable pain.

Shuddering, as, in the gloomy whirlwind's pause
Through the malign, distempered atmosphere,
The second circle's purple blackness, passed
The pitying Florentine, who saw the shades
Of poor Francesca and her paramour;
The princess o'er the ghastly relics stepped,
Listening the frightful clamour; till a gleam,
Whose sickly and phosphoric lustre seemed
Kindled from these decaying bones, lit up

The sable river. Then a pageant came
Over its obscure tides, of stately barks,
Gigantic, with their prows of quaint device,
Tall masts, and ghostly canvass, huge and high,
Hung in the unnatural light and lifeless air.
Grim bearded men, with stern and angry looks,
Strange robes, and uncouth armour, stood behind
Their galleries and bulwarks. One ship bore
A broad sheet pendant, where, inwrought with gold,
She marked the symbol that adorned the brow
Of her mysterious guide. Down the dark stream
Swept on the spectral fleet, in the false light
Flickering and fading. Louder then uprose
The roar of voices from the accursed strand.

WAKING OF PAPANTZIN IN THE SEPULCHRE.

She woke in darkness and in solitude.
Slow passed her lethargy away, and long
To her half-dreaming eye that brilliant sign
Distinct appeared. Then damp and close she felt
The air around, and knew the poignant smell
Of spicy herbs collected and confined.
As those awakening from some troubled trance
Are wont, she would have learned by touch if yet
The spirit to the body was allied.
Strange hindrances prevented. O'er her face
A mask thick-plated lay—and round her swathed
Was many a costly and encumbering robe,
Such as she wore on some high festival,
O'erspread with precious gems, rayless and cold,
That now pressed hard and sharp against her touch.
The cumbrous collar round her slender neck,
Of gold thick studded with each valued stone
Earth and the sea-depths yield for human pride—
The bracelets and the many-twisted rings
That girt her taper limbs, coil upon coil—
What were they in this dungeon's solitude?

The plumy coronal that would have sprung
Light from her fillet in the purer air,
Waving in mockery of the rainbow tints,
Now drooping low, and steeped in clogging dews,
Oppressive hung. Groping in dubious search,
She found the household goods, the spindle, broom,
Gicalli quaintly sculptured, and the jar
That held the useless beverage for the dead.
By these, and by the jewel to her lip
Attached, the emerald symbol of the soul,
In its green life immortal, soon she knew
Her dwelling was a sepulchre.

She loosed
The mask, and from her feathery bier uprose,
Casting away the robe, which like long alb
Wrapped her; and with it many an aloe leaf,
Inscribed with Azteck characters and signs,
To guide the spirit where the serpent hissed,
Hills towered, and deserts spread, and keen winds blew,
And many a "flower of death;" though their frail leaves
Were yet unwithered. For the living warmth
Which in her dwelt, their freshness had preserved;
Else, if corruption had begun its work,
The emblems of quick change would have survived
Her beauty's semblance. What is beauty worth,
If the cropp'd flower retains its tender bloom
When foul decay has stolen the latest lines
Of loveliness in death? Yet even now
Papantzin knew that her exuberant locks—
Which, unconfined, had round her flowed to earth,
Like a stream rushing down some rocky steep,
Threaded ten thousand channels—had been shorn
Of half their waving length, and liked it not.
But through a crevice soon she marked a gleam
Of rays uncertain; and, with staggering steps,
But strong in reckless dreaminess, while still

Presided o'er the chaos of her thoughts
The revelation that upon her soul
Dwelt with its power, she gained the cavern's throat,
And pushed the quarried stone aside, and stood
In the free air, and in her own domain.

But now obscurely o'er her vision swam
The beauteous landscape, with its thousand tints
And changeful views; long alleys of bright trees
Bending beneath their fruits; espaliers gay
With tropic flowers and shrubs that filled the breeze
With odorous incense, basins vast, where birds
With shining plumage sported, smooth canals
Leading the glassy wave, or towering grove
Of forest veterans. On a rising bank,
Her seat accustomed, near a well hewn out
From ancient rocks into which waters gushed
From living springs, where she was wont to bathe,
She threw herself to muse. Dim on her sight
The imperial city and its causeways rose,
With the broad lake and all its floating isles
And glancing shallops, and the gilded pomp
Of princely barges, canopied with plumes
Spread fanlike, or with tufted pageantry
Waving magnificent. Unmarked around
The frequent huitzilin, with murmuring hum
Of ever-restless wing, and shrill sweet note,
Shot twinkling, with the ruby star that glowed
Over his tiny bosom, and all hues
That loveliest seem in heaven, with ceaseless change,
Flashing from his fine films. And all in vain
Untiring, from the rustling branches near,
Poured the Centzontli all his hundred strains
Of imitative melody. Not now
She heeded them. Yet pleasant was the shade
Of palms and cedars; and through twining boughs
And fluttering leaves, the subtle god of air, [crept,
The serpent armed with plumes, most welcome
And fanned her cheek with kindest ministry.

A dull and dismal sound came booming on;
A solemn, wild, and melancholy noise,
Shaking the tranquil air; and afterward
A clash and jangling, barbarously prolonged,
Torturing the unwilling ear, rang dissonant.
Again the unnatural thunder rolled along,
Again the crash and clamour followed it.
Shuddering she heard, who knew that every peal
From the dread gong, announced a victim's heart
Torn from his breast, and each triumphant clang,
A mangled corse down the great temple's stairs
Hurled headlong; and she knew, as lately taught,
How vengeance was ordained for cruelty;
How pride would end; and uncouth soldiers tread
Through bloody furrows o'er her pleasant groves
And gardens; and would make themselves a road
Over the dead, choking the silver lake,
And cast the battered idols down the steps
That climbed their execrable towers, and raze
Sheer from the ground Ahuitzol's mighty pile.

GOOD-NIGHT.

Good-night to all the world! there's none,
Beneath the "over-going" sun,
To whom I feel, or hate, or spite,
And so to all a fair good-night.

Would I could say good-night to pain,
Good-night to conscience and her train,
To cheerless poverty, and shame
That I am yet unknown to fame!

Would I could say good-night to dreams
That haunt me with delusive gleams,
That through the sable future's veil
Like meteors glimmer, but to fail.

Would I could say a long good-night
To halting between wrong and right,
And, like a giant with new force,
Awake prepared to run my course!

But time o'er good and ill sweeps on,
And when few years have come and gone,
The past will be to me as naught,
Whether remembered or forgot.

Yet let me hope one faithful friend
O'er my last couch in tears shall bend;
And, though no day for me was bright,
Shall bid me then a long good-night.

THE DEAD OF 1832.

Oh Time and Death! with certain pace,
  Though still unequal, hurrying on,
O'erturning in your awful race,
  The cot, the palace, and the throne!

Not always in the storm of war,
  Nor by the pestilence that sweeps
From the plague-smitten realms afar,
  Beyond the old and solemn deeps:

In crowds the good and mighty go,
  And to those vast dim chambers hie:
Where, mingled with the high and low,
  Dead Cæsars and dead Shakspeares lie!

Dread ministers of God! sometimes
  Ye smite at once to do his will,
In all earth's ocean-severed climes,
  Those—whose renown ye cannot kill!

When all the brightest stars that burn
  At once are banished from their spheres,
Men sadly ask, when shall return
  Such lustre to the coming years?

For where is he*—who lived so long—
  Who raised the modern Titan's ghost,
And showed his fate in powerful song,
  Whose soul for learning's sake was lost?

Where he—who backward to the birth
  Of Time itself, adventurous trod,
And in the mingled mass of earth
  Found out the handiwork of God?†

Where he—who in the mortal head,‡
  Ordained to gaze on heaven, could trace
The soul's vast features, that shall tread
  The stars, when earth is nothingness?

Where he—who struck old Albyn's lyre,§
  Till round the world its echoes roll,
And swept, with all a prophet's fire,
  The diapason of the soul?

Where he—who read the mystic lore,||
  Buried, where buried Pharaohs sleep;
And dared presumptuous to explore
  Secrets four thousand years could keep?

Where he—who, with a poet's eye¶
  Of truth, on lowly nature gazed,
And made even sordid Poverty
  Classic, when in HIS numbers glazed?

Where—that old sage so hale and staid,**
  The "greatest good" who sought to find,
Who in his garden mused, and made
  All forms of rule for all mankind?

* Goethe and his Faust. † Cuvier. ‡ Spurzheim.
§ Scott. || Champollion. ¶ Crabbe. ** Jeremy Bentham.

And thou—whom millions far removed*
  Revered—the hierarch meek and wise,
Thy ashes sleep, adored, beloved,
  Near where thy Wesley's coffin lies.

He too—the heir of glory—where†
  Hath great Napoleon's scion fled?
Ah! glory goes not to an heir!
  Take him, ye noble, vulgar dead!

But hark! a nation sighs! for he,‡
  Last of the brave who perilled all
To make an infant empire free,
  Obeys the inevitable call!

They go—and with them is a crowd,
  For human rights who THOUGHT and DID,
We rear to them no temples proud,
  Each hath his mental pyramid.

All earth is now their sepulchre,
  The MIND, their monument sublime—
Young in eternal fame they are—
  Such are YOUR triumphs, Death and Time.

James A. Hillhouse.

DESCENT OF THE JUDGE AND HIS ANGELS.

METHOUGHT I journeyed o'er a boundless plain
Unbroke by hill or vale, on all sides stretched,
Like circling ocean to the low-browed sky;
Save in the midst a verdant mount, whose sides
Flowers of all hues and fragrant breath adorned
Lightly I trod, as on some joyous quest,

* Adam Clarke. † The Duke of Reichstadt.
‡ Charles Carroll.

Beneath the azure vault and early sun;
But while my pleased eyes ranged the circuit green,
New light shone round; a murmur came confused,
Like many voices and the rush of wings.
Upward I gazed, and mid the glittering skies,
Begirt by flying myriads, saw a throne,
Whose thousand splendours blazed upon the earth,
Refulgent as another sun. Through clouds
They came, and vapours coloured by Aurora,
Mingling in swell sublime, voices and harps,
And sounding wings and hallelujahs sweet.
Sudden a Seraph, that before them flew,
Pausing upon his wide-unfolded plumes,
Put to his mouth the likeness of a trump,
And towards the four winds four times fiercely breathed.
Doubling along the arch, the mighty peal
To Heaven resounded, Hell returned a groan,
And shuddering Earth a moment reeled, confounded
From her fixed pathway, as the staggering ship,
Stunned by some mountain billow, reels. The isles
With heaving ocean, rocked: the mountains shook
Their ancient coronets: the avalanche
Thundered: silence succeeded through the nations.
Earth never listened to a sound like this.
It struck the general pulse of nature still,
And broke for ever the dull sleep of death.
  Now o'er the mount the radiant legions hung,
Like plumy travellers from climes remote
On some sequestered isle about to stoop.
Gently its flowery head received the throne;
Cherubs and Seraphs, by ten thousands, round
Skirted it far and wide, like a bright sea;
Fair forms and faces, crowns, and coronets,
And glistering wings furled white and numberless.
About their Lord were those Seven glorious Spirits
Who in the Almighty's presence stand. Four leaned
On golden wands, with folded wings, and eyes
Fixed on the throne: one bore the dreadful Books,

The arbiters of life: another waved
The blazing ensign terrible, of yore,
To rebel angels in the wars of Heaven:
What seemed a trump the other Spirit grasped,
Of wondrous size, wreathed multiform and strange.
Illustrious stood the Seven, above the rest
Towering, and like a constellation glowing,
What time the sphere-instructed huntsman, taught
By Atlas, his star-studded belt displays
Aloft, bright-glittering, in the winter sky

ADAM, CÆSAR, AND ABRAHAM AT THE RESURRECTION.

Nearest the mount, of that mixed phalanx first,
Our general Parent stood; not as he looked
Wandering at eve amid the shady bowers
And odorous groves of that delicious garden,
Or flowery banks of some soft rolling stream,
Pausing to list its lulling murmur, hand
In hand with peerless Eve, the rose too sweet,
Fatal to Paradise. Fled from his cheek
The bloom of Eden; his hyacinthine locks
Were turned to gray; with years and sorrows bowed
He seemed, but through his ruined form still shone
The majesty of his Creator: round
Upon his sons a grieved and pitying look
He cast, and in his vesture hid his face.
Close at his side appeared a martial form
Of port majestic, clad in massive arms,
Cowering above whose helm, with outspread wings,
The Roman eagle flew; around its brim
Was charactered the name at which Earth's Queen
Bowed from her sevenfold throne and owned her lord.
In his dilated eye amazement stood;
Terror, surprise, and blank astonishment
Blanched his firm cheek, as when of old, close hemmed
Within the Capitol, amid the crowd

Of traitors, fearless else, he caught the gleam
Of Brutus' steel. Daunted, yet on the pomp
Of towering seraphim, their wings, their crowns,
Their dazzling faces, and upon the Lord,
He fixed a steadfast look of anxious note,
Like that Pharsalia's hurtling squadrons drew
When all his fortunes hung upon the hour.
 Near him, for wisdom famous through the East
Abraham rested on his staff; in guise
A Chaldee shepherd, simple in his raiment
As when at Mamre in his tent he sat,
The host of angels. Snow-white were his locks
And silvery beard that to his girdle rolled.
Fondly his meek eye dwelt upon his Lord,
Like one that, after long and troubled dreams,
A night of sorrows, dreary, wild, and sad,
Beholds, at last, the dawn of promised joys.

LAST SETTING OF THE SUN.

By this the sun his westering car drove low;
Round his broad wheels full many a lucid cloud
Floated, like happy isles in seas of gold:
Along the horizon castled shapes were piled,
Turrets and towers, whose fronts embattled gleamed
With yellow light: smit by the slanting ray,
A ruddy beam the canopy reflected;
With deeper light the ruby blushed; and thick
Upon the Seraphs' wings the glowing spots
Seemed drops of fire. Uncoiling from its staff,
With fainter wave, the gorgeous ensign hung,
Or, swelling with the swelling breeze, by fits
Cast off, upon the dewy air, huge flakes
Of golden lustre. Over all the hill,
The heavenly legions, the assembled world,
Evening her crimson tint for ever drew.
 But while at gaze, in solemn silence, men
And angels stood, and many a quaking heart

With expectation throbbed; about the throne
And glittering hill-top slowly wreathed the clouds,
Erewhile like curtains for adornment hung,
Involving Shiloh and the Seraphim
Beneath a snowy tent. The bands around
Eying the gonfalon that through the smoke
Tower'd into air, resembled hosts who watch
The king's pavilion where, ere battle hour,
A council sits. What their consult might be,
Those seven dread Spirits and their Lord, I mused,
I marvelled. Was it grace and peace? or death?
Was it of man? Did pity for the Lost
His gentle nature wring, who knew, who felt
How frail is this poor tenement of clay?
Arose there from the misty tabernacle
A cry like that upon Gethsemane?
What passed in Jesus' bosom none may know,
But close the cloudy dome invested him;
And, weary with conjecture, round I gazed
Where in the purple west, no more to dawn,
Faded the glories of the dying day.
Mild-twinkling through a crimson-skirted cloud
The solitary star of evening shone.
While gazing wistful on that peerless light
Thereafter to be seen no more (as oft
In dreams strange images will mix), sad thoughts
Passed o'er my soul. Sorrowing I cried, "Farewell,
Pale, beauteous planet, that displayest so soft,
Amid yon glowing streak, thy transient beam,
A long, a last farewell! Seasons have changed,
Ages and empires rolled, like smoke, away,
But thou, unaltered, beam'st as silver fair
As on thy birthnight! Bright and watchful eyes,
From palaces and bowers, have hailed thy gem
With secret transport! Natal star of love,
And souls that love the shadowy hour of fancy,
How much I owe thee, how I bless thy ray!
How oft thy rising o'er the hamlet green,
Signal of rest, and social converse sweet,

Beneath some patriarchal tree, has cheered
The peasant's heart, and drawn his benison!
Pride of the West! beneath thy placid light
The tender tale shall never more be told,
Man's soul shall never wake to joy again:
Thou set'st for ever—lovely orb, farewell!"

SCENE FROM HADAD.

The terraced roof of ABSALOM'S *house by night; adorned with vases of flowers and fragrant shrubs; an awning over part of it.* TAMAR *and* HADAD.

Tam. No, no, I well remember—proofs, you said
Unknown to Moses.
Had. Well, my love, thou know'st
I've been a traveller in various climes;
Trod Ethiopia's scorching sands, and scaled
The snow-clad mountains; trusted to the deep;
Traversed the fragrant islands of the sea,
And with the wise conversed of many nations.
Tam. I know thou hast.
Had. Of all mine eyes have seen,
The greatest, wisest, and most wonderful
Is that dread sage, the Ancient of the Mountain.
Tam. Who?
Had. None knows his lineage, age, or name: his [locks
Are like the snows of Caucasus; his eyes
Beam with the wisdom of collected ages.
In green unbroken years he sees, 'tis said,
The generations pass, like autumn fruits,
Garner'd, consumed, and springing fresh to life,
Again to perish, while he views the sun,
The seasons roll, in rapt serenity,
And high communion with celestial powers.
Some say 'tis Shem, our father, some say Enoch,
And some Melchizedek.

Tam. I've heard a tale
Like this, but ne'er believed it.
Had. I have proved it.
Through perils dire, dangers most imminent,
Seven days and nights mid rocks and wildernesses,
And boreal snows, and never-thawing ice,
Where not a bird, a beast, a living thing,
Save the far-soaring vulture, comes, I dared
My desperate way, resolved to know or perish.
Tam. Rash, rash advent'rer!
Had. On the highest peak
Of stormy Caucasus there blooms a spot
On which perpetual sunbeams play, where flowers
And verdure never die; and there he dwells.
Tam. But didst thou see him?
Had. Never did I view
Such awful majesty: his reverend locks
Hung like a silver mantle to his feet,
His raiment glistered saintly white, his brow
Rose like the gate of Paradise, his mouth
Was musical as its bright guardians' songs.
Tam. What did he tell thee? Oh! what wisdom
From lips so hallowed? [fell
Had. Whether he possess
The Tetragrammaton—the powerful name
Inscribed on Moses' rod, by which he wrought
Unheard-of wonders, which constrains the heavens
To shower down blessings, shakes the earth, and
The strongest spirits; or if God hath given [rules
A delegated power, I cannot tell.
But 'twas from him I learned their fate, their fall,
Who erewhile wore resplendent crowns in Heaven;
Now scattered through the earth, the air, the sea.
Them he compels to answer, and from them
Has drawn what Moses, nor no mortal ear,
Has ever heard.
Tam. But did he tell it thee?
Had. He told me much—more than I dare reveal;
For with a dreadful oath he sealed my lips.

Tam. But canst thou tell me nothing? Why un-
So much, if I must hear no more? [fold
Had. You bade
Explain my words, almost reproached me, sweet,
For what by accident escaped me.
Tam. Ah!
A little—something tell me—sure not all
Were words inhibited.
Had. Then promise never,
Never to utter of this conference
A breath to mortal.
Tam. Solemnly I vow.
Had. Even then, 'tis little I can say, compared
With all the marvels he related.
Tam. Come,
I'm breathless. Tell me how they sinn'd, how fell.
Had. Their head, their prince involved them in his ruin.
Tam. What black offence on his devoted head
Drew endless punishment?
Had. The wish to be
Like the All-Perfect.
Tam. Arrogating that
Due only to his Maker! awful crime!
But what their doom? their place of punishment?
Had. Above, about, beneath; earth, sea, and air;
Their habitations various as their minds,
Employments, and desires.
Tam. But are they round us, Hadad? not confined
In penal chains and darkness?
Had. So he said,
And so your holy books infer. What saith
Your Prophet? what the Prince of Uz?
Tam. I shudder,
Lest some dark minister be near us now.
Had. You wrong them. They are bright intelligences,
Robbed of some native splendour, and cast down,
'Tis true, from Heaven; but not deformed, and foul,

Revengeful, malice-working fiends, as fools
Suppose They dwell, like princes, in the clouds;
Sun their bright pinions in the middle sky;
Or arch their palaces beneath the hills,
With stones inestimable studded so,
That sun or stars were useless there.
Tam. Good heavens!
Had. He bade me look on rugged Caucasus,
Crag piled on crag beyond the utmost ken,
Naked and wild, as if creation's ruins
Were heaped in one immeasurable chain
Of barren mountains, beaten by the storms
Of everlasting winter. But within
Are glorious palaces and domes of light,
Irradiate halls and crystal colonnades,
Vaults set with gems the purchase of a crown,
Blazing with lustre past the noontide beam,
Or, with a milder beauty, mimicking
The mystic signs of changeful Mazzaroth.
Tam. Unheard-of splendour!
Had. There they dwell, and muse,
And wander; beings beautiful, immortal,
Minds vast as heaven, capacious as the sky,
Whose thoughts connect past, present, and to come,
And glow with light intense, imperishable.
Thus, in the sparry chambers of the sea
And air-pavilions, rainbow tabernacles,
They study Nature's secrets, and enjoy
No poor dominion.
Tam. Are they beautiful,
And powerful far beyond the human race?
Had. Man's feeble heart cannot conceive it. When
The sage described them, fiery eloquence
Flowed from his lips, his bosom heaved, his eyes
Grew bright and mystical; moved by the theme,
Like one who feels a deity within.
Tam. Wondrous! What intercourse have they with men?
Had. Sometimes they deign to intermix with man,
But oft with woman.

Tam. Ha! with woman?
Had. She
Attracts them with her gentler virtues, soft,
And beautiful, and heavenly, like themselves.
They have been known to love her with a passion
Stronger than human.
Tam. That surpasses all
You yet have told me.
Had. This the sage affirms;
And Moses, darkly.
Tam. How do they appear?
How manifest their love?
Had. Sometimes 'tis spiritual, signified
By beatific dreams, or more distinct
And glorious apparition. They have stooped
To animate a human form, and love
Like mortals.
Tam. Frightful to be so beloved!
Who could endure the horrid thought! What makes
Thy cold hand tremble? or is't mine
That feels so deathy?
Had. Dark imaginations haunt me
When I recall the dreadful interview.
Tam. Oh, tell them not: I would not hear them.
Had. But why contemn a spirit's love? so high,
So glorious, if he haply deigned?
Tam. Forswear
My Maker! love a demon!
Had. No—oh, no—
My thoughts but wandered. Oft, alas! they wander.
Tam. Why dost thou speak so sadly now? And
Thine eyes are fixed again upon Arcturus. [lo!
Thus ever, when thy drooping spirits ebb,
Thou gazest on that star. Hath it the power
To cause or cure thy melancholy mood?
[*He appears lost in thought.*
Tell me, ascrib'st thou influence to the stars?
Had. (*starting.*) The stars! What know'st thou
of the stars?

Tam. I know that they were made to rule the night.

Had. Like palace lamps! Thou echoest well thy grandsire.
Woman! the stars are living, glorious,
Amazing, infinite!

Tam. Speak not so wildly.
I know them numberless, resplendent, set
As symbols of the countless, countless years
That make eternity.

Had. Eternity!
Oh! mighty, glorious, miserable thought!
Had ye endured like those great sufferers,
Like them, seen ages, myriad ages roll;
Could ye but look into the void abyss
With eyes experienced, unobscured by torments,
Then mightst thou name it, name it feelingly.

Tam. What ails thee, Hadad? Draw me not so close.

Had. Tamar! I need thy love—more than thy love—

Tam. Thy cheek is wet with tears—Nay, let us part—
'Tis late—I cannot, must not linger.
[*Breaks from him, and exit.*

Had. Loved and abhorred! Still, still accursed!
[*He paces twice or thrice up and down with passionate gestures; then turns his face to the sky, and stands a moment in silence.*]
Oh! where,
In the illimitable space, in what
Profound of untried misery, when all
His worlds, his rolling orbs of light, that fill
With life and beauty yonder infinite,
Their radiant journey run, for ever set,
Where, where, in what abyss shall I be groaning?
[*Exit.*

Timothy Dwight.

THE COUNTRY SCHOOLMASTER.

Where yonder humbler spire salutes the eye,
It's vane slow turning in the liquid sky,
Where, in light gambols, healthy striplings sport,
Ambitious learning builds her outer court;
A grave preceptor, there, her usher stands,
And rules without a rod her little bands.
Some half-grown sprigs of learning graced his brow:
Little he knew, though much he wish'd to know,
Enchanted hung o'er Virgil's honey'd lay,
And smiled to see desipient Horace play;
Glean'd scraps of Greek; and, curious, traced afar,
Through Pope's clear glass, the bright Mæonian star
Yet oft his students at his wisdom stared,
For many a student to his side repair'd,
Surprised, they heard him Dilworth's knots untie,
And tell what lands beyond the Atlantic lie.

Many his faults; his virtues small, and few;
Some little good he did, or strove to do,
Laborious still, he taught the early mind,
And urged to manners meek and thoughts refined;
Truth he impress'd, and every virtue praised;
While infant eyes in wondering silence gazed;
The worth of time would day by day unfold,
And tell them every hour was made of gold.

THE SOCIAL VISIT.

Ye Muses! dames of dignified renown,
Revered alike in country and in town,
Your bard the mysteries of a visit show,
For sure your ladyships those mysteries know:
What is it, then, obliging Sisters! say,
The debt of social visiting to pay?

'Tis not to toil before the idol pier;
To shine the first in fashion's lunar sphere;
By sad engagements forced abroad to roam,
And dread to find the expecting fair at home!
To stop at thirty doors in half a day,
Drop the gilt card, and proudly roll away;
To alight, and yield the hand with nice parade;
Up stairs to rustle in the stiff brocade;
Swim through the drawing-room with studied air,
Catch the pink'd beau, and shade the rival fair;
To sit, to curb, to toss with bridled mien,
Mince the scant speech, and lose a glance between;
Unfurl the fan, display the snowy arm,
And ope, with each new motion, some new charm:
Or sit in silent solitude, to spy
Each little failing with malignant eye;
Or chatter with incessancy of tongue,
Careless if kind, or cruel, right or wrong;
To trill of us and ours, of mine and me,
Our house, our coach, our friends, our family,
While all th' excluded circle sit in pain,
And glance their cool contempt or keen disdain:
T' inhale from proud Nanking a sip of tea,
And wave a court'sy trim and flirt away:
Or waste at cards peace, temper, health, and life,
Begin with sullenness, and end in strife;
Lose the rich feast by friendly converse given,
And backward turn from happiness and heaven.

It is in decent habit, plain and neat,
To spend a few choice hours in converse sweet,
Careless of forms, to act th' unstudied part,
To mix in friendship, and to blend the heart;
To choose those happy themes which all must feel
The moral duties and the household weal,
The tale of sympathy, the kind design,
Where rich affections soften and refine;
T' amuse, to be amused, to bless, be bless'd,
And tune to harmony the common breast;

To cheer, with mild good-humour's sprightly ray,
And smooth life's passage o'er its thorny way;
To circle round the hospitable board,
And taste each good our generous climes afford:
To court a quick return with accents kind.
And leave, at parting, some regret behind.

THE DESTRUCTION OF THE PEQUODS.

AH me! while up the long, long vale of time,
Reflection wanders towards th' eternal vast,
How starts the eye at many a change sublime,
Unbosom'd dimly by the ages pass'd!
What Mausoleums crowd the mournful waste!
The tombs of empires fallen! and nations gone!
Each, once inscribed in gold with "AYE TO LAST,"
Sate as a queen; proclaim'd the world her own,
And proudly cried, "By me no sorrows shall be known."

Soon fleets the sunbright form by man adored.
Soon fell the head of gold, to Time a prey;
The arms, the trunk, his cankering tooth devour'd,
And whirlwinds blew the iron dust away.
Where dwelt imperial Timur? far astray,
Some lonely-musing pilgrim now inquires:
And, rack'd by storms, and hastening to decay,
Mohammed's mosque foresees its final fires,
And Rome's more lordly temple day by day expires.

As o'er proud Asian realms the traveller winds,
His manly spirit, hush'd by terror, falls;
When some deceased town's lost site he finds,
Where ruin wild his pondering eye appals;
Where silence swims along the moulder'd walls,
And broods upon departed Grandeur's tomb.
Through the lone, hollow aisles sad Echo calls
At each slow step; deep sighs the breathing gloom,
And weeping fields around bewail their empress' doom.

Where o'er a hundred realms the throne uprose,
The screech-owl nests, the panther builds his home;
Sleep the dull newts, the lazy adders doze,
Where pomp and luxury danced the golden room.
Low lies in dust the sky-resembled dome;
Tall grass around the broken column waves;
And brambles climb, and lonely thistles bloom:
The moulder'd arch the weedy streamlet laves,
And low resound, beneath, unnumber'd sunken graves.

Soon fleets the sunbright form by man adored,
And soon man's demon chiefs from memory fade.
In musty volume now must be explored,
Where dwelt imperial nations, long decay'd.
The brightest meteors angry clouds invade;
And where the wonders glitter'd, none explain.
Where Carthage, with proud hand, the trident sway'd,
Now mud-wall'd cots sit sullen on the plain,
And wandering, fierce and wild, sequester'd Arabs reign.

In thee, oh Albion! queen of nations, live
Whatever splendours earth's wide realms have known;
In thee proud Persia sees her pomp revive,
And Greece her arts, and Rome her lordly throne:
By every wind thy Tyrian fleets are blown;
Supreme, on Fame's dread roll, thy heroes stand;
All ocean's realms thy naval sceptre own;
Of bards, of sages, how august thy band!
And one rich Eden blooms around thy garden'd land.

But oh, how vast thy crimes! Through Heaven's great year,
When few centurial suns have traced their way;
When Southern Europe, worn by feuds severe,
Weak, doting, fallen, has bow'd to Russian sway,
And setting Glory beam'd her farewell ray,
To wastes, perchance, thy brilliant fields shall turn;
In dust thy temples, towers, and towns decay;

The forest howl, where London's turrets burn,
And all thy garlands deck thy sad, funereal urn.

Some land, scarce glimmering in the light of fame,
Scepter'd with arts and arms (if I divine),
Some unknown wild, some shore without a name,
In all thy pomp shall then majestic shine.
As silver-headed Time's slow years decline,
Not ruins only meet th' inquiring eye : [twine,
Where round yon mouldering oak vain brambles
The filial stem, already towering high, [sky.
Ere long shall stretch his arms, and nod in yonder

Where late resounded the wild woodland roar,
Now heaves the palace, now the temple smiles;
Where frown'd the rude rock and the desert shore,
Now pleasure sports, and business want beguiles,
And Commerce wings her flight to thousand isles;
Culture walks forth; gay laugh the loaded fields:
And jocund Labour plays his harmless wiles;
Glad Science brightens; Art her mansion builds;
And Peace uplifts her wand, and HEAVEN his blessing yields.

O'er these sweet fields, so lovely now and gay,
Where modest Nature finds each want supplied,
Where homeborn Happiness delights to play,
And counts her little flock with household pride,
Long frown'd, from age to age, a forest wide:
Here hung the slumbering bat; the serpent dire
Nested his brood, and drank th' impoison'd tide;
Wolves peal'd the dark, drear night in hideous choir,
Nor shrunk th' unmeasured howl from Sol's terrific fire.

No charming cot imbank'd the pebbly stream;
No mansion tower'd, nor garden teem'd with good,
No lawn expanded to the April beam,
Nor mellow harvest hung its bending load;
Nor science dawn'd, nor life with beauty glow'd,

Nor temple whiten'd in th' enchanting dell;
In clusters wild the sluggish wigwam stood;
And, borne in snaky paths, the Indian fell [yell.
Now aim'd the death unseen, now screamed the tiger-

Even now, perhaps, on human dust I tread,
Pondering with solemn pause the wrecks of time;
Here sleeps, perchance, among the vulgar dead,
Some chief, the lofty theme of Indian rhyme,
Who loved Ambition's cloudy steep to climb,
And smiled, deaths, dangers, rivals to engage;
Who roused his followers' souls to deeds sublime,
Kindling to furnace heat vindictive rage,
And soar'd Cæsarean heights, the Phœnix of his age.

In yon small field that dimly steals from sight
(From yon small field these meditations grow),
Turning the sluggish soil from morn to night,
The plodding hind, laborious, drives his plough,
Nor dreams a nation sleeps his foot below.
There, undisturbed by the roaring wave,
Released from war, and far from deadly foe,
Lies down in endless rest a nation brave,
And trains in tempests born there find a quiet grave

Oft have I heard the tale, when matron sere
Sung to my infant ear the song of wo;
Of maiden meek consumed with pining care,
Around whose tomb the wild-rose loved to blow:
Or told, with swimming eyes, how, long ago,
Remorseless Indians, all in midnight dire,
The little sleeping village did o'erthrow,
Bidding the cruel flames to heaven aspire, [fire.
And scalp'd the hoary head, and burn'd the babe with

Then, fancy-fired, her memory wing'd its flight
To long-forgotten wars and dread alarms,
To chiefs obscure, but terrible in fight,
Who mock'd each foe, and laugh'd at deadliest harms,
Sidneys in zeal, and Washingtons in arms.

By instinct tender to the woes of man,
My heart bewildering with sweet pity's charms,
Through solemn scenes, with Nature's step she ran,
And hushed her audience small, and thus the tale
began.

"Through verdant banks, where Thames's branches
Long held the Pequods an extensive sway; [glide,
Bold, savage, fierce, of arms the glorious pride,
And bidding all the circling realms obey.
Jealous, they saw the tribes beyond the sea
Plant in their climes; and towns and cities rise;
Ascending castles foreign flags display;
Mysterious art new scenes of life devise; [skies.
And steeds insult the plains, and cannon rend the

"They saw, and soon the strangers' fate decreed,
And soon of war disclosed the crimson sign;
First, hapless Stone! they bade thy bosom bleed,
A guiltless offering at th' infernal shrine:
Then, gallant Norton! the hard fate was thine,
By ruffians butcher'd, and denied a grave:
Thee, generous Oldham! next the doom malign
Arrested; nor could all thy courage save;
Forsaken, plunder'd, cleft, and buried in the wave

"Soon the sad tidings reach'd the general ear,
And prudence, pity, vengeance, all inspire:
Invasive war their gallant friends prepare;
And soon a noble band, with purpose dire,
And threatening arms, the murderous fiends require:
Small was the band, but never taught to yield;
Breasts faced with steel, and souls instinct with fire:
Such souls from Sparta Persia's world repell'd,
When nations paved the ground, and Xerxes flew
the field.

"The rising clouds the savage chief descried,
And round the forest bade his heroes arm;
To arms the painted warriors proudly hied,
And through surrounding nations rung th' alarm.

The nations heard; but smiled to see the storm,
With ruin fraught, o'er Pequod mountains driven;
And felt infernal joy the bosom warm,
To see their light hang o'er the skirts of even,
And other suns arise, to gild a kinder heaven.

" Swift to the Pequod fortress Mason sped,
Far in the wildering wood's impervious gloom;
A lonely castle, brown with twilight dread,
Where oft th' embowell'd captive met his doom,
And frequent heaved around the hollow tomb;
Scalps hung in rows, and whitening bones were strew'd;
Where, round the broiling babe, fresh from the womb,
With howls the Powaw fill'd the dark abode,
And screams and midnight prayers invoked the evil god.

" There too, with awful rites, the hoary priest,
Without, beside the moss-grown altar stood,
His sable form in magic cincture dress'd,
And heap'd the mingled offering to his god,
What time, with golden light, calm evening glow'd
The mystic dust, the flower of silver bloom,
And spicy herb, his hand in order strew'd;
Bright rose the curling flame; and rich perfume
On smoky wings upflew, or settled round the tomb.

" Then o'er the circus danced the maddening throng,
As erst the Thyas roam'd dread Nysa round,
And struck to forest notes th' ecstatic song,
While slow beneath them heaved the wavy ground.
With a low, lingering groan of dying sound,
The woodland rumbled; murmur'd deep each stream;
Shrill sung the leaves; all ether sigh'd profound;
Pale tufts of purple topped the silver flame,
And many-colour'd forms on evening breezes came.

" Thin, twilight forms, attired in changing sheen
Of plumes high-tinctured in the western ray;
Bending, they peep'd the fleecy folds between,
Their wings light-rustling in the breath of May.

Soft-hovering round the fire, in mystic play,
They snuff'd the incense waved in clouds afar,
Then, silent, floated towards the setting day:
Eve redden'd each fine form, each misty car,
And through them faintly gleam'd, at times, the western star.

"Then (so tradition sings) the train behind,
In plumy zones of rainbow'd beauty dress'd,
Rode the Great Spirit in th' obedient wind,
In yellow clouds slow-sailing from the west.
With dawning smiles the God his votaries bless'd,
And taught where deer retired to ivy dell;
What chosen chief with proud command t' invest;
Where crept th' approaching foe, with purpose fell,
And where to wind the scout, and war's dark storm dispel.

"There, on her lover's tomb, in silence laid,
While still and sorrowing shower'd the moon's pale beam,
At times expectant, slept the widow'd maid,
Her soul far-wandering on the sylph-wing'd dream.
Wafted from evening skies on sunny stream,
Her darling youth with silver pinions shone;
With voice of music, tuned to sweetest theme,
He told of shell-bright bowers beyond the sun,
Where years of endless joy o'er Indian lovers run.

"But now nor awful rites nor potent spell
To silence charm'd the peals of coming war;
Or told the dread recesses of the dell,
Where glowing Mason led his bands from far:
No spirit, buoyant on his airy car,
Controll'd the whirlwind of invading fight:
Deep died in blood, dun evening's falling star
Sent sad o'er western hills its parting light,
And no returning morn dispersed the long dark night

"On the drear walls a sudden splendour glow'd,
There Mason shone, and there his veterans pour'd.

Anew the hero claim'd the fiends of blood, [er'd,
While answering storms of arrows round him show-
And the war-scream the ear with anguish gored.
Alone he burst the gate : the forest round
Re-echoed death ; the peal of onset roar'd ;
In rush'd the squadrons ; earth in blood was drown'd ;
And gloomy spirits fled, and corses hid the ground

"Not long in dubious fight the host had striven,
When, kindled by the musket's potent flame,
In clouds and fire the castle rose to heaven,
And gloom'd the world with melancholy beam.
Then hoarser groans with deeper anguish came,
And fiercer fight the keen assault repell'd :
Nor even these ills the savage breast could tame ;
Like hell's deep caves the hideous region yell'd,
'Till death and sweeping fire laid waste the hostile
field.

"Soon the sad tale their friends surviving heard,
And Mason, Mason, rung in every wind :
Quick from their rugged wilds they disappear'd,
Howl'd down the hills, and left the blast behind.
Their fastening foes by generous Stoughton join'd,
Hung o'er the rear, and every brake explored ;
But such dire terror seized the savage mind,
So swift and black a storm behind them lower'd,
On wings of raging fear, through spacious realms
they scoured.

* * * * * * * *

"Amid a circling marsh expanded wide,
To a lone hill the Pequods wound their way ;
And none but Heaven the mansion had descried,
Close-tangled, wild, impervious to the day ;
But one poor wanderer, loitering long astray,
Wilder'd in labyrinths of pathless wood,
In a tall tree imbower'd, obscurely lay : [show'd
Straight summon'd down, the trembling suppliant
Where lurk'd his vanish'd friends within their drear
abode.

"To death the murderers were anew required,
A pardon proffer'd, and a peace assured;
And, though with vengeful heat their foes were fired,
Their lives, their freedom, and their lands secured.
Some yielding heard. In fastness strong immured,
The rest the terms refused with brave disdain;
Near and more near the peaceful herald lured,
Then bade a shower of arrows round him rain,
And wing'd him swift from danger to the distant plain.

"Through the sole, narrow way, to vengeance led,
To final fight our generous heroes drew;
And Stoughton now had pass'd the moor's black shade,
When hell's terrific region scream'd anew.
Undaunted on their foes they fiercely flew;
As fierce, the dusky warriors crowd the fight;
Despair inspires; to combat's face they glue;
With groans and shouts they rage, unknowing flight,
And close their sullen eyes in shades of endless night."

Indulge, my native land! indulge the tear,
That steals impassion'd o'er a nation's doom:
To me each twig from Adam's stock is near,
And sorrows fall upon an Indian's tomb.
And oh, ye chiefs! in yonder starry home,
Accept the humble tribute of this rhyme.
Your gallant deeds in Greece or haughty Rome,
By Maro sung or Homer's harp sublime,
Had charm'd the world's wide round, and triumph'd over time.

John Trumbull.

CHARACTER OF M'FINGAL.

When Yankees, skill'd in martial rule,
First put the British troops to school;
Instructed them in warlike trade,
And new manœuvres of parade;
The true war-dance of Yankee-reels,
And *manual exercise* of heels;
Made them give up, like saints complete,
The arm of flesh, and trust the feet,
And work, like Christians undissembling,
Salvation out by fear and trembling;
Taught Percy fashionable races,
And modern modes of Chevy-Chaces:*
From Boston, in his best array,
Great Squire M'Fingal took his way,
And, graced with ensigns of renown,
Steer'd homeward to his native town.
His high descent our heralds trace
To Ossian's famed Fingalian race;
For though their name some part may lack,
Old Fingal spelt it with a Mac;
Which great M'Pherson, with submission,
We hope will add the next edition.
His fathers flourish'd in the Highlands
Of Scotia's fog-benighted islands;
Whence gain'd our squire two gifts by right,
Rebellion and the second-sight.
Of these the first, in ancient days,
Had gain'd the noblest palms of praise,
'Gainst kings stood forth, and many a crown'd
With terror of its might confounded; [head

* Lord Percy commanded the party that was first opposed by the Americans at Lexington. This allusion to the family renown of Chevy-Chace arose from the precipitate manner of his quitting the field of battle, and returning to Boston.

Till rose a king with potent charm
His foes by goodness to disarm;
Whom ev'ry Scot and Jacobite
Straight fell in love with—at first sight;
Whose gracious speech, with aid of pensions,
Hush'd down all murmurs of dissensions,
And with the sound of potent metal,
Brought all their blust'ring swarms to settle;
Who rain'd his ministerial mannas,
Till loud Sedition sung hosannas;
The good lords-bishops and the kirk
United in the public work;
Rebellion from the northern regions,
With Bute and Mansfield swore allegiance,
And all combined to raze, as nuisance,
Of church and state, the constitutions;
Pull down the empire, on whose ruins
They meant to edify their new ones;
Enslave the Amer'can wildernesses,
And tear the provinces in pieces.
For these our squire, among the valient'st,
Employ'd his time, and tools, and talents;
And in their cause, with manly zeal,
Used his first virtue to rebel;
And found this new rebellion pleasing
As his old king-destroying treason.
  Nor less avail'd his optic sleight,
And Scottish gift of second-sight.
No ancient sibyl famed in rhyme,
Saw deeper in the womb of time;
No block in old Dodona's grove
Could ever more orac'lar prove.
Nor only saw he all that was,
But much that never came to pass;
Whereby all prophets far outwent he,
Though former days produced a plenty:
For any man with half an eye,
What stands before him may espy;

But optics sharp it needs, I ween,
To see what is not to be seen.
As in the days of ancient fame,
Prophets and poets were the same,
And all the praise that poets gain
Is but for what th' invent and feign:
So gain'd our squire his fame by seeing
Such things as never would have being.
Whence he for oracles was grown
The very tripod of his town.
Gazettes no sooner rose a lie in,
But straight he fell to prophesying;
Made dreadful slaughter in his course,
O'erthrew provincials, foot and horse;
Brought armies o'er by sudden pressings
Of Hanoverians, Swiss, and Hessians;
Feasted with blood his Scottish clan,
And hang'd all rebels to a man;
Divided their estates and pelf,
And took a goodly share himself.*
All this with spirit energetic,
He did by second-sight prophetic.
Thus stored with intellectual riches,
Skill'd was our squire in making speeches.
Where strength of brains united centres
With strength of lungs surpassing Stentor's.
But as some muskets so contrive it,
As oft to miss the mark they drive at,
And, though well aim'd at duck or plover,
Bear wide and kick their owners over:
So fared our squire, whose reas'ning toil
Would often on himself recoil,

* This prophecy, like some of the prayers of Homer's heroes, was but half accomplished. The Hanoverians, &c., indeed came over, and much were they feasted with blood; but the hanging of the rebels and the dividing their estates remain unfulfilled. This, however, cannot be the fault of our hero, but rather the British minister, who left off the war before the work was completed.

And so much injured more his side,
The stronger arg'ments he applied;
As old war-elephants, dismay'd,
Trod down the troops they came to aid,
And hurt their own side more in battle
Than less and ordinary cattle:
Yet at town meetings ev'ry chief
Pinn'd faith on great M'Fingal's sleeve,
And, as he motioned all by rote,
Raised sympathetic hands to vote.
The town, our hero's scene of action,
Had long been torn by feuds of faction;
And as each party's strength prevails,
It turn'd up diff'rent heads or tails;
With constant rattling, in a trice
Show'd various sides, as oft as dice:
As that famed weaver, wife t' Ulysses,
By night each day's work pick'd in pieces·
And though she stoutly did bestir her,
Its finishing was ne'er the nearer:
So did this town with steadfast zeal,
Weave cobwebs for the public weal,
Which, when completed, or before,
A second vote in pieces tore.
They met, made speeches full long-winded,
Resolved, protested, and rescinded;
Addresses sign'd, then chose committees,
To stop all drinking of Bohea-teas;
With winds of doctrine veer'd about,
And turn'd all Whig committees out.
Meanwhile our hero, as their head,
In pomp the Tory faction led,
Still following, as the squire should please,
Successive on. like files of geese.

St. John Honeywood.

INEFFICACY OF PUNISHMENTS.

With stronger force than fear temptations draw,
And cunning thinks to parry with the law.
"My brother swung, poor novice in his art,
He blindly stumbled on a hangman's cart;
But wiser I, assuming every shape,
As Proteus erst, am certain to escape."
The knave, thus jeering, on his skill relies,
For never villain deemed himself unwise. [wide,
When earth convulsive heaved, and, yawning
Ingulfed in darkness Lisbon's spiry pride,
At that dread hour of ruin and dismay
'Tis famed the harden'd felon prowled for prey;
Nor trembling earth nor thunders could restrain
His daring feet, which trod the sinking fane;
Whence, while the fabric to its centre shook,
By impious stealth the hallowed vase he took.
What time the gaping, vulgar throng to see
The wretch expire on Tyburn's fatal tree,
Fast by the crowd the luckier villain clings,
And pilfers while the hapless culprit swings.

William Clifton.

ANCIENT AND MODERN LITERATURE.

When Truth in classic majesty appear'd,
And Greece on high the dome of Science rear'd,
Patience and Perseverance, Care and Pain,
Alone the steep, the rough ascent could gain:
None but the great the sun-clad summit found;
The weak were baffled, and the strong were crown'd.
The tardy transcript's high-wrought page confined
To one pursuit the undivided mind.

No venal critic fattened on the trade,
Books for delight, and not for sale were made;
Then shone superior in the realms of thought,
The chief who govern'd, and the sage who taught;
The drama then with deathless bays was wreath'd,
The statue quicken'd, and the canvass breathed.
The poet, then, with unresisted art,
Sway'd every impulse of the captive heart.
Touch'd with a beam of Heaven's creative mind,
His spirit kindled, and his taste refined:
Incessant toil inform'd his rising youth;
Thought grew to thought, and truth attracted truth,
Till, all complete, his perfect soul display'd
Some bloom of genius that could never fade.
So the sage oak, to Nature's mandate true,
Advanced but slow, and strengthen'd as he grew!
But when at length (full many a season o'er)
His head the blossoms of high promise bore;
When steadfast were his roots, and sound his heart,
He bade oblivion and decay depart;
And, storm and time defying, still remains
The never-dying glory of the plains.

Then, if some thoughtless Bavius dared appear,
Short was his date, and limited his sphere;
He could but please the changeling mob a day,
Then, like his noxious labours, pass away:
So, near a forest tall, some worthless flower
Enjoys the triumphs of its gaudy hour,
Scatters its little poison through the skies,
Then droops its empty, hated head, and dies.

Still, as from famed Ilyssus' classic shore,
To Mincius' banks the Muse her laurel bore,
The sacred plant to hands divine was given,
And deathless Maro nursed the boon of Heaven.
Exalted bard! to hear thy gentler voice,
The valleys listen, and their swains rejoice;
But when, on some wild mountain's awful form,
We hear thy spirit chanting to the storm,

Of battling chiefs, and armies laid in gore,
We rage, we sigh, we wonder and adore.
Thus Rome with Greece in rival splendour shone,
But claim'd immortal satire for her own:
While Horace pierced full oft the wanton breast
With sportive censure and resistless jest;
And that Etrurian, whose indignant lay
Thy kindred genius* can so well display,
With many a well-aimed thought and pointed line,
Drove the bold villain from his black design.
For as those mighty masters of the lyre,
With temper'd dignity or quenchless ire,
Through all the various paths of science trod,
Their school was Nature, and their teacher God.

Nor did the Muse decline, till o'er her head
The savage tempest of the North was spread
Till arm'd with desolation's bolt it came,
And wrapp'd her temple in funereal flame.

But soon the Arts once more a dawn diffuse,
And Petrarch hail'd it with his morning muse;
Boccace and Dante join'd the choral lay,
And Arno glisten'd with returning day.
Thus Science rose; and, all her troubles pass'd,
She hoped a steady, tranquil reign at last;
But Faustus came: (indulge the painful thought),
Were not his countless volumes dearly bought;
For, while to every clime and class they flew,
Their worth diminish'd as their numbers grew.
Some pressman, rich in Homer's wealthy page,
Could give ten epics to one wondering age;
A single thought supplied the great design,
And clouds of Iliads spread from every line.
Nor Homer's glowing page, nor Virgil's fire,
Could one lone breast with equal flame inspire;

* These lines were addressed to the English satirist William Gifford

But, lost in books, irregular and wild,
The poet wonder'd, and the critic smiled:
The friendly smile a bulkier work repays;
For fools will print, while greater fools will praise.

Washington Allston.

THE SYLPH OF SPRING.

Then spake the Sylph of Spring serene.
'Tis *I* thy joyous heart, I ween,
With sympathy shall move:
For I with living melody
Of birds in choral symphony,
First waked thy soul to poesy,
To piety and love.

When thou, at call of vernal breeze,
And beck'ning bough of budding trees,
Hast left thy sullen fire;
And stretch'd thee in some mossy dell,
And heard the browsing wether's bell,
Blythe echoes rousing from their cell
To swell the tinkling quire:

Or heard from branch of flow'ring thorn
The song of friendly cuckoo warn
The tardy-moving swain;
Hast bid the purple swallow hail;
And seen him now through ether sail,
Now sweeping downward o'er the vale,
And skimming now the plain;

Then, catching with a sudden glance
The bright and silver-clear expanse
Of some broad river's stream,
Beheld the boats adown it glide,
And motion wind again the tide,
Where, chain'd in ice by Winter's pride,
Late roll'd the heavy team:

Or, lured by some fresh-scented gale,
That woo'd the moored fishers' sail
    To tempt the mighty main,
Hast watch'd the dim receding shore,
Now faintly seen the ocean o'er,
Like hanging cloud, and now no more
    To bound the sapphire plain;

Then, wrapped in night, the scudding bark
(That seem'd, self-poised amid the dark,
    Through upper air to leap),
Beheld, from thy most fearful height,
The rapid dolphin's azure light
Cleave, like a living meteor bright,
    The darkness of the deep:

'Twas mine the warm, awakening hand
That made thy grateful heart expand,
    And feel the high control
Of Him, the mighty Power, that moves
Amid the waters and the groves,
And through his vast creation proves
    His omnipresent soul.

Or, brooding o'er some forest rill,
Fringed with the early daffodil,
    And quiv'ring maiden-hair,
When thou hast mark'd the dusky bed,
With leaves and water-rust o'erspread,
That seem'd an amber light to shed
    On all was shadow'd there;

And thence, as by its murmur call'd,
The current traced to where it brawl'd
    Beneath the noontide ray;
And there beheld the checker'd shade
Of waves, in many a sinuous braid,
That o'er the sunny channel play'd,
    With motion ever gay:

'Twas I to these the magic gave,
That made thy heart, a willing slave,
To gentle Nature bend;
And taught thee how with tree and flower,
And whispering gale, and dropping shower,
In converse sweet to pass the hour,
As with an early friend.

That mid the noontide sunny haze,
Did in thy languid bosom raise
The raptures of the boy;
When, waked as if to second birth,
Thy soul through every pore look'd forth,
And gazed upon the beauteous Earth
With myriad eyes of joy:

That made thy heart, like His above,
To flow with universal love
For every living thing.
And oh! if I, with ray divine,
Thus tempering, did thy soul refine,
Then let thy gentle heart be mine,
And bless the Sylph of Spring.

THE PAINT-KING.

Fair Ellen was long the delight of the young,
No damsel could with her compare;
Her charms were the theme of the heart and the tongue,
And bards without number in ecstasies sung,
The beauties of Ellen the fair.

Yet cold was the maid; and though legions advanced,
All drill'd by Ovidean art,
And languish'd and ogled, protested and danced,
Like shadows they came, and like shadows they glanced
From the hard-polish'd ice of her heart.

Yet still did the heart of fair Ellen implore
  A something that could not be found;
Like a sailor she seem'd on a desolate shore,
With nor house, nor a tree, nor a sound but the roar
  Of breakers high dashing around.

From object to object still, still would she veer,
  Though nothing, alas! could she find;
Like the moon, without atmosphere, brilliant and clear,
Yet doom'd, like the moon, with no being to cheer
  The bright barren waste of her mind.

But rather than sit like a statue so still
  When the rain made her mansion a *pound*,
Up and down would she go, like the sails of a mill,
And pat every stair, like a woodpecker's bill,
  From the tiles of the roof to the ground.

One morn, as the maid from her casement inclined,
  Pass'd a youth with a frame in his hand.
The casement she closed—not the eye of her mind;
For, do all she could, no, she could not be blind;
  Still before her she saw the youth stand.

"Ah, what can he do," said the languishing maid,
  "Ah, what with that frame can he do?"
And she knelt to the goddess of Secrets and pray'd,
When the youth pass'd again, and again he display'd
  The frame and a picture to view.

"Oh, beautiful picture!" the fair Ellen cried,
  "I must see thee again or I die."
Then under her white chin her bonnet she tied,
And after the youth and the picture she hied,
  When the youth, looking back, met her eye.

"Fair damsel," said he (and he chuckled the while),
  "This picture I see you admire:
Then take it, I pray you, perhaps 'twill beguile
Some moments of sorrow (nay, pardon my smile);
  Or at least keep you home by the fire."

Then Ellen the gift with delight and surprise
From the cunning young stripling received.
But she knew not the poison that enter'd her eyes,
When, sparkling with rapture, they gazed on her
Thus, alas, are fair maidens deceived! [prize—

'Twas a youth o'er the form of a statue inclined,
And the sculptor he seem'd of the stone;
Yet he languish'd as though for its beauty he pined,
And gazed as the eyes of the statue so blind
Reflected the beams of his own.

'Twas the tale of the sculptor Pygmalion of old;
Fair Ellen remember'd and sigh'd;
"Ah, couldst thou but lift from that marble so cold,
Thine eyes too imploring, thy arms should enfold,
And press me this day as thy bride."

She said: when, behold, from the canvass arose
The youth, and he stepp'd from the frame:
With a furious transport his arms did enclose
The love-plighted Ellen: and, clasping, he froze
The blood of the maid with his flame!

She turn'd and beheld on each shoulder a wing.
"Oh, heaven!" cried she, "who art thou?" [ring,
From the roof to the ground did his fierce answer
As, frowning, he thunder'd "I am the PAINT-KING!
And mine, lovely maid, thou art now!"

Then high from the ground did the grim monster lift
The loud-screaming maid like a blast;
And he sped through the air like a meteor swift,
While the clouds, wand'ring by him, did fearfully
To the right and the left as he pass'd. [drift

Now suddenly sloping his hurricane flight,
With an eddying whirl he descends;
The air all below him becomes black as night,
And the ground where he treads, as if moved with
affright,
Like the surge of the Caspian bends.

"I am here!" said the fiend, and he thundering
At the gates of a mountainous cave; [knock'd
The gates open flew, as by magic unlock'd,
While the peaks of the mount, reeling to and fro,
Like an island of ice on the wave. [rock'd

"Oh, mercy!" cried Ellen, and swoon'd in his arms,
But the PAINT-KING he scoff'd at her pain.
"Prithee, love," said the monster, "what mean these
alarms?"
She hears not, she sees not the terrible charms,
That work her to horror again.

She opens her lids, but no longer her eyes
Behold the fair youth she would woo;
Now appears the PAINT-KING in his natural guise;
His face, like a palette of villanous dyes,
Black and white, red and yellow, and blue.

On the scull of a Titan, that Heaven defied,
Sat the fiend, like the grim giant Gog,
While aloft to his mouth a huge pipe he applied,
Twice as big as the Eddystone lighthouse, descried
As it looms through an easterly fog.

And anon, as he puff'd the vast volumes, were seen,
In horrid festoons on the wall,
Legs and arms, heads and bodies emerging between,
Like the drawing-room grim of the Scotch Sawney
By the devil dress'd out for a ball. [Beane,

"Ah me!" cried the damsel, and fell at his feet.
"Must I hang on these walls to be dried?" [seat,
"Oh, no!" said the fiend, while he sprung from his
"A far nobler fortune thy person shall meet;
Into paint will I grind thee, my bride!"

Then seizing the maid by her dark auburn hair,
An oil jug he plunged her within.
Seven days, seven nights, with the shrieks of despair,
Did Ellen in torment convulse the dun air,
All covered with oil to the chin.

On the morn of the eighth, on a huge sable stone,
  Then Ellen, all reeking, he laid;
With a rock for his muller he crush'd every bone,
But, though ground to jelly, still, still did she groan,
  For life had forsook not the maid.

Now reaching his palette, with masterly care
  Each tint on its surface he spread;
The blue of her eyes, and the brown of her hair,
And the pearl and the white of her forehead so fair,
  And her lips' and her cheeks' rosy red.

Then, stamping his foot, did the monster exclaim,
  " Now I brave, cruel Fairy, thy scorn!"
When lo! from a chasm wide-yawning there came
A light tiny chariot of rose-colour'd flame,
  By a team of ten glow-worms upborne.

Enthroned in the midst on an emerald bright,
  Fair Geraldine sat without peer;
Her robe was a gleam of the first blush of light,
And her mantle the fleece of a noon-cloud white,
  And a beam of the moon was her spear.

In an accent that stole on the still charmed air
  Like the first gentle language of Eve,
Thus spake from her chariot the fairy so fair:
" I come at thy call, but, oh Paint-King, beware,
  Beware if again you deceive."

" 'Tis true," said the monster, " thou queen of my heart,
  Thy portrait I oft have essay'd;
Yet ne'er to the canvass could I with my art
The least of thy wonderful beauties impart;
  And my failure with scorn you repaid.

" Now I swear by the light of the Comet-King's tail!"
  And he tower'd with pride as he spoke,
" If again with these magical colours I fail,
The crater of Etna shall hence be my jail,
  And my food shall be sulphur and smoke.

"But if I succeed, then, oh, fair Geraldine!
  Thy promise with justice I claim,
And thou, queen of fairies, shalt ever be mine,
The bride of my bed; and thy portrait divine
  Shall fill all the earth with my fame."

He spake; when, behold, the fair Geraldine's form
  On the canvass enchantingly glow'd;
His touches—they flew like the leaves in a storm;
And the pure pearly white and the carnation warm
  Contending in harmony flow'd.

And now did the portrait a twin-sister seem
  To the figure of Geraldine fair:
With the same sweet expression did faithfully teem
Each muscle, each feature; in short, not a gleam
  Was lost of her beautiful hair.

'Twas the fairy herself! but alas! her blue eyes
  Still a pupil did ruefully lack;
And who shall describe the terrific surprise
That seized the PAINT-KING when, behold, he descries
  Not a speck on his palette of black!

"I am lost!" said the fiend, and he shook like a leaf;
  When, casting his eyes to the ground,
He saw the lost pupils of Ellen with grief
In the jaws of a mouse, and the sly little thief
  Whisk away from his sight with a bound.

"I am lost!" said the fiend, and he fell like a stone;
  Then rising, the fairy, in ire,
With a touch of her finger she loosen'd her zone
(While the limbs on the wall gave a terrible groan),
  And she swelled to a column of fire.

Her spear now a thunder-bolt flash'd in the air,
  And sulphur the vault fill'd around:
She smote the grim monster; and now by the hair,
High-lifting, she hurl'd him in speechless despair
  Down the depths of the chasm profound.

Then over the picture thrice waving her spear,
  " Come forth !" said the good Geraldine ;
When, behold, from the canvass descending, appear
Fair Ellen, in person more lovely than e'er,
  With grace more than ever divine !

ROSALIE.

Oh, pour upon my soul again
    That sad, unearthly strain,
That seems from other worlds to plain ;
Thus falling, falling from afar,
As if some melancholy star
Had mingled with her light her sighs
    And dropped them from the skies.

No—never came from aught below
    This melody of wo,
That makes my heart to overflow
As from a thousand gushing springs
Unknown before : that with it brings
This nameless light—if light it be—
    That veils the world I see.

For all I see around me wears
    The hue of other spheres ;
And something blent of smiles and tears
Comes from the very air I breathe.
Oh, nothing, sure, the stars beneath,
Can mould a sadness like to this—
    So like angelic bliss.

So, at that dreamy hour of day
    When the last lingering ray
Stops on the highest cloud to play—
So thought the gentle Rosalie
As on her maiden revery
First fell the strain of him who stole
    In music to her soul.

RICHARD H. DANA.

MURDER OF A SPANISH LADY BY A PIRATE.

A sound is in the Pyrenees!
Whirling and dark, comes roaring down
A tide, as of a thousand seas,
Sweeping both cowl and crown.
On field and vineyard thick and red it stood.
Spain's streets and palaces are full of blood;

And wrath and terror shake the land;
The peaks shine clear in watchfire lights;
Soon comes the tread of that stout band—
Bold Arthur and his knights.
Awake ye, Merlin! Hear the shout from Spain!
The spell is broke! Arthur is come again!

Too late for thee, thou young, fair bride;
The lips are cold, the brow is pale,
That thou didst kiss in love and pride.
He cannot hear thy wail, [sound—
Whom thou didst lull with fondly murmur'd
His couch is cold and lonely in the ground.

He fell for Spain—her Spain no more;
For he was gone who made it dear;
And she would seek some distant shore,
At rest from strife and fear,
And wait amid her sorrows till the day
His voice of love should call her thence away.

Lee feign'd him grieved, and bow'd him low.
'Twould joy his heart could he but aid
So good a lady in her wo,
He meekly, smoothly said.
With wealth and servants she is soon aboard,
And that white steed she rode beside her lord.

The sun goes down upon the sea;
The shadows gather round her home.
"How like a pall are ye to me!
My home, how like a tomb!
Oh! blow, ye flowers of Spain, above his head:
Ye will not blow o'er me when I am dead."

And now the stars are burning bright;
Yet still she looks towards the shore,
Beyond the waters black in night.
"I ne'er shall see thee more!
Ye're many, waves, yet lonely seems your flow,
And I'm alone—scarce know I where I go."

Sleep, sleep, thou sad one, on the sea!
The wash of waters lulls thee now;
His arm no more will pillow thee,
Thy hand upon his brow.
He is not near, to hush thee or to save.
The ground is his, the sea must be thy grave.

The moon comes up, the night goes on.
Why in the shadow of the mast,
Stands that dark, thoughtful man alone?
Thy pledge, man; keep it fast!
Bethink thee of her youth and sorrows, Lee:
Helpless alone—and then her trust in thee!

When told the hardships thou hadst borne,
Her words were to thee like a charm.
With uncheer'd grief her heart is worn.
Thou wilt not do her harm!
He looks out on the sea that sleeps in light,
And growls an oath: "It is too still to-night!"

He sleeps; but dreams of massy gold,
And heaps of pearl. He stretch'd his hands.
He hears a voice: "Ill man, withhold."
A pale one near him stands:
Her breath comes deathly cold upon his cheek;
Her touch is cold. He wakes with piercing shriek.

He wakes; but no relentings wake
Within his angry, restless soul.
"What, shall a dream Matt's purpose shake?
The gold will make all whole.
Thy merchant trade had nigh unmann'd thee, lad!
What, balk thy chance because a woman's sad?"

He cannot look on her mild eye—
Her patient words his spirit quell.
Within that evil heart there lie
The hates and fears of hell.
His speech is short; he wears a surly brow.
There's none will hear her shriek. What fear ye now?

The workings of the soul ye fear;
Ye fear the power that goodness hath;
Ye fear the Unseen One, ever near,
Walking his ocean path.
From out the silent void there comes a cry:
"Vengeance is mine! Lost man, thy doom is nigh!"

Nor dread of ever-during wo,
Nor the sea's awful solitude,
Can make thee, wretch, thy crime forego.
Then, bloody hand—to blood!
The scud is driving wildly over head;
The stars burn dim; the ocean moans its dead.

Moan for the living—moan our sins—
The wrath of man, more fierce than thine.
Hark! still thy waves! The work begins:
He makes the deadly sign.
The crew glide down like shadows. Eye and hand
Speak fearful meanings through that silent band.

They're gone. The helmsman stands alone,
And one leans idly o'er the bow.
Still as a tomb the ship keeps on;
Nor sound nor stirring now.

Hush, hark! as from the centre of the deep,
Shrieks! fiendish yells! They stab them in their
sleep.

The scream of rage, the groan, the strife,
The blow, the gasp, the horrid cry,
The panting, stifled prayer for life,
The dying's heaving sigh, [glare,
The murderer's curse, the dead man's fix'd, still
And Fear's, and Death's cold sweat—they all are
there!

On pale, dead men, on burning cheek,
On quick, fierce eyes, brows hot and damp,
On hands that with the warm blood reek,
Shines the dim cabin lamp.
Lee look'd. "They sleep so sound," he laughing
said,
"They'll scarcely wake for mistress or for maid."

A crash! They've forced the door; and then
One long, long, shrill, and piercing scream
Comes thrilling through the growl of men.
'Tis hers! Oh God, redeem [child!
From worse than death thy suffering, helpless
That dreadful cry again—sharp, sharp, and wild!

It ceased. With speed o' th' lightning's flash,
A loose-robed form, with streaming hair,
Shoots by. A leap! a quick, short splash!
'Tis gone! There's nothing there!
The waves have swept away the bubbling tide.
Bright-crested waves, how proudly on ye ride!

She's sleeping in her silent cave,
Nor hears the stern, loud roar above,
Or strife of man on land or wave.
Young thing! thy home of love
Thou soon hast reach'd! Fair, unpolluted thing,
They harm'd thee not! Was dying suffering?

Oh, no! To live when joy was dead;
To go with one, lone, pining thought—
To mournful love thy being wed—
Feeling what death had wrought;
To live the child of wo, yet shed no tear,
Bear kindness, and yet share no joy nor fear;

To look on man, and deem it strange
That he on things of earth should brood,
When all its throng'd and busy range
To thee was solitude—
Oh, this was bitterness! Death came and press'd
Thy wearied lids, and brought thy sick heart rest.

THE HUSBAND'S AND WIFE'S GRAVE.

Husband and wife! No converse now ye hold,
As once ye did in your young days of love,
On its alarms, its anxious hours, delays,
Its silent meditations, its glad hopes,
Its fears, impatience, quiet sympathies;
Nor do ye speak of joy assured, and bliss
Full, certain, and possess'd. Domestic cares
Call you not now together. Earnest talk
On what your children may be, moves you not.
Ye lie in silence, and an awful silence;
'Tis not like that in which ye rested once
Most happy—silence eloquent, when heart
With heart held speech, and your mysterious frames,
Harmonious, sensitive, at every beat
Touch'd the soft notes of love.

Stillness profound,
Insensible, unheeding, folds you round;
And darkness, as a stone, has seal'd you in.
Away from all the living, here ye rest:
In all the nearness of the narrow tomb,
Yet feel ye not each other's presence now.
Dread fellowship! together, yet alone.

Is this thy prison-house, thy grave, then, Love?
And doth death cancel the great bond that holds
Commingling spirits? Are thoughts that know no
bounds,
But, self-inspired, rise upward, searching out
The eternal Mind—the Father of all thought—
Are they become mere tenants of a tomb?
Dwellers in darkness, who th' illuminate realms
Of uncreated light have visited and lived?
Lived in the dreadful splendour of that throne,
Which One, with gentle hand the veil of flesh
Lifting, that hung 'twixt man and it, reveal'd
In glory? throne, before which even now
Our souls, moved by prophetic power, bow down
Rejoicing, yet at their own natures awed?
Souls that Thee know by a mysterious sense,
Thou awful, unseen presence—are they quenched,
Or burn they on, hid from our mortal eyes
By that bright day which ends not, as the sun
His robe of light flings round the glittering stars?

And with our frames do perish all our loves?
Do those that took their root and put forth buds,
And their soft leaves unfolded in the warmth
Of mutual hearts, grow up and live in beauty,
Then fade and fall, like fair unconscious flowers?
Are thoughts and passions that to the tongue give
speech,
And make it send forth winning harmonies,
That to the cheek do give its living glow,
And vision in the eye the soul intense
With that for which there is no utterance—
Are these the body's accidents? no more?
To live in it, and when that dies, go out
Like the burnt taper's flame?

Oh, listen, man!
A voice within us speaks that startling word,
"Man, thou shalt never die!" Celestial voices
Hymn it unto our souls: according harps,

By angel fingers touch'd when the mild stars
Of morning sang together, sound forth still
The song of our great immortality:
Thick clustering orbs, and this our fair domain,
The tall, dark mountains, and the deep-toned seas
Join in this solemn, universal song.
Oh, listen, ye, our spirits; drink it in
From all the air! 'Tis in the gentle moonlight;
'Tis floating midst day's setting glories; Night,
Wrapped in her sable robe, with silent step
Comes to our bed and breathes it in our ears:
Night, and the dawn, bright day, and thoughtful eve,
All time, all bounds, the limitless expanse,
As one vast mystic instrument, are touch'd
By an unseen, living Hand, and conscious chords
Quiver with joy in this great jubilee.
The dying hear it; and as sounds of earth
Grow dull and distant, wake their passing souls
To mingle in this heavenly harmony.

Why is it that I linger round this tomb?
What holds it? Dust that cumber'd those I mourn.
They shook it off, and laid aside earth's robes,
And put on those of light. They're gone to dwell
In love—their God's and angels'. Mutual love,
That bound them here, no longer needs a speech
For full communion; nor sensations strong,
Within the breast, their prison, strive in vain
To be set free, and meet their kind in joy.
Changed to celestials, thoughts that rise in each,
By natures new, impart themselves, though silent.
Each quick'ning sense, each throb of holy love,
Affections sanctified, and the full glow
Of being, which expand and gladden one,
By union all mysterious, thrill and live
In both immortal frames: Sensation all,
And thought, pervading, mingling sense and thought!
Ye pair'd, yet one! wrapped in a consciousness
Twofold, yet single—this is love, this life!

Why call we, then, the square-built monument,
The upright column, and the low-laid slab,
Tokens of death, memorials of decay?
Stand in this solemn, still assembly, man,
And learn thy proper nature; for thou see'st,
In these shaped stones and letter'd tables, figures
Of life: More are they to thy soul than those
Which he who talk'd on Sinai's mount with God
Brought to the old Judeans—types are these,
Of thine eternity.

I thank thee, Father,
That at this simple grave, on which the dawn
Is breaking, emblem of that day which hath
No close, Thou kindly unto my dark mind
Hast sent a sacred light, and that away
From this green hillock, whither I had come
In sorrow, Thou art leading me in joy

DAYBREAK.

"The Pilgrim they laid in a large upper chamber, whose window opened towards the sun rising: the name of the chamber was Peace; where he slept till break of day, and then he awoke and sang."—*The Pilgrim's Progress.*

Now, brighter than the host that all night long,
In fiery armour, up the heavens high
Stood watch, thou comest to wait the morning's song,
Thou comest to tell me day again is nigh.
Star of the dawning, cheerful is thine eye,
And yet in the broad day it must grow dim.
Thou seem'st to look on me, as asking why
My mourning eyes with silent tears do swim;
Thou bid'st me turn to God, and seek my rest in Him.

"Canst thou grow sad," thou say'st, "as earth grows bright?
And sigh, when little birds begin discourse
In quick, low voices, ere the streaming light
Pours on their nests, as sprung from day's fresh source?

With creatures innocent thou must perforce
A sharer be, if that thine heart be pure.
And holy hour like this, save sharp remorse,
Of ills and pains of life must be the cure,
And breathe in kindred calm, and teach thee to endure."

I feel its calm. But there's a sombrous hue
Along that eastern cloud of deep, dull red;
Nor glitters yet the cold and heavy dew;
And all the woods and hilltops stand outspread
With dusky lights, which warmth nor comfort shed.
Still—save the bird that scarcely lifts its song—
The vast world seems the tomb of all the dead—
The silent city emptied of its throng,
And ended, all alike, grief, mirth, love, hate, and wrong.

But wrong, and hate, and love, and grief, and mirth
Will quicken soon; and hard, hot toil and strife,
With headlong purpose, shake this sleeping earth
With discord strange, and all that man calls life.
With thousand scatter'd beauties nature's rife;
And airs, and woods, and streams breathe harmonies:
Man weds not these, but taketh art to wife;
Nor binds his heart with soft and kindly ties:
He, feverish, blinded, lives, and, feverish, sated, dies.

And 'tis because man useth so amiss
Her dearest blessings, Nature seemeth sad;
Else why should she in such fresh hour as this
Not lift the veil, in revelation glad,
From her fair face? It is that man is mad!
Then chide me not, clear star, that I repine
When Nature grieves: nor deem this heart is bad.
Thou look'st towards earth; but yet the heavens are thine,
While I to earth am bound: When will the heavens be mi–

If man would but his finer nature learn,
And not in life fantastic lose the sense
Of simpler things; could Nature's features stern
Teach him be thoughtful; then, with soul intense,
I should not yearn for God to take me hence,
But bear my lot, albeit in spirit bow'd,
Remembering humbly why it is, and whence:
But when I see cold man, of reason proud,
My solitude is sad—I'm lonely in the crowd.

But not for this alone, the silent tear
Steals to mine eyes, while looking on the morn,
Nor for this solemn hour: fresh life is near;
But all my joys! they died when newly born.
Thousands will wake to joy; while I, forlorn,
And, like the stricken dear, with sickly eye, [torn;
Shall see them pass. Breathe calm—my spirit's
Ye holy thoughts, lift up my soul on high! [nigh.
Ye hopes of things unseen, the far-off world bring

And when I grieve, oh rather let it be
That I, whom Nature taught to sit with her
On her proud mountains, by her rolling sea;
Who, when the winds are up, with mighty stir
Of woods and waters, feel the quick'ning spur
To my strong spirit; who, as mine own child,
Do love the flower, and in the ragged bur
A beauty see: that I this mother mild [and wild!
Should leave, and go with care, and passions fierce

How suddenly that straight and glittering shaft
Shot 'thwart the earth! In crown of living fire
Up comes the Day! As if they conscious quaff'd
The sunny flood, hill, forest, city, spire
Laugh in the wakening light. Go, vain Desire!
The dusky lights have gone; go thou thy way!
And pining Discontent, like them, expire!
Be call'd my chamber, PEACE, when ends the day;
And let me with the dawn, like PILGRIM, sing and
pray!

Nathaniel P. Willis.

THE BAPTISM OF CHRIST.

It was a green spot in the wilderness,
Touch'd by the river Jordan. The dark pine
Never had dropp'd its tassels on the moss
Tufting the leaning bank, nor on the grass
Of the broad circle stretching evenly
To the straight larches, had a heavier foot
Than the wild heron's trodden. Softly in
Through a long aisle of willows, dim and cool,
Stole the clear waters with their muffled feet,
And hushing as they spread into the light,
Circled the edges of the pebbled tank
Slowly, then rippled through the woods away.

Hither had come th' apostle of the wild,
Winding the river's course. 'Twas near the flush
Of eve, and, with a multitude around,
Who from the cities had come out to hear,
He stood breast high amid the running stream,
Baptizing as the Spirit gave him power.
His simple raiment was of camel's hair,
A leathern girdle close about his loins,
His beard unshorn, and his daily meat
The locust and wild honey of the wood;
But like the face of Moses on the mount
Shone his rapt countenance, and in his eye
Burn'd the mild fire of love, as he spoke
The ear lean'd to him, and persuasion swift
To the chain'd spirit of the listener stole.

Silent upon the green and sloping bank
The people sat, and while the leaves were shook
With the birds dropping early to their nests,
And the gray eve came on, within their hearts
They mused if he were Christ. The rippling stream

Still turn'd its silver courses from his breast
As he divined their thought. "I but baptize,"
He said, "with water; but there cometh One
The latchet of whose shoes I may not dare
Even to unloose. He will baptize with fire
And with the Holy Ghost." And lo! while yet
The words were on his lips, he raised his eyes,
And on the bank stood Jesus. He had laid
His raiment off, and with his loins alone
Girt with a mantle, and his perfect limbs,
In their angelic slightness, meek and bare,
He waited to go in. But John forbade,
And hurried to his feet and stay'd him there,
And said, "Nay, Master! I have need of *thine*,
Not thou of *mine!*" And Jesus, with a smile
Of heavenly sadness, met his earnest looks,
And answered, "Suffer it to be so now;
For thus it doth become me to fulfil
All righteousness." And, leaning to the stream,
He took around him the apostle's arm,
And drew him gently to the midst.

The wood
Was thick with the dim twilight as they came
Up from the water. With his clasp'd hands
Laid on his breast, th' apostle silently
Followed his Master's steps; when lo! a light,
Bright as the tenfold glory of the sun,
Yet lambent as the softly burning stars,
Enveloped them, and from the heavens away
Parted the dim blue ether like a veil;
And as a voice, fearful exceedingly,
Broke from the midst, "THIS IS MY MUCH-LOVED SON,
IN WHOM I AM WELL PLEASED," a snow-white dove,
Floating upon its wings, descended through,
And, shedding a swift music from its plumes,
Circled and flutter'd to the Saviour's breast.

SPRING.

"L'onda del mar divisa
Bagna la valle e l'monte,
Va passegiera
In fiume,
Va prigionera
In fonte,
Mormora sempre e geme
Fin che non torna al mar."
METASTASIO.

THE Spring is here, the delicate-footed May,
With its slight fingers full of leaves and flowe
And with it comes a thirst to be away,
Wasting in wood-paths its voluptuous hours :
A feeling that is like a sense of wings,
Restless to soar above these perishing things.

We pass out from the city's feverish hum,
To find refreshment in the silent woods ;
And Nature, that is beautiful and dumb,
Like a cool sleep upon the pulses broods :
Yet even there a restless thought will steal,
To teach the indolent heart it still must *feel.*

Strange, that the audible stillness of the noon,
The waters tripping with their silver feet,
The turning to the light leaves in June,
And the light whisper as their edges meet :
Strange, that they fill not, with their tranquil tone,
The spirit, walking in their midst alone.

There's no contentment in a world like this,
Save in forgetting the immortal dream ;
We may not gaze upon the stars of bliss,
That through the cloud-rifts radiantly stream ;
Bird-like, the prisoned soul *will* lift its eye,
And pine till it is hooded from the sky.

H

APRIL.

"A violet by a mossy stone
 Half hidden from the eye,
Fair as a star, when only one
 Is shining in the sky."
WORDSWORTH.

I HAVE found violets. April hath come on,
And the cool winds feel softer, and the rain
Falls in the beaded drops of summer time.
You may hear birds at morning, and at eve
The tame dove lingers till the twilight falls,
Cooing upon the eaves, and drawing in
His beautiful bright neck, and, from the hills,
A murmur like the hoarseness of the sea
Tells the release of waters, and the earth
Sends up a pleasant smell, and the dry leaves
Are lifted by the grass; and so I know
That Nature, with her delicate ear, hath heard
The dropping of the velvet foot of Spring.
Take of my violets! I found them where
The liquid South stole o'er them, on a bank
That leaned to running water. There's to me
A daintiness about these early flowers
That touches me like poetry. They blow
With such a simple loveliness among
The common herbs of pasture, and breathe out
Their lives so unobtrusively, like hearts
Whose beatings are too gentle for the world.
I love to go in the capricious days
Of April and hunt violets; when the rain
Is in the blue cups trembling, and they nod
So gracefully to the kisses of the wind.
It may be deem'd too idle, but the young
Read nature like the manuscript of heaven,
And call the flowers its poetry. Go out!
Ye spirits of habitual unrest,
And read it when the "fever of the world"
Hath made your hearts impatient, and, if life

Hath yet one spring unpoisoned, it will be
Like a beguiling music to its flow,
And you will no more wonder that I love
To hunt for violets in the April time.

THE BELFRY PIGEON.

"Mine eyes are sick of this perpetual flow
Of people, and my heart of one sad thought."
SHELLEY.

On the cross beam under the Old South bell
The nest of a pigeon is builded well.
In summer and winter that bird is there,
Out and in with the morning air:
I love to see him track the street,
With his wary eye and active feet;
And I often watch him as he springs,
Circling the steeple with easy wings,
Till across the dial his shade has passed,
And the belfry edge is gained at last.
'Tis a bird I love, with its brooding note,
And the trembling throb in its mottled throat;
There's a human look in its swelling breast,
And the gentle curve of its lowly crest;
And I often stop with the fear I feel—
He runs so close to the rapid wheel.

Whatever is rung on that noisy bell—
Chime of the hour or funeral knell—
The dove in the belfry must hear it well.
When the tongue swings out to the midnight moon—
When the sexton cheerly rings for noon—
When the clock strikes clear at morning light—
When the child is waked with "nine at night"—
When the chimes play soft in the Sabbath air,
Filling the spirit with tones of prayer—
Whatever tale in the bell is heard,
He broods on his folded feet unstirred,

Or rising half in his rounded nest,
He takes the time to smooth his breast,
Then drops again with filmed eyes,
And sleeps as the last vibration dies.

Sweet bird! I would that I could be
A hermit in the crowd like thee!
With wings to fly to wood and glen,
Thy lot, like mine, is cast with men;
And daily, with unwilling feet,
I tread, like thee, the crowded street;
But, unlike me, when day is o'er,
Thou canst dismiss the world and soar,
Or, at a half-felt wish for rest,
Canst smooth thy feathers on thy breast,
And drop, forgetful, to thy nest.

I would that in such wings of gold
I could my weary heart upfold;
I would I could look down unmoved
(Unloving as I am unloved),
And while the world throngs on beneath,
Smooth down my cares and calmly breathe;
And never sad with others' sadness,
And never glad with others' gladness
Listen, unstirred, to knell or chime,
And, lapp'd in quiet, bide my time.

JOSEPH RODMAN DRAKE.

JOURNEY OF THE CULPRIT FAY.

THE goblin marked his monarch well;
He spake not, but he bowed him low,
Then plucked a crimson colen-bell,
And turned him round in act to go.

The way is long, he cannot fly,
  His soiled wing has lost its power,
And he winds adown the mountain high,
  For many a sore and weary hour.
Through dreary beds of tangled fern,
Through groves of nightshade dark and dern,
Over the grass and through the brake,
Where toils the ant and sleeps the snake;
  Now o'er the violet's azure flush
He skips along in lightsome mood;
  And now he thrids the bramble bush,
Till its points are dyed in fairy blood.
He has leaped the bog, he has pierced the brier,
He has swum the brook, and waded the mire,
Till his spirits sank, and his limbs grew weak,
And the red waxed fainter in his cheek.
He had fallen to the ground outright,
  For rugged and dim was his onward track,
But there came a spotted toad in sight,
  And he laughed as he jumped upon her back:
He bridled her mouth with a silk-weed twist;
  He lashed her sides with an osier thong;
And now, through evening's dewy mist,
  With leap and spring they bound along,
Till the mountain's magic verge is pass'd,
And the beach of sand is reached at last.

Soft and pale is the moony beam,
Moveless still the glassy stream,
The wave is clear, the beach is bright
  With snowy shells and sparkling stones;
The shore-surge comes in ripples light,
  In murmurings faint and distant moans;
And ever afar in the silence deep
Is heard the splash of the sturgeon's leap,
And the bend of his graceful bow is seen—
A glittering arch of silver sheen,
Spanning the wave of burnished blue,
And dripping with gems of the river dew.

The elfin cast a glance around,
  As he lighted down from his courser toad,
Then round his breast his wings he wound,
  And close to the river's brink he strode;
He sprang on a rock, he breathed a prayer,
  Above his head his arms he threw,
Then tossed a tiny curve in air,
  And headlong plunged in the waters blue.

Up sprung the spirits of the waves,
From sea-silk beds in their coral caves,
With snail-plate armour snatched in haste,
They speed their way through the liquid waste,
Some are rapidly borne along
On the mailed shrimp or the prickly prong,
Some on the blood-red leeches glide,
Some on the stony starfish ride,
Some on the back of the lancing squab,
Some on the sideling soldier-crab;
And some on the jellied quarl, that flings
At once a thousand streamy stings—
They cut the wave with the living oar,
And hurry on to the moonlight shore,
To guard their realms and chase away
The footsteps of the invading Fay.

Fearlessly he skims along,
His hope is high and his limbs are strong,
He spreads his arms like the swallow's wing,
And throws his feet with a frog-like fling;
His locks of gold on the waters shine,
  At his breast the tiny foam-beads rise,
His back gleams bright above the brine,
  And the wake-line foam behind him lies.
But the water-sprites are gathering near,
  To check his course along the tide;
Their warriors come in swift career,
  And hem him round on every side;
On his thigh the leech has fixed his hold,
The quarl's long arms are round him roll'd,

The prickly prong has pierced his skin,
And the squab has thrown his javelin;
The gritty star has rubbed him raw,
And the crab has struck with his giant claw;
He howls with rage, and he shrieks with pain,
He strikes around, but his blows are vain;
Hopeless is the unequal fight,
Fairy! naught is left but flight.

He turned him round and fled amain
With hurry and dash to the beach again,
He twisted over from side to side,
And laid his cheek to the cleaving tide.
The strokes of his plunging arms are fleet,
And with all his might he flings his feet,
But the water-sprites are round him still,
To cross his path and work him ill.
They bade the wave before him rise;
They flung the sea-fire in his eyes,
And they stunned his ears with the scallop stroke,
With the porpoise heave and the drumfish croak.
Oh! but a weary wight was he
When he reached the foot of the dogwood tree:
Gashed and wounded, and stiff and sore,
He laid him down on the sandy shore;
He blessed the force of the charmed line,
  And he banned the water-goblins' spite,
For he saw around in the sweet moonshine,
Their little wee faces above the brine,
  Giggling and laughing with all their might
  At the piteous hap of the Fairy wight.

Soon he gathered the balsam dew
  From the sorrel leaf and the henbane bud;
Over each wound the balm he drew,
  And with cobweb lint he stanched the blood.
The mild west wind was soft and low,
It cooled the heat of his burning brow,
And he felt new life in his sinews shoot,
As he drank the juice of the cal'mus root:

And now he treads the fatal shore,
As fresh and vigorous as before.

Wrapped in musing stands the sprite
'Tis in the middle wane of night,
  His task is hard, his way is far,
But he must do his errand right
  Ere dawning mounts her beamy car,
And rolls her chariot wheels of light;
And vain are the spells of fairy-land,
He must work with a human hand.

He cast a saddened look around,
  But he felt new joy his bosom swell,
When, glittering on the shadowed ground,
  He saw a purple muscle shell;
Thither he ran, and he bent him low,
He heaved at the stern and he heaved at the bow,
And he pushed her over the yielding sand,
Till he came to the verge of the haunted land.
She was as lovely a pleasure boat
  As ever fairy had paddled in,
For she glowed with purple paint without,
  And shone with silvery pearl within;
A sculler's notch in the stern he made,
An oar he shaped of the bootle blade;
Then sprung to his seat with a lightsome step,
And launched afar on the calm blue deep.

The imps of the river yell and rave;
They had no power above the wave,
But they heaved the billow before the prow,
  And they dashed the surge against her side,
And they struck her keel with jerk and blow,
  Till the gunwale bent to the rocking tide.
She wimpled about in the pale moonbeam,
Like a feather that floats on a wind-tossed stream;
And momently athwart her track
The quarl upreared his island back,

And the fluttering scallop behind would float,
And patter the water about the boat;
But he bailed her out with his colen-bell,
  And he kept her trimmed with a wary tread,
While on every side like lightning fell
  The heavy strokes of his bootle-blade.

Onward still he held his way,
Till he came where the column of moonshine lay
And saw beneath the surface dim
The brown-backed sturgeon slowly swim:
Around him were the goblin train;
But he sculled with all his might and main,
And followed wherever the sturgeon led,
Till he saw him upward point his head;
Then he dropped his paddle blade,
And held his colen goblet up
To catch the drop in its crimson cup.

With sweeping tail and quivering fin,
  Through the wave the sturgeon flew,
And, like the heaven-shot javelin,
  He sprung above the waters blue.
Instant as the star-fall light,
  He plunged him in the deep again,
But left an arch of silver bright,
  The rainbow of the moony main.
It was a strange and lovely sight
  To see the puny goblin there;
He seemed an angel form of light,
  With azure wing and sunny hair,
  Throned on a cloud of purple fair,
Circled with blue and edged with white,
And sitting at the fall of even
Beneath the bow of summer heaven.

A moment, and its lustre fell;
  But, ere it met the billow blue,
He caught within his crimson bell
  A droplet of its sparkling dew—

Joy to thee, Fay! thy task is done,
Thy wings are pure, for the gem is won:
Cheerily ply thy dripping oar,
And haste away to the elfin shore.

BRONX.

I SAT me down upon a green bank-side,
Skirting the smooth edge of a gentle river,
Whose waters seemed unwillingly to glide,
Like parting friends who linger while they sever;
Enforced to go, yet seeming still unready,
Backward they wind their way in many a wistful eddy.

Gray o'er my head the yellow-vested willow
Ruffled its hoary top in the fresh breezes,
Glancing in light, like spray on a green billow,
Or the fine frostwork which young winter freezes·
When first his power in infant pastime trying,
Congeals sad autumn's tears on the dead branches lying.

From rocks around hung the loose ivy dangling,
And in the clefts sumach of liveliest green,
Bright ising-stars the little beach was spangling,
The gold-cup sorrel from his gauzy screen
Shone like a fairy crown, enchased and beaded,
Left on some morn, when light flashed in their eyes unheeded.

The humbird shook his sun-touch'd wings around,
The bluefinch caroll'd in the still retreat;
The antic squirrel capered on the ground
Where lichens made a carpet for his feet:
Through the transparent waves, the ruddy minkle
Shot up in glimmering sparks his red fin's tiny twinkle.

There were dark cedars with loose mossy tresses,
White powdered dog-trees, and stiff hollies flaunt-
Gaudy as rustics in their May-day dresses, [ing
Blue pelloret from purple leaves upslanting
A modest gaze, like eyes of a young maiden
Shining beneath dropp'd lids the evening of her
wedding.

The breeze fresh springing from the lips of morn,
Kissing the leaves, and sighing so to lose 'em,
The winding of the merry locust's horn, [som:
The glad spring gushing from the rock's bare bo-
Sweet sights, sweet sounds, all sights, all sounds ex-
celling, [ing.
Oh! 'twas a ravishing spot formed for a poet's dwell-

And did I leave thy loveliness, to stand
Again in the dull world of earthly blindness?
Pained with the pressure of unfriendly hands,
Sick of smooth looks, agued with icy kindness?
Left I for this thy shades, where none intrude,
To prison wandering thought and mar sweet solitude?

Yet I will look upon thy face again,
My own romantic Bronx, and it will be
A face more pleasant than the face of men.
Thy waves are old companions, I shall see
A well-remembered form in each old tree,
And hear a voice long loved in thy wild minstrelsy

William Leggett.

A SACRED MELODY.

If yon bright stars which gem the night
Be each a blissful dwelling sphere,
Where kindred spirits reunite,
Whom death has torn asunder here;

How sweet it were at once to die,
And leave this blighted orb afar—
Mixed soul with soul, to cleave the sky,
And soar away from star to star.

But oh! how dark, how drear, how lone
Would seem the brightest world of bliss,
If, wandering through each radiant one,
We failed to find the loved of this!
If there no more the ties should twine,
Which death's cold hand alone can sever,
Ah! then these stars in mockery shine,
More hateful as they shine for ever.

It cannot be! each hope and fear
That lights the eye or clouds the brow,
Proclaims there is a happier sphere
Than this bleak world that holds us now!
There is a voice which sorrow hears,
When heaviest weighs life's galling chain;
'Tis heaven that whispers, "Dry thy tears:
The pure in heart shall meet again!"

John G. C. Brainard.

THE FALL OF NIAGARA.

Labitur et labetur.

The thoughts are strange that crowd into my brain
While I look upward to thee. It would seem
As if God pour'd thee from his "hollow hand,"
And hung his bow upon thine awful front;
And spoke in that loud voice, which seem'd to him
Who dwelt in Patmos for his Saviour's sake,
"The sound of many waters;" and had bade
Thy flood to chronicle the ages back,
And notch His cent'ries in the eternal rocks.

Deep calleth unto deep. And what are we,
That hear the question of that voice sublime?
Oh! what are all the notes that ever rung
From war's vain trumpet, by thy thundering side!
Yea, what is all the riot man can make
In his short life, to thy unceasing roar!
And yet, bold babbler, what art thou to HIM,
Who drown'd a world, and heap'd the waters far
Above its loftiest mountains? a light wave
That breaks, and whispers of its Maker's might.

MR. MERRY'S LAMENT FOR "LONG TOM."

"Let us think of them that sleep,
Full many a fathom deep,
By thy wild and stormy steep,
Elsinore."

THY cruise is over now,
Thou art anchor'd by the shore,
And never more shalt thou
Hear the storm around thee roar;
Death has shaken out the sands of thy glass.
Now around thee sports the whale,
And the porpoise snuffs the gale,
And the night-winds wake their wail,
As they pass.

The sea-grass round thy bier
Shall bend beneath the tide,
Nor tell the breakers near
Where thy manly limbs abide;
But the granite rock thy tombstone shall be.
Though the edges of thy grave
Are the combings of the wave,
Yet unheeded they shall rave
Over thee.

At the piping of all hands,
When the judgment signal's spread—
When the islands, and the lands,
And the seas give up their dead,
And the south and the north shall come;
When the sinner is betray'd,
And the just man is afraid,
Then Heaven be thy aid,
Poor Tom.

THE INDIAN SUMMER.

What is there sadd'ning in the Autumn leaves?
Have they that "green and yellow melancholy"
That the sweet poet spake of? Had he seen
Our variegated woods, when first the frost
Turns into beauty all October's charms—
When the dread fever quits us—when the storms
Of the wild Equinox, with all its wet,
Has left the land, as the first deluge left it,
With a bright bow of many colours hung
Upon the forest tops—he had not sigh'd.

The moon stays longest for the Hunter now:
The trees cast down their fruitage, and the blithe
And busy squirrel hoards his winter store:
While man enjoys the breeze that sweeps along
The bright blue sky above him, and that bends
Magnificently all the forest's pride,
Or whispers through the evergreens, and asks,
"What is there sadd'ning in the Autumn leaves?"

"The dead leaves strow the forest walk,
And wither'd are the pale wild-flowers;
The frost hangs blackening on the stalk,
The dewdrops fall in frozen showers.

Gone are the spring's green sprouting bowers,
Gone summer's rich and mantling vines,
And Autumn, with her yellow hours,
On hill and plain no longer shines.

I learn'd a clear and wild-toned note,
That rose and swell'd from yonder tree.
A gay bird, with too sweet a throat,
There perch'd and raised her song for me.
The winter comes, and where is she?
Away—where summer wings will rove,
Where buds are fresh, and every tree
Is vocal with the notes of love.

Too mild the breath of southern sky,
Too fresh the flower that blushes there,
The northern breeze that rustles by,
Finds leaves too green and buds too fair;
No forest-tree stands stripp'd and bare,
No stream beneath the ice is dead,
No mountain-top, with sleety hair,
Bends o'er the snows its reverend head.

Go there with all the birds, and seek
A happier clime, with livelier flight,
Kiss, with the sun, the evening's cheek,
And leave me lonely with the night.
I'll gaze upon the cold north light,
And mark where all its glories shone—
See!—that it all is fair and bright,
Feel—that it all is cold and gone."

William Gilmore Simms.

SCENE FROM ATALANTIS.

Scene changes to the Ship—Leon *reclining on a cushion —to him, enter* Isabel.

Isa. What wraps you thus, sweet brother? why so sad,
When thus, so trimly, speeds our swan-like bark
Upon the placid waters? You are sick,
And in your eye a dim abstraction lies,
Lacking all sense; and, as it were, at search
For airy speculations in the deep.
Leon. Why, thou art right: a speculation true,
For I behold naught that may speak for it,
And tell me whence it comes.
Isa. What is't thou say'st?
Leon. Stay but a moment! as I live, I heard it
Steal by me, like the whispers of a lute
From thy own lattice, Isabel.
Isa. Heard what?
What is it that thou speak'st of?
Leon. A sound—a strain,
Even as the softest music, heard afar,
At twilight, o'er our Andalusian hills,
From melancholy maiden, by me crept,
But now, upon the waters. They were tones
Slight as a spirit's whisperings; and, as far
As met my sense, they had a gentle voice,
Tremulous as an echo faintly made,
The replication of an infant's cry,
Thrown back from some rude mountain.
Isa. Thou dreamest.
Whence should such music come?
Leon. Ay, where or whence,
But from some green-haired maiden of the sea?
If thou believ'st me, Isabel, 'tis true;
I heard it even now, and syllabled

Into familiar sounds, that conjured up
My boyhood's earliest dreams: of isles, that lie
In farthest depths of ocean; girt with all
Of natural wealth and splendour—jewell'd isles—
Boundless in unimaginable spoils,
That earth is stranger to.
Isa. Thou dreamest still:
Thy boyhood's legends carry thee away,
Till thou forgett'st the mighty difference [toils,
'Twixt those two worlds—the one, where nature
The other she but dreams of.
Leon. I dream not:
I heard it visibly to the sense, and hark!
It comes again: dost thou not hear it now?
List now, dear Isabel.
Isa. I hear naught.
Leon. Surely I marked it then; I could not dream:
'Twas like the winds among a bed of reeds,
And spoke a deep, heart-melancholy sound,
That made me sigh when I heard it.
Isa. No more!
Thou art too led away by idle thoughts,
Dear Leon; and, I fear me, thou dost take
Too much the colour of the passing cloud,
Filling thy heart with shadowings, that mislead
Thy roving thoughts, already too much prone
To empty speculation.
Leon. I said not wrong:
My spirit trick'd me not: my sense was true.
I hear it now again. Far, far off, fine—
So delicate, as if some spirit form
Were for the first time murmuring into life,
And this its first complaining. Hearken now—
Nay, Isabel! thou dost not longer doubt—
Thy ears are traitors if they did not feel
The music as it came by us but now.
Isa. I heard a murmur truly, but so slight,
A breath of the wind might make it, or a sail
Drawn suddenly.

Leon. Now, now, thou hast it there:
Thou dost not longer question. It is there

Spirit sings.

O'er the wide world of ocean
  My home is afar,
Beyond its commotion,
  I laugh at its war;
Yet by destiny bidden,
  I cannot deny,
All night I have ridden
  From my home in the sky.

In the billow before thee
  My form is conceal'd,
In the breath that comes o'er thee
  My thought is reveal'd;
Strown thickly beneath me
  The coral rocks grow,
And the waves that enwreath me
  Are working thee wo.

Leon. Did'st hear the strain it utter'd, Isabel?
Isa. All, all! It spoke, methought, of peril near,
From rocks and wiles of the ocean: did it not?
Leon. It did, but idly! Here can lurk no rocks;
For, by the chart which now before me lies,
Thy own unpractised eye may well discern
The wide extent of the ocean—shoreless all.
The land, for many a league, to th' eastward hangs,
And not a point beside it.
Isa. Wherefore, then,
Should come this voice of warning?
Leon. From the deep:
It hath its demons as the earth and air,
All tributaries to the master-fiend
That sets their springs in motion. This is one,
That, doubting to mislead us, plants this wile,
So to divert our course, that we may strike
The very rocks he fain would warn us from.

Isa. A subtle sprite: and, now I think of it,
Dost thou remember the old story told
By Diaz Ortis, the lame mariner,
Of an adventure in the Indian Seas,
Where he made one with John of Portugal,
Touching a woman of the ocean wave,
That swam beside the barque, and sang strange songs
Of riches in the waters; with a speech
So winning on the senses, that the crew
Grew all infected with the melody;
And, but for a good father of the church,
Who made the sign of the cross, and offer'd up
Befitting pray'rs, which drove the fiend away,
They had been tempted by her cunning voice
To leap into the ocean.
Leon. I do, I do!
And, at the time, I do remember me,
I made much mirth of the extravagant tale,
As a deceit of the reason: the old man
Being in his second childhood, and at fits
Wild, as you know, on other themes than this.
Isa. I never more shall mock at marvellous things,
Such strange conceits hath after-time found true,
That once were themes for jest. I shall not smile
At the most monstrous legend.
Leon. Nor will I:
To any tale of mighty wonderment
I shall bestow my ear, nor wonder more;
And every fancy that my childhood bred,
In vagrant dreams of frolic, I shall look
To have, without rebuke, my sense approve.
Thus, like a little island in the sea,
Girt in by perilous waters, and unknown
To all adventure, may be yon same cloud,
Specking, with fleecy bosom, the blue sky,
Lit by the rising moon. There we may dream,
And find no censure in an after day—
Throng the assembled fairies, perch'd on beams,
And riding on their way triumphantly.

There gather the coy spirits. Many a fay,
Roving the silver sands of that same isle,
Floating in azure ether, plumes her wing
Of ever-frolicsome fancy, and pursues—
While myriads, like herself, do watch the chase—
Some truant sylph, through the infinitude
Of their uncircumscribed and rich domain.
There sport they through the night, with mimicry
Of strife and battle; striking their tiny shields
And gathering into combat; meeting fierce,
With lip compress'd and spear aloft, and eye
Glaring with fight and desperate circumstance;
Then sudden—in a moment all their wrath,
Mellow'd to friendly terms of courtesy—
Throwing aside the dread array, and linked,
Each, in his foe's embrace. Then comes the dance
The grateful route, the wild and musical pomp,
The long procession o'er fantastic realms [night,
Of cloud and moonbeam, through th' enamoured
Making it all one revel. Thus the eye,
Breathed on by fancy, with enlarged scope,
Through the protracted and deep hush of night
May note the fairies, coursing the lazy hours
In various changes and without fatigue.
A fickle race, who tell their time by flow'rs,
And live on zephyrs, and have stars for lamps,
And night-dews for ambrosia; perch'd on beams,
Speeding through space, even with the scattering
On which they feed and frolic. [light

Isa. A sweet dream:
And yet, since this same tale we laughed at once,
The story of old Ortis, is made sooth—
Perchance not all a dream. I will not doubt.

Leon. And yet there may be, dress'd in subtle guise
Of unsuspected art, some gay deceit
Of human conjuration mix'd with this.
Some cunning seaman having natural skill—
As, from the books, we learn may yet be done—
Hath 'yond our vessel's figure pitched his voice,
Leading us wantonly.

Isa. It is not so,
Or does my sense deceive? Look there: the wave
A perch beyond our barque. What dost thou see?
Leon. A marvellous shape, that with the billow [curls,
In gambols of the deep, and yet is not
Its wonted burden; for beneath the waves
I mark a gracious form, though nothing clear
Of visage I discern. Again it speaks.

THE EDGE OF THE SWAMP.

'Tis a wild spot and hath a gloomy look;
The bird sings never merrily in the trees,
And the young leaves seem blighted. A rank growth
Spreads poisonously round, with pow'r to taint,
With blistering dews, the thoughtless hand that dares
To penetrate the covert. Cypresses
Crowd on the dank, wet earth; and, stretched at length,
The cayman—a fit dweller in such home—
Slumbers, half buried in the sedgy grass,
Beside the green ooze where he shelters him.
A whooping crane erects his skeleton form,
And shrieks in flight. Two summer ducks, aroused
To apprehension as they hear his cry,
Dash up from the lagoon with marvellous haste,
Following his guidance. Meetly taught by these,
And startled at our rapid, near approach,
The steel-jawed monster, from his grassy bed,
Crawls slowly to his slimy, green abode,
Which straight receives him. You behold him now,
His ridgy back uprising as he speeds
In silence to the centre of the stream,
Whence his head peers alone. A butterfly,
That, travelling all the day, has counted climes
Only by flowers, to rest himself a while,
Lights on the monster's brow. The surly mute
Straightway goes down. so suddenly, that he,

The dandy of the summer flow'rs and woods,
Dips his light wings and spoils his golden coat
With the rank water of that turbid pond.
Wondering and vex'd, the pluméd citizen
Flies, with an hurried effort, to the shore,
Seeking his kindred flow'rs; but seeks in vain:
Nothing of genial growth may there be seen,
Nothing of beautiful! Wild, ragged trees,
That look like felon spectres—fetid shrubs,
That taint the gloomy atmosphere—dusk shades,
That gather, half a cloud and half a fiend
In aspect, lurking on the swamp's wild edge—
Gloom with their sternness and forbidding frowns
The general prospect. The sad butterfly,
Waving his lacker'd wings, darts quickly on,
And, by his free flight, counsels us to speed
For better lodgings, and a scene more sweet
Than these drear borders offer us to-night.

Rufus Dawes.

TO AN INFANT SLEEPING IN A GARDEN.

Sleep on, sweet babe! the flowers that wake
 Around thee are not half so fair;
Thy dimpling smiles unconscious break,
 Like sunlight on the vernal air.

Sleep on! no dreams of care are thine,
 No anxious thoughts that may not rest;
For angel arms around thee twine,
 To make thy infant slumbers bless'd.

Perchance *her* spirit hovers near,
 Whose name thy infant beauty bears,
To guard thine eyelids from the tear
 That every child of sorrow shares.

Oh! may thy life like hers endure,
  Unsullied to its spotless close;
And bend to earth as calm and pure
  As ever bowed the summer rose.

SUNRISE FROM MOUNT WASHINGTON.

The laughing hours have chased away the night,
Plucking the stars out from her diadem:
And now the blue-eyed Morn, with modest grace,
Looks through her half-drawn curtains in the east,
Blushing in smiles and glad as infancy.
And see, the foolish Moon, but now so vain
Of borrowed beauty, how she yields her charms,
And, pale with envy, steals herself away!
The clouds have put their gorgeous livery on,
Attendant on the day: the mountain tops
Have lit their beacons, and the vales below
Send up a welcoming: no song of birds,
Warbling to charm the air with melody,
Floats on the frosty breeze; yet Nature hath
The very soul of music in her looks!
The sunshine and the shade of poetry.

  I stand upon thy lofty pinnacle,
Temple of Nature! and look down with awe
On the wide world beneath me, dimly seen;
Around me crowd the giant sons of earth,
Fixed on their old foundations, unsubdued;
Firm as when first rebellion bade them rise
Unrifted to the Thunderer: now they seem
A family of mountains, clustering round
Their hoary patriarch, emulously watching
To meet the partial glances of the day.
Far in the glowing east the flickering light,
Mellow'd by distance, with the blue sky blending,
Questions the eye with ever-varying forms.

The sun comes up! away the shadows fling
From the broad hills; and, hurrying to the West,
Sport in the sunshine till they die away.
The many beauteous mountain streams leap down,
Out-welling from the clouds, and sparkling light
Dances along with their perennial flow.
And there is beauty in yon river's path,
The glad Connecticut! I know her well,
By the white veil she mantles o'er her charms:
At times she loiters by a ridge of hills,
Sportfully hiding; then again with glee,
Out-rushes from her wild-wood lurking-place,
Far as the eye can bound, the ocean-waves,
And hills and rivers, mountains, lakes, and woods,
And all that hold the faculty entranced,
Bathed in a flood of glory, float in air,
And sleep in the deep quietude of joy.

There is an awful stillness in this place,
A Presence, that forbids to break the spell,
Till the heart pour its agony in tears.
But I must drink the vision while it lasts;
For even now the curling vapours rise,
Wreathing their cloudy coronals, to grace
These towering summits—bidding me away;
But often shall my heart turn back again,
Thou glorious eminence! and when oppress'd,
And aching with the coldness of the world,
Find a sweet resting-place and home with thee.

Lucretia Maria Davidson.

THE PROPHECY.*

Let me gaze a while on that marble brow,
On that full dark eye, on that cheek's warm glow,

* Written in her sixteenth year.

Let me gaze for a moment, that, ere I die,
I may read thee, maiden, a prophecy.
That brow may beam in glory a while;
That cheek may bloom, and that lip may smile;
That full, dark eye may brightly beam
In life's gay morn, in hope's young dream;
But clouds shall darken that brow of snow,
And sorrow blight thy bosom's glow.
I know by that spirit so haughty and high,
I know by that brightly-flashing eye,
That, maiden, there's that within thy breast,
Which hath mark'd thee out for a soul unbless'd:
The strife of love with pride shall wring
Thy youthful bosom's tenderest string;
And the cup of sorrow, mingled for thee,
Shall be drained to the dregs in agony.
Yes, maiden, yes, I read in thine eye
A dark and a doubtful prophecy.
Thou shalt love, and that love shall be thy curse;
Thou wilt need no heavier, thou shalt feel no worse
I see the cloud and the tempest near;
The voice of the troubled tide I hear;
The torrent of sorrow, the sea of grief,
The rushing waves of a wretched life;
Thy bosom's bark on the surge I see,
And, maiden, thy loved one is there with thee.
Not a star in the heavens, not a light on the wave.
Maiden, I've gazed on thine early grave.
When I am cold, and the hand of Death
Hath crown'd my brow with an icy wreath;
When the dew hangs damp on this motionless lip
When this eye is closed in its long, last sleep,
Then, maiden, pause, when thy heart beats high,
And think on my last sad prophecy.

TO A LADY WHOSE SINGING RESEMBLED THAT OF AN ABSENT SISTER.*

Oh! touch the chord yet once again,
  Nor chide me though I weep the while;
Believe me, that deep seraph strain
  Bore with it memory's moonlight smile.

It murmur'd of an absent friend;
  The voice, the air, 'twas all her own;
And hers those wild, sweet notes, which blend
  In one mild, murmuring, touching tone.

And days and months have darkly pass'd
  Since last I listen'd to her lay;
And Sorrow's cloud its shade hath cast,
  Since then, across my weary way.

Yet still the strain comes sweet and clear,
  Like seraph-whispers lightly breathing;
Hush, busy Memory, Sorrow's tear
  Will blight the garland thou art weaving.

'Tis sweet, though sad—yes, I will stay,
  I cannot tear myself away.
I thank thee, lady, for the strain,
  The tempest of my soul is still;
Then touch the chord yet once again,
  For thou canst calm the storm at will.

* Written in her fifteenth year.

MARGARET MILLER DAVIDSON.

HOME.*

I WOULD fly from the city, would fly from its care,
To my own native plants and my flow'rets so fair,
To the cool grassy shade and the rivulet bright,
Which reflects the pale moon in its bosom of light;
Again would I view the old cottage so dear,
Where I sported a babe, without sorrow or fear;
I would leave this great city, so brilliant and gay,
For a peep at my home on this fair summer day.
I have friends whom I love, and would leave with regret,
But the love of my home, oh! 'tis tenderer yet;
There a sister reposes unconscious in death,
'Twas there she first drew, and there yielded her breath.
A father I love is away from me now,
Oh! could I but print a sweet kiss on his brow,
Or smooth the gray locks to my fond heart so dear,
How quickly would vanish each trace of a tear.
Attentive I listen to pleasure's gay call,
But my own happy home—it is dearer than all.

TO MY MOTHER.†

OH, mother, would the power were mine
To wake the strain thou lovest to hear,
And breathe each trembling new-born thought
Within thy fondly-listening ear,
As when in days of health and glee,
My hopes and fancies wandered free.

* Written at the age of nine years.

† This poem was written in the author's sixteenth year, and was her last composition.

But, mother, now a shade hath pass'd
Athwart my brightest visions here;
A cloud of darkest gloom hath wrapp'd
The remnant of my brief career;
No song, no echo can I win,
The sparkling fount hath dried within.

The torch of earthly hope burns dim,
And fancy spreads her wings no more,
And oh, how vain and trivial seem
The pleasures that I prized before;
My soul, with trembling steps and slow,
Is struggling on through doubt and strife
Oh, may it prove, as time rolls on,
The pathway to eternal life!
Then when my cares and fears are o'er,
I'll sing thee as in "days of yore."

I said that Hope had passed from earth,
'Twas but to fold her wings in heaven,
To whisper of the soul's new birth,
Of sinners saved and sins forgiven;
When mine are washed in tears away,
Then shall my spirit swell my lay.

When God shall guide my soul above,
By the soft chords of heavenly love—
When the vain cares of earth depart,
And tuneful voices swell my heart—
Then shall each word, each note I raise
Burst forth in pealing hymns of praise,
And all not offered at His shrine,
Dear mother, I will place on thine.

Carlos Wilcox.

SPRING IN NEW-ENGLAND.

Long swoln in drenching rain, seeds, germes, and
Start at the touch of vivifying beams. [buds
Moved by their secret force, the vital lymph
Diffusive runs, and spreads o'er wood and field
A flood of verdure. Clothed, in one short week,
Is naked Nature in her full attire.
On the first morn, light as an open plain
Is all the woodland, filled with sunbeams, poured
Through the bare tops, on yellow leaves below,
With strong reflection: on the last, 'tis dark
With full-grown foliage, shading all within.
In one short week the orchard buds and blooms;
And now, when steep'd in dew or gentle showers,
It yields the purest sweetness to the breeze,
Or all the tranquil atmosphere perfumes.
E'en from the juicy leaves of sudden growth,
And the rank grass of steaming ground, the air,
Filled with a watery glimmering, receives
A grateful smell, exhaled by warming rays.
Each day are heard, and almost every hour,
New notes to swell the music of the groves.
And soon the latest of the feather'd train
At evening twilight come; the lonely snipe,
O'er marshy fields, high in the dusky air,
Invisible, but with faint, tremulous tones,
Hovering or playing o'er the listener's head;
And, in mid-air, the sportive night-hawk, seen
Flying a while at random, uttering oft
A cheerful cry, attended with a shake
Of level pinions, dark, but when upturned
Against the brightness of the western sky,
One white plume showing in the midst of each,
Then far down diving with loud hollow sound;
And, deep at first within the distant wood,

The whip-poor-will, her name her only song.
She, soon as children from the noisy sport
Of hooping, laughing, talking with all tones,
To hear the echoes of the empty barn,
Are by her voice diverted and held mute,
Comes to the margin of the nearest grove;
And when the twilight, deepened into night,
Calls them within, close to the house she comes,
And on its dark side, haply on the step
Of unfrequented door, lighting unseen,
Breaks into strains articulate and clear,
The closing sometimes quickened as in sport.
Now, animate throughout, from morn to eve
All harmony, activity, and joy,
Is lovely Nature, as in her bless'd prime.
The robin to the garden or green yard,
Close to the door, repairs to build again
Within her wonted tree; and at her work
Seems doubly busy for her past delay.
Along the surface of the winding stream,
Pursuing every turn, gay swallows skim,
Or round the borders of the spacious lawn
Fly in repeated circles, rising o'er
Hillock and fence with motion serpentine,
Easy, and light. One snatches from the ground
A downy feather, and then upward springs,
Followed by others, but oft drops it soon,
In playful mood, or from too slight a hold,
When all at once dart at the falling prize.
The flippant blackbird, with light yellow crown,
Hangs fluttering in the air, and chatters thick
Till her breath fail, when, breaking off, she drops
On the next tree, and on its highest limb
Or some tall flag, and gently rocking, sits,
Her strain repeating. With sonorous notes
Of every tone, mixed in confusion sweet,
All chanted in the fulness of delight,
The forest rings: where, far around enclosed
With bushy sides. and covered high above

With foliage thick, supported by bare trunks,
Like pillars rising to support a roof,
It seems a temple vast, the space within
Rings loud and clear with thrilling melody.
Apart, but near the choir, with voice distinct,
The merry mocking-bird together links
In one continued song their different notes,
Adding new life and sweetness to them all.
Hid under shrubs, the squirrel that in fields
Frequents the stony wall and briery fence,
Here chirps so shrill that human feet approach
Unheard till just upon him, when, with cries
Sudden and sharp, he darts to his retreat
Beneath the mossy hillock or aged tree;
But oft a moment after reappears,
First peeping out, then starting forth at once
With a courageous air, yet in his pranks
Keeping a watchful eye, nor venturing far
Till left unheeded. In rank pastures graze,
Singly and mutely, the contented herd;
And on the upland rough the peaceful sheep;
Regardless of the frolic lambs, that, close
Beside them, and before their faces prone,
With many an antic leap and butting feint,
Try to provoke them to unite in sport
Or grant a look, till tired of vain attempts;
When, gathering in one company apart,
All vigour and delight, away they run,
Straight to the utmost corner of the field,
The fence beside; then, wheeling, disappear
In some small sandy pit, then rise to view;
Or crowd together up the heap of earth
Around some upturned root of fallen tree,
And on its top a trembling moment stand,
Then to the distant flock at once return.
Exhilarated by the general joy,
And the fair prospect of a fruitful year,
The peasant, with light heart and nimble step,
His work pursues, as it were pastime sweet.

With many a cheering word, his willing team,
For labour fresh, he hastens to the field
Ere morning lose its coolness; but at eve,
When loosened from the plough and homeward
He follows slow and silent, stopping oft [turn'd,
To mark the daily growth of tender grain
And meadows of deep verdure, or to view
His scatter'd flock and herd, of their own will
Assembling for the night by various paths,
The old now freely sporting with the young,
Or labouring with uncouth attempts at sport.

SEPTEMBER.

The sultry summer past, September comes,
Soft twilight of the slow-declining year.
All mildness, soothing loneliness, and peace;
The fading season ere the falling come,
More sober than the buxom blooming May,
And therefore less the favourite of the world,
But dearest month of all to pensive minds.
'Tis now far spent; and the meridian sun,
Most sweetly smiling with attempered beams,
Sheds gently down a mild and grateful warmth.
Beneath its yellow lustre groves and woods,
Checker'd by one night's frost with various hues,
While yet no wind has swept a leaf away,
Shine doubly rich. It were a sad delight
Down the smooth stream to glide, and see it tinged
Upon each brink with all the gorgeous hues,
The yellow, red, or purple of the trees
That singly, or in tufts, or forests thick
Adorn the shores; to see, perhaps, the side
Of some high mount reflected far below
With its bright colours, intermix'd with spots
Of darker green. Yes, it were sweetly sad
To wander in the open fields, and hear,

E'en at this hour, the noonday hardly past,
The lulling insects of the summer's night;
To hear, where lately buzzing swarms were heard,
A lonely bee long roving here and there
To find a single flower, but all in vain;
Then rising quick and with a louder hum,
In widening circles round and round his head,
Straight by the listener flying clear away,
As if to bid the fields a last adieu;
To hear within the woodland's sunny side,
Late fall of music, nothing save perhaps
The sound of nutshells by the squirrel dropp'd
From some tall beech fast falling through the leaves.

THE CASTLE OF IMAGINATION.

Just in the centre of that wood was rear'd
Her castle, all of marble, smooth and white;
Above the thick young trees, its top appear'd
Among the naked trunks of towering height;
And here at morn and eve it glitter'd bright,
As often by the far-off traveller seen
In level sunbeams, or at dead of night,
When the low moon shot in her rays between
That wide-spread roof and floor of solid foliage green.

Through this wide interval the roving eye
From turrets proud might trace the waving line
Where meet the mountains green and azure sky,
And view the deep when sun-gilt billows shine;
Fair bounds to sight, that never thought confine,
But tempt it far beyond, till by the charm
Of some sweet wood-note or some whispering pine
Call'd home again, or by the soft alarm
Of Love's approaching step, and her encircling arm.

Through this wide interval, the mountain side
Showed many a sylvan slope and rocky steep:
Here roaring torrents in dark forests hide;
There silver streamlets rush to view, and leap
Unheard from lofty cliffs to valleys deep:
Here rugged peaks look smooth in sunset glow,
Along the clear horizon's western sweep;
There from some eastern summit moonbeams flow
Along o'er level wood, far down to plains below.

Now stretch'd a blue, and now a golden zone
Round that horizon; now o'er mountains proud
Dim vapours rest, or bright ones move alone:
An ebon wall, a smooth portentous cloud,
First muttering low, anon with thunder loud,
Now rises quick, and brings a sweeping wind
O'er all that wood in waves before it bowed;
And now a rainbow, with its top behind
A spangled veil of leaves, seems heaven and earth to bind.

Above the canopy, so thick and green,
And spread so high o'er that enchanted vale,
Through scatter'd openings oft were glimpses seen
Of fleecy clouds, that, linked together, sail
In moonlight clear before the gentle gale:
Sometimes a shooting meteor draws a glance;
Sometimes a twinkling star, or planet pale,
Long holds the lighted eye, as in a trance;
And oft the milky-way gleams through the white expanse.

That castle's open windows, though half hid
With flowering vines, showed many a vision fair;
A face all bloom, or light young forms that thrid
Some maze within, or lonely ones that wear

The garb of joy with sorrow's thoughtful air,
Oft caught the eye a moment: and the sound
Of low, sweet music often issued there,
And by its magic held the listener bound,
And seem'd to hold the winds and forests far around.

Within, the queen of all, in pomp or mirth,
While glad attendants at her glance unfold
Their shining wings, and fly through heaven and earth,
Oft took her throne of burning gems and gold,
Adorn'd with emblems that of empire told,
And rising in the midst of trophies bright,
That bring her memory from the days of old,
And help prolong her reign, and with the flight
Of every year increase the wonders of her might.

In all her dwelling, tales of wild romance,
Of terror, love, and mystery dark or gay,
Were scatter'd thick to catch the wandering glance,
And stop the dreamer on his unknown way;
There too was every sweet and lofty lay,
The sacred, classic, and romantic, sung
As that Enchantress moved in might or play;
And there was many a harp but newly strung,
Yet with its fearless notes the whole wide valley rung.

There, from all lands and ages of her fame,
Were marble forms, array'd in order due,
In groups and single, all of proudest name;
In them the high, the fair, and tender, grew
To life intense in love's impassion'd view,
And from each air and feature, bend and swell,
Each shapely neck, and lip, and forehead, threw
O'er each enamour'd sense so deep a spell,
The thoughts but with the past or bright ideal dwell.

The walls around told all the pencil's power;
There proud creations of each mighty hand
Shone with their hues and lines as in the hour,
When the last touch was given at the command
Of the same genius that at first had plann'd,
Exulting in its great and glowing thought:
Bright scenes of peace and war, of sea and land,
Of love and glory, to new life were wrought,
From history, from fable, and from nature brought.

With these were others all divine, drawn all
From ground where oft, with signs and accents
The lonely prophet doom'd to sudden fall [dread,
Proud kings and cities, and with gentle tread
Bore life's quick triumph to the humble dead,
And where strong angels flew to blast or save,
Where martyr'd hosts of old, and youthful bled,
And where their mighty Lord o'er land and wave
Spread life and peace till death, then spread them
through the grave.

From these fix'd visions of the hallow'd eye,
Some kindling gleams of their ethereal glow,
Would ofttimes fall, as from the opening sky,
On eyes delighted, glancing to and fro,
Or fasten'd till their orbs dilated grow;
Then would the proudest seem with joy to learn
Truths they had feared or felt ashamed to know,
The skeptic would believe, the lost return;
And all the cold and low would seem to rise and burn.

Theirs was devotion kindled by the vast,
The beautiful, impassion'd, and refined;
And in the deep enchantment o'er them cast,
They look'd from earth, and soar'd above their
To the bless'd calm of an abstracted mind, [kind
And its communion with things all its own,
Its forms sublime and lovely; as the blind,
Mid earthly scenes, forgotten, or unknown,
Live in ideal worlds, and wander there alone.

Such were the lone enthusiasts, wont to dwell
With all whom that Enchantress held subdued,
As in the holiest circle of her spell,
Where meaner spirits never dare intrude,
They dwelt in calm and silent solitude,
Rapt in the love of all the high and sweet,
In thought, and art, and nature, and imbued
With its devotion to life's inmost seat,
As drawn from all the charms which in that valley meet.

ROSSEAU AND COWPER.

Rosseau could weep—yes, with a heart of stone
The impious sophist could recline beside
The pure and peaceful lake, and muse alone
On all its loveliness at even tide:
On its small running waves in purple dyed
Beneath bright clouds or all the glowing sky,
On the white sails that o'er its bosom glide,
And on surrounding mountains wild and high,
Till tears unbidden gush'd from his enchanted eye.

But his were not the tears of feeling fine
Of grief or love; at fancy's flash they flow'd,
Like burning drops from some proud lonely pine
By lightning fired; his heart with passion glow'd
Till it consumed his life, and yet he show'd
A chilling coldness both to friend and foe,
As Etna, with its centre an abode
Of wasting fire, chills with the icy snow
Of all its desert brow the living world below.

Was he but justly wretched from his crimes?
Then why was Cowper's anguish oft as keen,
With all the heaven-born virtue that sublimes
Genius and feeling, and to things unseen

Lifts the pure heart through clouds that roll between
The earth and skies, to darken human hope?
Or wherefore did those clouds thus intervene
To render vain faith's lifted telescope,
And leave him in thick gloom his weary way to grope?

He too could give himself to musing deep,
By the calm lake at evening he could stand,
Lonely and sad, to see the moonlight sleep
On all its breast by not an insect fanned,
And hear low voices on the far-off strand,
Or through the still and dewy atmosphere
The pipe's soft tones waked by some gentle hand,
From fronting shore and woody island near
In echoes quick return'd more mellow and more clear.

And he could cherish wild and mournful dreams,
In the pine grove, when low the full moon fair
Shot under lofty tops her level beams,
Stretching the shades of trunks erect and bare,
In stripes drawn parallel with order rare,
As of some temple vast or colonnade,
While on green turf made smooth without his care
He wander'd o'er its stripes of light and shade,
And heard the dying day-breeze all the boughs pervade.

'Twas thus in nature's bloom and solitude
He nursed his grief till nothing could assuage;
'Twas thus his tender spirit was subdued,
Till in life's toils it could no more engage;
And his had been a useless pilgrimage,
Had he been gifted with no sacred power,
To send his thoughts to every future age;
But he is gone where grief will not devour,
Where beauty will not fade, and skies will never lower.

THE CURE OF MELANCHOLY.

AND thou to whom long worshipp'd nature lends
No strength to fly from grief or bear its weight,
Stop not to rail at foes or fickle friends,
Nor set the world at naught, nor spurn at fate;
None seek thy misery, none thy being hate;
Break from thy former self, thy life begin;
Do thou the good thy thoughts oft meditate,
And thou shalt feel the good man's peace within,
And at thy dying day his wreath of glory win.

With deeds of virtue to embalm his name,
He dies in triumph or serene delight;
Weaker and weaker grows his mortal frame
At every breath, but in immortal might
His spirit grows, preparing for its flight:
The world recedes and fades like clouds of even,
But heaven comes nearer fast, and grows more bright,
All intervening mists far off are driven;
The world will vanish soon, and all will soon be heaven.

Wouldst thou from sorrow find a sweet relief?
Or is thy heart oppress'd with woes untold?
Balm wouldst thou gather for corroding grief?
Pour blessings round thee like a shower of gold:
'Tis when the rose is wrapp'd in many a fold
Close to its heart, the worm is wasting there
Its life and beauty; not, when all unrolled,
Leaf after leaf its bosom rich and fair
Breathes freely its perfumes throughout the ambient air.

Wake thou that sleepest in enchanted bowers,
Lest these lost years should haunt thee on the night
When death is waiting for thy number'd hours
To take their swift and everlasting flight;

Wake ere the earthborn charm unnerve thee quite,
And be thy thoughts to work divine address'd;
Do something—do it soon—with all thy might;
An angel's wing would droop if long at rest,
And God himself inactive were no longer bless'd.

Some high or humble enterprise of good
Contemplate till it shall possess thy mind,
Become thy study, pastime, rest, and food,
And kindle in thy heart a flame refined;
Pray Heaven for firmness thy whole soul to bind
To this thy purpose—to begin, pursue,
With thoughts all fix'd and feelings purely kind,
Strength to complete, and with delight review,
And grace to give the praise where all is ever due.

Fitz-Greene Halleck.

BURNS.

To a rose, brought from near Alloway Kirk, in Ayreshire, in the autumn of 1822.

Wild Rose of Alloway! my thanks:
Thou 'mindst me of that autumn noon
When first we met upon "the banks
And braes o' bonny Doon."

Like thine, beneath the thorn-tree's bough,
My sunny hour was glad and brief,
We've cross'd the winter sea, and thou
Art wither'd—flower and leaf.

And will not thy death-doom be mine—
The doom of all things wrought of clay—
And wither'd my life's leaf like thine,
Wild rose of Alloway?

Not so his memory, for whose sake
  My bosom bore thee far and long,
His—who a humbler flower could make
  Immortal as his song.

The memory of Burns—a name
  That calls, when brimm'd her festal cup,
A nation's glory, and her shame,
  In silent sadness up.

A nation's glory—be the rest
  Forgot—she's canonized his mind;
And it is joy to speak the best
  We may of human kind.

I've stood beside the cottage bed
  Where the Bard-peasant first drew breath;
A straw-thatch'd roof above his head,
  A straw-wrought couch beneath.

And I have stood beside the pile,
  His monument—that tells to Heaven
The homage of earth's proudest isle
  To that Bard-peasant given!

Bid thy thoughts hover o'er that spot,
  Boy-Minstrel, in thy dreaming hour;
And know, however low his lot,
  A Poet's pride and power.

The pride that lifted Burns from earth,
  The power that gave a child of song
Ascendancy o'er rank and birth,
  The rich, the brave, the strong;

And if despondency weigh down
  Thy spirit's fluttering pinions then,
Despair—thy name is written on
  The roll of common men.

There have been loftier themes than his,
  And longer scrolls, and louder lyres,
And lays lit up with Poesy's
  Purer and holier fires:

Yet read the names that know not death;
  Few nobler ones than Burns are there;
And few have won a greener wreath
  Than that which binds his hair.

His is that language of the heart,
  In which the answering heart would speak,
Thought, word, that bids the warm tear start,
  Or the smile light the cheek;

And his that music, to whose tone
  The common pulse of man keeps time.
In cot or castle's mirth or moan,
  In cold or sunny clime.

And who hath heard his song, nor knelt
  Before its spell with willing knee,
And listen'd, and believed, and felt
  The Poet's mastery.

O'er the mind's sea, in calm and storm,
  O'er the heart's sunshine and its showers,
O'er Passion's moments, bright and warm,
  O'er Reason's dark, cold hours;

On fields where brave men "die or do,"
  In halls where rings the banquet's mirth,
Where mourners weep, where lovers woo,
  From throne to cottage hearth;

What sweet tears dim the eyes unshed,
  What wild vows falter on the tongue,
When "Scots wha hae wi' Wallace bled,"
  Or "Auld Lang Syne" is sung!

Pure hopes, that lift the soul above,
  Come with his Cotter's hymn of praise,
And dreams of youth, and truth, and love,
  With "Logan's" banks and braes.

And when he breathes his master-lay
  Of Alloway's witch-haunted wall,
All passions in our frames of clay
  Come thronging at his call.

Imagination's world of air,
  And our own world, its gloom and glee,
Wit, pathos, poetry, are there,
  And death's sublimity.

And Burns—though brief the race he ran,
  Though rough and dark the path he trod—
Lived—died—in form and soul a Man,
  The image of his God.

Through care, and pain, and want, and wo,
  With wounds that only death could heal,
Tortures—the poor alone can know,
  The proud alone can feel;

He kept his honesty and truth,
  His independent tongue and pen,
And moved, in manhood and in youth,
  Pride of his fellow-men.

Strong sense, deep feeling, passions strong,
  A hate of tyrant and of knave,
A love of right, a scorn of wrong,
  Of coward, and of slave;

A kind, true heart, a spirit high,
  That could not fear and would not bow,
Were written in his manly eye,
  And on his manly brow.

Praise to the bard! his words are driven,
  Like flower-seeds by the far winds sown,
Where'er, beneath the sky of heaven,
  The birds of fame have flown.

Praise to the man! a nation stood
  Beside his coffin with wet eyes,
Her brave, her beautiful, her good,
  As when a loved one dies.

And still, as on his funeral day,
  Men stand his cold earth-couch around,
With the mute homage that we pay
  To consecrated ground.

And consecrated ground it is,
  The last, the hallow'd home of one
Who lives upon all memories,
  Though with the buried gone.

Such graves as his are pilgrim-shrines,
  Shrines to no code or creed confined—
The Delphian vales, the Palestines,
  The Meccas of the mind.

Sages, with Wisdom's garland wreathed,
  Crown'd kings, and mitred priests of power,
And warriors with their bright swords sheathed,
  The mightiest of the hour;

And lowlier names, whose humble home
  Is lit by Fortune's dimmer star,
Are there—o'er wave and mountain come,
  From countries near and far;

Pilgrims, whose wandering feet have press'd
  The Switzer's snow, the Arab's sand,
Or trod the piled leaves of the West,
  My own green forest-land.

All ask the cottage of his birth,
  Gaze on the scenes he loved and sung,
And gather feelings not of earth
  His fields and streams among.

They linger by the Doon's low trees,
  And pastoral Nith, and wooded Ayr,
And round thy sepulchres, Dumfries!
  The Poet's tomb is there.

But what to them the sculptor's art,
  His funeral columns, wreaths, and urns?
Wear they not graven on the heart
  The name of Robert Burns?

RED JACKET.

A chief of the Indian Tribes, the Tuscaroras.

Cooper, whose name is with his country's woven,
  First in her files, her pioneer of mind,
A wanderer now in other climes, has proven
  His love for the young land he left behind;

And throned her in the Senate Hall of Nations,
  Robed like the deluge rainbow, heaven-wrought,
Magnificent as his own mind's creations,
  And beautiful as its green world of thought.

And faithful to the Act of Congress, quoted
  As law-authority—it passed nem. con.—
He writes that we are, as ourselves have voted,
  The most enlighten'd people ever known.

That all our week is happy as a Sunday
  In Paris, full of song, and dance, and laugh;
And that, from Orleans to the Bay of Fundy,
  There's not a bailiff nor an epitaph

And, furthermore, in fifty years or sooner,
We shall export our poetry and wine;
And our brave fleet, eight frigates and a schooner,
Will sweep the seas from Zembla to the Line.

If he were with me, King of Tuscarora,
Gazing as I, upon thy portrait now,
In all its medall'd, fringed, and beaded glory,
Its eyes dark beauty, and its thoughtful brow—

Its brow, half martial and half diplomatic,
Its eye, upsoaring like an eagle's wings;
Well might he boast that we, the Democratic,
Outrival Europe—even in our kings.

For thou wert monarch born. Tradition's pages
Tell not the planting of thy parent tree,
But that the forest tribes have bent for ages,
To thee, and to thy sires, the subject knee.

Thy name is princely. Though no poet's magic
Could make Red Jacket grace an English rhyme,
Unless he had a genius for the tragic,
And introduced it in a pantomime;

Yet it is music in the language spoken
Of thine own land; and on her herald-roll,
As nobly fought for, and as proud a token
As Cœur de Lion's, of a warrior's soul.

Thy garb — though Austria's bosom-star would frighten
That medal pale, as diamonds the dark mine,
And George the Fourth wore, in the dance at Brighton,
A more becoming evening dress than thine;

Yet 'tis a brave one, scorning wind and weather,
And fitted for thy couch on field and flood,
As Rob Roy's tartans for the Highland heather,
Or forest green for England's Robin Hood.

Is strength a monarch's merit? (like a whaler's)
Thou art as tall, as sinewy, and as strong
As earth's first kings—the Argo's gallant sailors,
Heroes in history, and gods in song.

Is eloquence? Her spell is thine that reaches
The heart, and makes the wisest head its sport;
And there's one rare, strange virtue in thy speeches,
The secret of their mastery—they are short.

Is beauty? Thine has with thy youth departed,
But the love-legends of thy manhood's years,
And she who perish'd, young and broken-hearted,
Are—but I rhyme for smiles, and not for tears.

The monarch mind—the mystery of commanding,
The godlike power, the art Napoleon,
Of winning, fettering, moulding, wielding, banding
The hearts of millions till they move as one;

Thou hast it. At thy bidding men have crowded
The road to death as to a festival;
And minstrel minds, without a blush, have shrouded
With banner-folds of glory their dark pall.

Who will believe—not I—for in deceiving
Lies the dear charm of life's delightful dream;
I cannot spare the luxury of believing
That all things beautiful are what they seem.

Who will believe that, with a smile whose blessing
Would, like the patriarch's, sooth a dying hour;
With voice as low, as gentle, and caressing
As e'er won maiden's lip in moonlight bower;

With look, like patient Job's, eschewing evil;
With motions graceful as a bird's in air;
Thou art, in sober truth, the veriest devil
That e'er clinched fingers in a captive's hair!

That in thy veins there springs a poison fountain,
  Deadlier than that which bathes the Upas-tree;
And in thy wrath, a nursing Cat o' Mountain
  Is calm as her babe's sleep compared with thee?

And underneath that face like summer's ocean's,
  Its lip as moveless, and its cheek as clear,
Slumbers a whirlwind of the heart's emotions,
  Love, hatred, pride, hope, sorrow—all, save fear,

Love—for thy land, as if she were thy daughter,
  Her pipes in peace, her tomahawk in wars;
Hatred—of missionaries and cold water;
  Pride—in thy rifle trophies and thy scars;

Hope—that thy wrongs will be by the Great Spirit
  Remember'd and revenged when thou art gone;
Sorrow—that none are left thee to inherit
  Thy name, thy fame, thy passions, and thy throne.

Henry Wadsworth Longfellow

THE LIGHT OF STARS.

The night is come, but not too soon;
  And sinking silently,
All silently, the little moon
  Drops down behind the sky.

There is no light in earth or heaven
  But the cold light of stars;
And the first watch of night is given
  To the red planet Mars.

Is it the tender star of love?
  The star of love and dreams?
Oh no! from that blue tent above,
  A hero's armour gleams.

And earnest thoughts within me rise,
  When I behold afar,
Suspended in the evening skies,
  The shield of that red star.

Oh star of strength! I see thee stand
  And smile upon my pain;
Thou beckonest with thy mailed hand,
  And I am strong again.

Within my breast there is no light
  But the cold light of stars:
I give the first watch of the night
  To the red planet Mars.

The star of the unconquer'd will,
  He rises in my breast,
Serene, and resolute, and still,
  And calm, and self-possess'd.

And thou, too, whosoe'er thou art,
  That readest this brief psalm,
As one by one thy hopes depart,
  Be resolute and calm.

Oh, fear not in a world like this,
  And thou shalt know ere long,
Know how sublime a thing it is
  To suffer and be strong.

FOOTSTEPS OF ANGELS.

When the hours of Day are number'd,
  And the voices of the Night
Wake the better soul that slumber'd,
  To a holy, calm delight;

Ere the evening lamps are lighted,
  And, like phantoms grim and tall,
Shadows from the fitful firelight
  Dance upon the parlour wall;

Then the forms of the departed
  Enter at the open door;
The beloved ones, the true-hearted,
  Come to visit me once more;

He, the young and strong, who cherish'd
  Noble longings for the strife,
By the roadside fell and perish'd,
  Weary with the march of life!

They, the holy ones and weakly,
  Who the cross of suffering bore,
Folded their pale hands so meekly,
  Spake with us on earth no more!

And with them the Being Beauteous,
  Who unto my youth was given,
More than all things else to love me,
  And is now a saint in heaven.

With a slow and noiseless footstep
  Comes that messenger divine,
Takes the vacant chair beside me,
  Lays her gentle hand in mine.

And she sits and gazes at me
  With those deep and tender eyes,
Like the stars, so still and saint-like,
  Looking downward from the skies.

Utter'd not, yet comprehended,
  Is the spirit's voiceless prayer,
Soft rebukes, in blessings ended,
  Breathing from her lips of air.

Oh, though oft depress'd and lonely,
All my fears are laid aside
If I but remember only
Such as these have lived and died!

THE SPIRIT OF POETRY.

There is a quiet spirit in these woods,
That dwells where'er the south wind blows;
Where, underneath the white-thorn, in the glade,
The wild flowers bloom, or, kissing the soft air,
The leaves above their sunny palms outspread.
With what a tender and impassion'd voice
It fills the nice and delicate ear of thought,
When the fast-ushering star of morning comes
O'er-riding the gray hills with golden scarf;
Or when the cowl'd and dusky-sandaled Eve,
In mourning weeds, from out the western gate,
Departs with silent pace! That spirit moves
In the green valley, where the silver brook,
From its full laver, pours the white cascade;
And, babbling low amid the tangled woods,
Slips down through moss-grown stones with endless laughter.
And frequent, on the everlasting hills,
Its feet go forth, when it doth wrap itself
In all the dark embroidery of the storm,
And shouts the stern, strong wind. And here, amid
The silent majesty of these deep woods,
Its presence shall uplift thy thoughts from earth,
As to the sunshine, and the pure bright air,
Their tops the green trees lift. Hence gifted bards
Have ever loved the calm and quiet shades.
For them there was an eloquent voice in all
The sylvan pomp of woods, the golden sun,
The flowers, the leaves, the river on its way,
Blue skies, and silver clouds, and gentle winds;

The swelling upland, where the sidelong sun
Aslant the wooded slope at evening goes;
Groves, through whose broken roof the sky looks in;
Mountain, and shatter'd cliff, and sunny vale,
The distant lake, fountains, and mighty trees,
In many a lazy syllable, repeating
Their old poetical legends to the wind.

And this is the sweet spirit that doth fill
The world; and, in these wayward days of youth,
My busy fancy oft imbodies it,
As the bright image of the light and beauty
That dwell in nature, of the heavenly forms
We worship in our dreams, and the soft hues
That stain the wild-bird's wing, and flush the clouds
When the sun sets. Within her eye
The heaven of April, with its changing light,
And when it wears the blue of May, is hung,
And on her lip the rich red rose. Her hair
Is like the summer tresses of the trees,
When twilight makes them brown, and on her cheek
Blushes the richness of an autumn sky,
With ever-shifting beauty. Then her breath,
It is so like the gentle air of Spring,
As, from the morning's dewy flowers, it comes
Full of their fragrance, that it is a joy
To have it round us, and her silver voice
Is the rich music of a summer bird,
Heard in the still night, with its passionate cadence.

Charles Sprague.

THE FORCE OF CURIOSITY.

How swells my theme! how vain my power I find,
To track the windings of the curious mind;
Let aught be hid, though useless, nothing boots,
Straightway it must be pluck'd up by the roots.

How oft we lay the volume down to ask
Of him, the victim in the Iron Mask;
The crusted medal rub with painful care,
To spell the legend out—that is not there;
With dubious gaze o'er mossgrown tombstones bend
To find a name—the herald never penned;
Dig through the lava-deluged city's breast,
Learn all we can, and wisely guess the rest:
Ancient or modern, sacred or profane,
All must be known, and all obscure made plain;
If 'twas a pippin tempted Eve to sin,
If glorious Byron drugged his muse with gin;
If Troy e'er stood, if Shakspeare stole a deer,
If Israel's missing tribes found refuge here;
If like a villain Captain Henry lied,
If like a martyr Captain Morgan died.
  Its aim oft idle, lovely in its end,
We turn to look, then linger to befriend;
The maid of Egypt thus was led to save
A nation's future leader from the wave:
New things to hear when erst the Gentiles ran,
Truth closed what Curiosity began.
How many a noble art, now widely known,
Owes its young impulse to this power alone:
Even in its slightest working we may trace
A deed that changed the fortunes of a race;
Bruce, banned and hunted on his native soil,
With curious eye surveyed a spider's toil;
Six times the little climber strove and failed;
Six times the chief before his foes had quailed;
"Once more," he cried, "in thine my doom I read,
Once more I dare the fight if thou succeed;"
'Twas done: the insect's fate he made his own:
Once more the battle waged, and gained a throne.
  Behold the sick man in his easy chair;
Barred from the busy crowd and bracing air,
How every passing trifle proves its power
To while away the long, dull, lazy hour.
As down the pane the rival rain-drops chase,
Curious he'll watch to see which wins the race

And let two dogs beneath his window fight,
He'll shut his Bible to enjoy the sight.
So with each newborn nothing rolls the day,
Till some kind neighbour, stumbling in his way,
Draws up his chair, the sufferer to amuse,
And makes him happy while he tells—The News.
The News! our morning, noon, and evening cry;
Day unto day repeats it till we die.
For this the cit, the critic, and the fop,
Dally the hour away in Tonsor's shop;
For this the gossip takes her daily route,
And wears your threshold and your patience out,
For this we leave the parson in the lurch,
And pause to prattle on the way to church;
Even when some coffin'd friend we gather round,
We ask, "What news?" then lay him in the ground;
To this the breakfast owes its sweetest zest,
For this the dinner cools, the bed remains unpress'd.

THE TRAVELLER'S FATE.

Undraw yon curtain, look within that room,
Where all is splendour, yet where all is gloom:
Why weeps that mother? why, in pensive mood,
Group noiseless round, that little, lovely brood?
The battledore is still, lain by each book,
And the harp slumbers in its 'custom'd nook.
Who hath done this? what cold, unpitying foe,
Hath made his house the dwelling-place of wo?
'Tis he, the husband, father, lost in care,
O'er that sweet fellow in his cradle there:
The gallant bark that rides by yonder strand,
Bears him to-morrow from his native land.
Why turns he, half unwilling, from his home,
To tempt the ocean and the earth to roam?
Wealth he can boast, a miser's sigh would hush,
And health is laughing in that ruddy blush;

Friends spring to greet him, and he has no foe—
So honour'd and so bless'd, what bids him go?
His eye must see, his foot each spot must tread,
Where sleeps the dust of earth's recorded dead;
Where rise the monuments of ancient time,
Pillar and pyramid in age sublime:
The pagan's temple and the churchman's tower,
War's bloodiest plain, and Wisdom's greenest bower;
All that his wonder woke in schoolboy themes,
All that his fancy fired in youthful dreams:
Where Socrates once taught he thirsts to stray,
Where Homer poured his everlasting lay;
From Virgil's tomb he longs to pluck one flower,
By Avon's stream to live one moonlight hour;
To pause where England "garners up" her great,
And drop a patriot's tear to Milton's fate;
Fame's living masters, too, he must behold,
Whose deeds shall blazon with the best of old:
Nations compare, their laws and customs scan,
And read, wherever spread, the book of Man;
For these he goes, self-banish'd from his hearth,
And wrings the hearts of all he loves on earth.
  Yet say, shall not new joy those hearts inspire,
When grouping round the future winter fire,
To hear the wonders of the world they burn,
And lose his absence in his glad return?
Return? alas! he shall return no more,
To bless his own sweet home, his own proud shore
Look once again: cold in his cabin now,
Death's finger-mark is on his pallid brow;
No wife stood by, her patient watch to keep,
To smile on him, then turn away to weep;
Kind woman's place rough mariners supplied,
And shared the wanderer's blessing when he died.
Wrapp'd in the raiment that it long must wear,
His body to the deck they slowly bear;
Even there the spirit that I sing is true,
The crew look on with sad but curious view;
The setting sun flings round his farewell rays,
O'er the broad ocean not a ripple plays;

How eloquent, how awful in its power,
The silent lecture of death's sabbath-hour:
One voice that silence breaks—the prayer is said,
And the last rite man pays to man is paid;
The plashing water marks his resting-place,
And fold him round in one long, cold embrace;
Bright bubbles for a moment sparkle o'er,
Then break, to be, like him, beheld no more;
Down, countless fathoms down, he sinks to sleep,
With all the nameless shapes that haunt the deep.

I SEE THEE STILL.

"I rocked her in the cradle,
And laid her in the tomb. She was the *youngest:*
What fireside circle hath not felt the charm
Of that sweet tie! The youngest ne'er grow old.
The fond endearments of our earlier days
We keep alive in them, and when they die,
Our youthful joys we bury with them."

I SEE thee still:
Remembrance, faithful to her trust,
Calls thee in beauty from the dust;
Thou comest in the morning light,
Thou'rt with me through the gloomy night;
In dreams I meet thee as of old;
Then thy soft arms my neck enfold,
And thy sweet voice is in my ear;
In every scene to memory dear,
I see thee still.

I see thee still,
In every hallow'd token round;
This little ring thy finger bound,
This lock of hair thy forehead shaded,
This silken chain by thee was braided,
These flowers, all withered now, like thee,
Sweet sister, thou didst cull for me;

This book was thine, here didst thou read;
This picture, ah! yes, here, indeed,
I see thee still.

I see thee still:
Here was thy summer noon's retreat,
Here was thy favourite fireside seat;
This was thy chamber—here, each day,
I sat and watch'd thy sad decay;
Here, on this bed, thou last didst lie,
Here, on this pillow, thou didst die:
Dark hour! once more its woes unfold;
As then I saw thee, pale and cold,
I see thee still.

I see thee still:
Thou art not in the grave confined—
Death cannot claim the immortal Mind;
Let Earth close o'er its sacred trust,
But goodness dies not in the dust;
Thee, oh! my sister, 'tis not thee
Beneath the coffin's lid I see;
Thou to a fairer land art gone:
There, let me hope, my journey done,
To see thee still!

THE FAMILY MEETING.

Written on occasion of the accidental meeting of all the surviving members of a family.

We are all here!
Father, Mother,
Sister, Brother,
All who hold each other dear.
Each chair is filled—we're all *at home:*
To-night let no cold stranger come:
It is not often thus around
Our old familiar hearth we're found:

Bless, then, the meeting and the spot;
For once be every care forgot;
Let gentle Peace assert her power,
And kind Affection rule the hour;
We're all—all here.

We're *not* all here!
Some are away—the dead ones dear,
Who thronged with us this ancient hearth,
And gave the hour to guiltless mirth.
Fate, with a stern, relentless hand,
Looked in and thinned our little band:
Some like a night-flash passed away,
And some sank, lingering, day by day;
The quiet graveyard—some lie there—
And cruel Ocean has his share—
We're *not* all here.

We *are* all here!
Even they—the dead—though dead, so dear;
Fond Memory, to her duty true,
Brings back their faded forms to view.
How life-like, through the mist of years,
Each well-remembered face appears!
We see them as in times long past,
From each to each kind looks are cast;
We hear their words, their smiles behold,
They're round us as they were of old—
We *are* all here.

We are all here!
Father, Mother,
Sister, Brother,
You that I love with love so dear.
This may not long of us be said;
Soon must we join the gathered dead;
And by the hearth we now sit round,
Some other circle will be found.
Oh! then, that wisdom may we know,
Which yields a life of peace below;

So, in the world to follow this,
May each repeat, in words of bliss,
We're all—all *here!*

THE WINGED WORSHIPPERS.

Two swallows, having flown into church during divine service, were apostrophized in the following stanzas.

GAY, guiltless pair,
What seek ye from the fields of heaven?
Ye have no need of prayer,
Ye have no sins to be forgiven.

Why perch ye here,
Where mortals to their Maker bend?
Can your pure spirits fear
The God ye never could offend?

Ye never knew
The crimes for which we come to weep:
Penance is not for you,
Bless'd wanderers of the *upper deep.*

To you 'tis given
To wake sweet nature's untaught lays;
Beneath the arch of heaven
To chirp away a life of praise.

Then spread each wing,
Far, far above, o'er lakes and lands,
And join the choirs that sing
In yon blue dome not rear'd with hands.

Or if ye stay
To note the consecrated hour,
Teach me the airy way,
And let me try your envied power.

Above the crowd,
On upward wings could I but fly,
I'd bathe in yon bright cloud,
And seek the stars that gem the sky.

'Twere heaven indeed,
Through fields of trackless light to soar,
On nature's charms to feed,
And nature's own great God adore.

Edward C. Pinkney.

THE INDIAN'S BRIDE.

Why is that graceful female here,
With yon red hunter of the deer?
Of gentle mien and shape, she seems
For civil halls design'd,
Yet with the stately savage walks
As she were of his kind.
Look on her leafy diadem,
Enrich'd with many a floral gem:
Those simple ornaments about
Her candid brow, disclose
The loitering Spring's last violet,
And Summer's earliest rose;
But not a flower lies breathing there,
Sweet as herself, or half so fair.
Exchanging lustre with the sun,
A part of day she strays;
A glancing, living, human smile,
On nature's face she plays.
Can none instruct me what are these
Companions of the lofty trees?

Intent to blend with his her lot,
Fate form'd her all that he was not;

And as by mere unlikeness thoughts
    Associate we see,
Their hearts from very difference caught
    A perfect sympathy.
The household goddess here to be
Of that one dusky votary,
She left her pallid countrymen,
    An earthling most divine,
And sought in this sequester'd wood
    A solitary shrine.
Behold them roaming hand in hand,
Like night and sleep, along the land;
Observe their movements: he for her
    Restrains his active stride,
While she assumes a bolder gait
    To ramble at his side:
Thus, even as the steps they frame,
Their souls fast alter to the same.
The one forsakes ferocity,
    And momently grows mild;
The other tempers more and more
    The artful with the wild.
She humanizes him, and he
Educates her to liberty.

Oh, say not they must soon be old,
Their limbs prove faint, their breasts feel cold!
Yet envy I that sylvan pair
    More than my words express,
The singular beauty of their lot,
    And seeming happiness.
They have not been reduced to share
The painful pleasures of despair:
Their sun declines not in the sky,
    Nor are their wishes cast,
Like shadows of the afternoon,
    Repining towards the past:
With naught to dread or to repent,
The present yields them full content.

In solitude there is no crime;
  Their actions are all free,
And passion lends their way of life
  The only dignity;
And how should they have any cares?
Whose interest contends with theirs?

The world, or all they know of it,
Is theirs: for them the stars are lit;
For them the earth beneath is green,
  The heavens above are bright:
For them the moon doth wax and wane,
  And decorate the night;
For them the branches of those trees
Wave music in the vernal breeze;
For them upon that dancing spray
  The free bird sits and sings,
And glitt'ring insects flit about
  Upon delighted wings;
For them that brook, the brakes among,
Murmurs its small and drowsy song;
For them the many-colour'd clouds
  Their shapes diversify,
And change at once, like smiles and frowns,
  Th' expression of the sky.
For them and by them all is gay,
And fresh and beautiful as they:
The images their minds receive,
  Their minds assimilate,
To outward forms imparting thus
  The glory of their state.
Could aught be painted otherwise
Than fair, seen through her star-bright eyes?
He too, because she fills his sight,
  Each object falsely sees;
The pleasure that he has in her
  Makes all things seem to please.
And this is love; and it is life
They lead, that Indian and his wife.

MEMORY.

How feels the guiltless dreamer, who
With idly curious gaze
Has let his mind's glance wander through
The relics of past days?
As feels the pilgrim that has scann'd,
Within their skirting wall,
The moonlit marbles of some grand
Disburied capital;
Masses of whiteness and of gloom,
The darkly bright remains
Of desolate palace, empty tomb,
And desecrated fanes:
For in the ruins of old hours
Remembrance haply sees
Temples, and tombs, and palaces,
Not different from these.

Emma C. Embury.

CHRIST IN THE TEMPEST.

Midnight was on the mighty deep,
  And darkness filled the boundless sky,
While mid the raging wind was heard
  The sea-bird's mournful cry;
For tempest clouds were mustering wrath
Across the seaman's trackless path.

It came at length: one fearful gust
  Rent from the mast the shivering sail,
And drove the helpless bark along,
  The plaything of the gale,
While fearfully the lightning's glare
Fell on the pale brows gather'd there.

But there was one o'er whose bright face
  Unmark'd the livid lightnings flash'd;
And on whose stirless, prostrate form,
  Unfelt the sea-spray dash'd;
For mid the tempest fierce and wild,
He slumber'd like a wearied child.

Oh! who could look upon that face,
  And feel the sting of coward fear?
Though hell's fierce demons raged around,
  Yet heaven itself was here;
For who that glorious brow could see,
Nor own a present Deity?

With hurried fear they press around
  The lowly Saviour's humble bed,
As if his very touch had power
  To shield their souls from dread;
While cradled on the raging deep,
He lay in calm and tranquil sleep.

Vainly they struggled with their fears,
  But wilder still the tempest woke,
Till from their full and o'erfraught hearts
  The voice of terror broke:
"Behold! we sink beneath the wave,
We perish, Lord! but thou canst save."

Slowly he rose; and mild rebuke
  Shone in his soft and heaven-lit eye:
"Oh ye of little faith," he cried,
  "Is not your master nigh?
Is not your hope of succour just?
Why know ye not in whom ye trust?"

He turn'd away, and conscious power
  Dilated his majestic form,
As o'er the boiling sea he bent,
  The ruler of the storm;

Earth to its centre felt the thrill,
As low he murmur'd, "Peace! Be still!"

Hark to the burst of meeting waves,
The roaring of the angry sea!
A moment more, and all is hush'd
In deep tranquillity;
While not a breeze is near to break
The mirror'd surface of the lake.

Then on the stricken hearts of all
Fell anxious doubt and holy awe,
As timidly they gazed on him
Whose will was nature's law:
"What man is this," they cry, "whose word
E'en by the raging sea is heard?"

·NES SUGGESTED BY THE MORAVIAN BURIAL-GROUND AT BETHLEHEM.

When in the shadow of the tomb
This heart shall rest,
Oh! lay me where spring flow'rets bloom
On earth's bright breast.

Oh! ne'er in vaulted chambers lay
My lifeless form;
Seek not of such mean, worthless prey
To cheat the worm.

In this sweet city of the dead
I fain would sleep,
Where flowers may deck my narrow bed,
And night dews weep.

But raise not the sepulchral stone
To mark the spot;
Enough, if by thy heart alone
'Tis ne'er forgot

Henry Pickering.

THE LAST DAYS OF AUTUMN

Hark to the sounding gale! how through the soul
It vibrates, and in thunder seems to roll
Along the mountains! Loud the forest moans,
And, naked to the blast, the o'ermastering spirit owns.

Rustling, the leaves are rudely hurried by,
Or in dark eddies whirl'd; while from on high
The ruffian Winds, as if in giant mirth,
Unseat the mountain pine, and headlong dash to earth!

With crest of foam, the uplifted flood no more
Flows placidly along the sylvan shore;
But, vex'd to madness, heaves its turbid wave,
Threatening to leap the banks it whilom loved lave:

And in the angry heavens, where, wheeling low,
The sun exhibits yet a fitful glow,
The clouds, obedient to the stormy power,
Or shatter'd fly along, or still more darkly lower

Amazement seizes all! within the vale
Shrinking, the mute herd snuff the shivering gale,
The while, with tossing head and streaming mane,
The horse affrighted bounds, or wildly skims the plain.

Whither, with charms to Fancy yet so dear,
Whither has fled the lovely infant year?
Where, too, the groves in greener pomp array'd?
The deep and solemn gloom of the inspiring shade?

The verdant heaven that once the woods o'er-
And underneath a pensive twilight shed, [spread,

Is shrivell'd all: dead the vine-mantled bowers,
And wither'd in their bloom the beautiful young
flowers!

Mute, too, the voice of Joy! no tuneful bird
Amid the leafless forest now is heard;
Nor more may ploughboy's laugh the bosom cheer,
Nor in the velvet glade Love's whisper charm the
ear.

But lo, the ruthless storm its force hath spent;
And see! where sinking 'neath yon cloudy tent,
The sun withdraws his last cold, feeble ray,
Abandoning to Night his short and dubious sway.

A heavier gloom pervades the chilly air!
Now in their northern caves the Winds prepare
The nitrous frost to sheet with dazzling white,
The long-deserted fields at the return of light:

Or with keen icy breath they may glass o'er
The restless wave, and on the lucid floor
Let fall the feathery shower, and far and wide
Involve in snowy robe the land and fetter'd tide!

Thus shut the varied scene! and thus, in turn,
Oh Autumn! thou within thine ample urn
Sweep'st all earth's glories. Ah, for one brief hour,
Spare the soft virgin's bloom and tender human
flower!

James G. Percival.

THE PATRIARCHAL AGE.

Oh! for those early days, when patriarchs dwelt
In pastoral tents, that rose beneath the palm,
When life was pure, and every bosom felt
Unwarp'd affection's sweetest, holiest balm,

And like the silent scene around them, calm,
Years stole along in one unruffled flow;
Their hearts aye warbled with devotion's psalm,
And as they saw their buds around them blow,
Their keenly glistening eye revealed the grateful glow.

They sat at evening, when their gather'd flocks
Bleated and sported by the palm-crowned well,
The sun was glittering on the pointed rocks,
And long and wide the deepening shadows fell;
They sang their hymn, and in a choral swell
They raised their simple voices to the Power
Who smiled along the fair sky; they would dwell
Fondly and deeply on his praise; that hour
Was to them, as to flowers that droop and fade, the shower.

He warm'd them in the sunbeams, and they gazed
In wonder on that kindling fount of light;
And as, hung on the glowing west, it blazed
In brighter glories, with a full delight
They pour'd their pealing anthem, and when night
Lifted her silver forehead, and the moon
Roll'd through the blue serenity, in bright
But softer radiance, they bless'd the boon
That gave those hours the charm without the fire of noon.

Spring of the living world, the dawn of nature,
When man walk'd forth the lord of all below,
Erect and godlike in his giant stature,
Before the tainted gales of vice 'gan blow:
His conscience spotless as the new-fallen snow,
Pure as the crystal spouting from the spring,
He aim'd no murderous dagger, drew no bow,
But at the soaring of the eagle's wing,
The gaunt wolf's stealthy step, the lion's ravening spring.

With brutes alone he arm'd himself for war;
  Free to the winds his long locks dancing flew,
And at his prowling enemy afar,
  He shot his death-shaft from the nervy yew;
  In morning's mist his shrill-voiced bugle blew,
And with the rising sun on tall rocks strode,
  And, bounding through the gemm'd and sparkling, dew,
The rose of health, that in his full cheek glow'd,
Told of the pure fresh stream that there enkindling flow'd.

This was the age when mind was all on fire,
  The days of inspiration when the soul,
Warm'd, heighten'd, lifted, burning with desire
  For all the great and lovely, to the goal
  Of man's essential glory rush'd; then stole
The sage his spark from heaven, the prophet spake
  His deep-toned words of thunder, as when roll
The peals amid the clouds: words that would break
The spirit's leaden sleep, and all its terrors wake.

THE SUN.

Centre of light and energy! thy way
  Is through the unknown void; thou hast thy throne,
Morning, and evening, and at noon of day,
  Far in the blue, untended and alone:
  Ere the first-waken'd airs of earth had blown,
On thou didst march, triumphant in thy light;
  Then thou didst send thy glance, which still hath flown
Wide through the never-ending worlds of night,
And yet thy full orb burns with flash as keen and bright.

We call thee Lord of Day, and thou dost give
  To Earth the fire that animates her crust,
And wakens all the forms that move and live,
  From the fine viewless mould which lurks in dust,
  To him who looks to Heaven, and on his bust
Bears stamp'd the seal of God, who gathers there
  Lines of deep thought, high feeling, daring trust
In his own centred powers, who aims to share
In all his soul can frame of wide, and great, and fair.

Thy path is high in Heaven; we cannot gaze
  On the intense of light that girds thy car;
There is a crown of glory in thy rays,
  Which bears thy pure divinity afar,
  To mingle with the equal light of star,
For thou, so vast to us, art in the whole
  One of the sparks of night that fire the air,
And as around thy centre planets roll,
So thou too hast thy path around the central soul.

I am no fond idolater to thee,
  One of the countless multitude, who burn,
As lamps, around the one Eternity,
  In whose contending forces systems turn
  Their circles round that seat of life, the urn
Where all must sleep, if matter ever dies:
  Sight fails me here, but fancy can discern
With the wide glance of her all-seeing eyes,
Where, in the heart of worlds, the ruling Spirit lies.

And thou, too, hast thy world, and unto thee
  We are as nothing; thou goest forth alone,
And movest through the wide aërial sea,
  Glad as a conqueror resting on his throne
  From a new victory, where he late had shown
Wider his power to nations; so thy light
  Comes with new pomp, as if thy strength had grown,
With each revolving day, or thou at night
Had lit again thy fires, and thus renew'd thy might.

Age o'er thee has no power: thou bringst the same
  Light to renew the morning, as when first,
If not eternal, thou, with front of flame,
  On the dark face of earth in glory burst,
  And warm'd the seas, and in their bosom nursed
The earliest things of life, the worm and shell;
  Till through the sinking ocean mountains pierced,
And then came forth the land whereon we dwell,
Rear'd like a magic fane above the watery swell.

And there thy searching heat awoke the seeds
  Of all that gives a charm to earth, and lends
An energy to nature; all that feeds
  On the rich mould, and then in bearing bends
  Its fruits again to earth, wherein it blends
The last and first of life; of all who bear
  Their forms in motion, where the spirit tends
Instinctive, in their common good to share, [there.
Which lies in things that breathe, or late were living

They live in thee: without thee all were dead
  And dark, no beam had lighted on the waste,
But one eternal night around had spread
  Funereal gloom, and coldly thus defaced
  This Eden, which thy fairy hand had graced
With such uncounted beauty; all that blows
  In the fresh air of Spring, and, growing, braced
Its form to manhood, when it stands and glows
In the full-temper'd beam, that gladdens as it goes.

Thou lookest on the Earth, and then it smiles;
  Thy light is hid, and all things droop and mourn;
Laughs the wide sea around her budding isles,
  When through their heaven thy changing car is
      borne;
  Thou wheel'st away thy flight, the woods are shorn
Of all their waving locks, and storms awake;
  All, that was once so beautiful, is torn
By the wild winds which plough the lonely lake,
And in their maddening rush the crested mountains

The earth lies buried in a shroud of snow;
Life lingers, and would die, but thy return
Gives to their gladden'd hearts an overflow
Of all the power that brooded in the urn [spurn
Of their chill'd frames, and then they proudly
All bands that would confine, and give to air
Hues, fragrance, shapes of beauty, till they burn,
When on a dewy morn thou dartest there [fair.
Rich waves of gold to wreath with fairer light the

The vales are thine; and when the touch of Spring
Thrills them, and gives them gladness, in thy light
They glitter, as the glancing swallow's wing
Dashes the water in his winding flight,
And leaves behind a wave that crinkles bright,
And widens outward to the pebbled shore—
The vales are thine: and when they wake from
night,
The dews that bend the grass tips, twinkling o'er
Their soft and oozy beds, look upward and adore.

The hills are thine: they catch thy newest beam,
And gladden in thy parting, where the wood
Flames out in every leaf, and drinks the stream
That flows from out thy fulness, as a flood
Bursts from an unknown land, and rolls the food
Of nations in its waters; so thy rays
Flow and give brighter tints, than ever bud,
When a clear sheet of ice reflects a blaze [plays.
Of many twinkling gems, as every gloss'd bough

Thine are the mountains, where they purely lift
Snows that have never wasted in a sky
Which hath no stain; below the storm may drift
Its darkness, and the thunder-gust roar by;
Aloft in thy eternal smile they lie,
Dazzling but cold; thy farewell glance looks there
And when below thy hues of beauty die,
Girt round them as a rosy belt, they bear
Into the high dark vault a brow that still is fair.

The clouds are thine, and all their magic hues
  Are pencill'd by thee; when thou bendest low,
Or comest in thy strength, thy hand imbues
  Their waving fold with such a perfect glow
  Of all pure tints, the fairy pictures throw
Shame on the proudest art; the tender stain
  Hung round the verge of Heaven, that has a bow
Girds the wide world, and in their blended chain
All tints to the deep gold that flashes in thy train:

These are thy trophies, and thou bendst thy arch,
  The sign of triumph, in a seven-fold twine,
Where the spent storm is hasting on its march,
  And there the glories of thy light combine,
  And form with perfect curve a lifted line,
Striding the earth and air; man looks and tells
  How Peace and Mercy in its beauty shine,
And how the heavenly messenger impels
Her glad wings on the path, that thus in ether swells.

The ocean is thy vassal: thou dost sway
  His waves to thy dominion, and they go
Where thou in Heaven dost guide them on their way,
  Rising and falling in eternal flow;
  Thou lookest on the waters, and they glow;
They take them wings, and spring aloft in air,
  And change to clouds, and then, dissolving, throw
Their treasures back to earth, and, rushing, tear
The mountain and the vale, as proudly on they bear.

I too have been upon thy rolling breast,
  Widest of waters! I have seen thee lie
Calm, as an infant pillow'd in its rest
  On a fond mother's bosom, when the sky,
  Not smoother, gave the deep its azure die,
Till a new Heaven was arch'd and glass'd below;
  And then the clouds, that, gay in sunset, fly,
Cast on it such a stain, it kindled so,
As in the cheek of youth the living roses grow.

I too have seen thee on thy surging path,
  When the night tempest met thee: thou didst dash
Thy white arms high in Heaven, as if in wrath
  Threatening the angry sky; thy waves did lash
  The labouring vessel, and with deadening crash
Rush madly forth to scourge its groaning sides;
  Onward thy billows came to meet and clash
In a wild warfare, till the lifted tides [rides.
Mingled their yesty tops, where the dark storm-cloud

In thee, first light, the bounding ocean smiles,
  When the quick winds uprear it in a swell,
That rolls in glittering green around the isles,
  Where ever-springing fruits and blossoms dwell:
  Oh! with a joy no gifted tongue can tell,
I hurry o'er the waters, when the sail
  Swells tensely, and the light keel glances well
Over the curling billow, and the gale
Comes off from spicy groves to tell its winning tale.

The soul is thine: of old thou wert the power
  Who gave the poet life, and I in thee
Feel my heart gladden at the holy hour
  When thou art sinking in the silent sea;
  Or when I climb the height, and wander free
In thy meridian glory, for the air
  Sparkles and burns in thy intensity,
I feel thy light within me, and I share
In the full glow of soul thy spirit kindles there.

THE DESERTED WIFE.

He comes not; I have watched the moon go down,
But yet he comes not. Once it was not so.
He thinks not how these bitter tears do flow,
The while he holds his riot in that town.
Yet he will come and chide, and I shall weep;
And he will wake my infant from its sleep,

To blend its feeble wailing with my tears
Oh! how I love a mother's watch to keep,
Over those sleeping eyes, that smile, which cheers
My heart, though sunk in sorrow, fix'd and deep.
I had a husband once, who loved me ; now
He ever wears a frown upon his brow,
And feeds his passion on a wanton's lip,
As bees, from laurel flowers, a poison sip;
But yet I cannot hate. Oh! there were hours,
When I could hang for ever on his eye,
And Time, who stole with silent swiftness by,
Strew'd, as he hurried on, his path with flowers.
I loved him then; he loved me too. My heart
Still finds its fondness kindle if he smile ;
The memory of our loves will ne'er depart;
And though he often sting me with a dart,
Venom'd and barb'd, and waste upon the vile
Caresses which his babe and mine should share—
Though he should spurn me, I will camly bear
His madness; and should sickness come, and lay
Its paralyzing hand upon him, then
I would, with kindness, all my wrongs repay,
Until the penitent should weep, and say
How injured and how faithful I had been.

THE CORAL GROVE.

Deep in the wave is a coral grove,
Where the purple mullet and goldfish rove,
Where the sea-flower spreads its leaves of blue,
That never are wet with falling dew,
But in bright and changeful beauty shine,
Far down in the green and glassy brine ;
The floor is of sand, like the mountain drift,
And the pearl shells spangle the flinty snow ;
From coral rocks the sea-plants lift
Their boughs, where the tides and billows flow;

The water is calm and still below,
For the winds and waves are absent there,
And the sands are bright as the stars that glow
In the motionless fields of upper air:
There with its waving blade of green,
The sea-flag streams through the silent water,
And the crimson leaf of the dulse is seen
To blush, like a banner bathed in slaughter:
There, with a light and easy motion,
The fan-coral sweeps through the clear deep sea;
And the yellow and scarlet tufts of ocean
Are bending like corn on the upland lea:
And life, in rare and beautiful forms,
Is sporting amid those bowers of stone,
And is safe, when the wrathful spirit of storms
Has made the top of the wave his own:
And when the ship from his fury flies,
Where the myriad voices of ocean roar,
When the wind-god frowns in the murky skies,
And demons are waiting the wreck on shore;
Then far below in the peaceful sea,
The purple mullet and goldfish rove,
Where the waters murmur tranquilly,
Through the bending twigs of the coral grove

CLOUDS.

Ye clouds, who are the ornament of heaven,
Who give to it its gayest shadowings,
And its most awful glories; ye who roll
In the dark tempest, or at dewy evening
Hang low in tenderest beauty; ye who, ever
Changing your Protean aspects, now are gather'd,
Like fleecy piles, when the mid sun is brightest,
Even in the height of heaven, and there repose,
Solemnly calm, without a visible motion,
Hour after hour, looking upon the earth

With a serenest smile : or ye who rather,
Heap'd in those sulphury masses, heavily
Jutting above their bases, like the smoke
Poured from a furnace or a roused volcano,
Stand on the dun horizon, threatening
Lightning and storm ; who, lifted from the hills,
March onward to the zenith, ever darkening,
And heaving into more gigantic towers
And mountainous piles of blackness ; who then roar
With the collected winds within your womb,
Or the far uttered thunders ; who ascend
Swifter and swifter, till wide overhead
Your vanguards curl and toss upon the tempest
Like the stirred ocean on a reef of rocks
Just topping o'er its waves, while deep below
The pregnant mass of vapour and of flame
Rolls with an awful pomp, and grimly lowers,
Seeming to the struck eye of fear the car
Of an offended spirit, whose swart features
Glare through the sooty darkness, fired with ven-
And ready with uplifted hand to smite [geance,
And scourge a guilty nation ; ye who lie,
After the storm is over, far away,
Crowning the drippling forests with the arch
Of beauty, such as lives alone in heaven,
Bright daughter of the sun, bending around
From mountain unto mountain like the wreath
Of victory, or like a banner telling
Of joy and gladness ; ye who round the moon
Assemble, when she sits in the mid sky
In perfect brightness, and encircle her
With a fair wreath of all aërial dyes ;
Ye who, thus hovering round her, shine like mount-
Whose tops are never darken'd, but remain, [ains
Centuries and countless ages, reared for temples
Of purity and light ; or ye who crowd
To hail the newborn day, and hang for him,
Above his ocean couch, a canopy
Of all inimitable hues and colours,

Such as are only pencill'd by the hands
Of the unseen ministers of earth and air,
Seen only in the tinting of the clouds,
And the soft shadowing of plumes and flowers
Or ye who, following in his funeral train,
Light up your torches at his sepulchre,
And open on us through the clefted hills
Far glances into glittering worlds beyond
The twilight of the grave, where all is light,
Golden and glorious light, too full and high
For mortal eye to gaze on, stretching out
Brighter and ever brighter, till it spread,
Like one wide radiant ocean without bounds,
One infinite sea of glory: Thus, ye clouds,
And in innumerable other shapes
Of greatness or of beauty, ye attend us,
To give to the wide arch above us Life
And all its changes. Thus it is to us
A volume full of wisdom, but without ye
One awful uniformity had ever,
With too severe a majesty, oppress'd us.

James Wallis Eastburn.

EVENING ON NARRAGANSET BAY*.

The sun is sinking from the sky
In calm and cloudless majesty;
And cooler hours, with gentle sway,
Succeed the fiery heat of day.

* This and the succeeding specimens of Eastburn's poetry are taken from the narrative poem of Yamoyden, written jointly by him and Sands. The different portions of that work have never been assigned to the respective authors, and the merit of these extracts must therefore be shared between them, except perhaps, in the case of the "Song of an Indian Mother," which we have somewhere seen claimed as the sole property of Eastburn.

Forest, and shore, and rippling tide,
Confess the evening's influence wide,
Seen lovelier in that fading light,
That heralds the approaching night;
That magic colouring nature throws,
To deck her beautiful repose;
When, floating on the breeze of even,
Long clouds of purple streak the heaven,
With brighter tints of glory blending,
And darker hues of night descending.
While hastening to its shady rest
Each weary songster seeks its nest,
Chanting a last, a farewell lay,
As gloomier falls the parting day.

Broad Narraganset's bosom blue
Has shone with every varying hue;
The mystic alchymy of even
Its rich delusions all has given.
The silvery sheet unbounded spread,
First melting from the waters fled;
Next the wide path of beaten gold
Flashing with fiery sparkles roll'd;
As all its gorgeous glories died,
An amber tinge blush'd o'er the tide;
Faint and more faint, as more remote,
The lessening ripples peaceful float;
And now, one ruby line alone
Trembles, is paler, and is gone;
And from the blue wave fades away
The last life-tint of dying day!
In darkness veil'd, was seen no more
Connanicut's extended shore;
Each little isle with bosom green,
Descending mists impervious screen;
One gloomy shade o'er all the woods
Of forest-fringed Aquetnet broods;
Where solemn oak was seen before
Beside the rival sycamore,

Or pine and cedar lined the height,
All in one livery brown were dight.

But lo! with orb serene on high,
The round moon climbs the eastern sky;
The stars all quench their feebler rays
Before her universal blaze.
Round moon! how sweetly dost thou smile,
Above that green reposing isle;
Soft cradled in the illumined bay,
Where from its banks the shadows seem
Melting in filmy light away.
Far does thy temper'd lustre stream,
Checkering the tufted groves on high,
While glens in gloom beneath them lie.
Oft sheeted with the ghostly beam,
Mid the thick forest's mass of shade,
The shingled roof is gleaming white,
Where labour, in the cultured glade,
Has all the wild a garden made.
And there with silvery tassels bright
The serried maize is waving slow,
While fitful shadows come and go,
Swift o'er its undulating seas,
As gently breathes the evening breeze.

Solemn it is, in green woods deep,
That magic light o'er nature's sleep;
Where in long ranks the pillars gray
Aloft their mingling structures bear—
Mingling, in gloom or tracery fair,
Where find the unbroken beams their way—
Or through close trellis flickering stray,
While sheeny leaflets here and there
Flutter, with momentary glow.
'Tis wayward life reveal'd below,
With checker'd gleams of joy and wo!
And those pure realms above that shine,
So chaste, so vivid, so divine,

Are the sole type that heaven has shown
Of those more lovely realms, its own!

There is no sound amid the trees,
Save the faint brush of rustling breeze;
Save insect sentinels, that still
Prolong their constant 'larum shrill,
And answer all, from tree to tree,
With one monotonous revelry.

SONG OF AN INDIAN MOTHER.

'Sleep, child of my love! be thy slumber as light
  As the redbird's that nestles secure on the spray;
Be the visions that visit thee fairy and bright
  As the dewdrops that sparkle around with the ray!
Oh, soft flows the breath from thine innocent breast;
  In the wild wood, sleep cradles in roses thy head;
But her who protects thee, a wanderer unbless'd,
  He forsakes, or surrounds with his phantoms of dread.
I fear for thy father! why stays he so long
  On the shores where the wife of the giant was thrown,
And the sailor oft linger'd to hearken her song,
  So sad o'er the wave, ere she harden'd to stone.
He skims the blue tide in his birchen canoe,
  Where the foe in the moonbeams his path may descry;
The ball to its scope may speed rapid and true,
  And lost in the wave be thy father's death cry!
The POWER that is round us, whose presence is near,
  In the gloom and the solitude felt by the soul,
Protect that frail bark in its lonely career,
  And shield *thee* when roughly life's billows shall roll."

PHILIP'S DREAM.

And on this night, whose parting shades
Shall see the avengers lift their blades,
And bring relentless fury, fraught
With many an insult's goading thought,
  The outlaw Sachem slept;
The while his scanty band around,
Low in the swamp's unequal ground,
  Their mournful vigils kept.
Tall trees o'erthrown their bulwark made,
While rude, luxuriant vines o'erspread,
  Conceal'd their lurking-place;
There, now to feeble numbers worn,
In strength o'erspent, in hope forlorn,
Shrunk, trembling for the coming morn,
  The Wampanoag race.

Mothers and widows sad were then
Hidden within that gloomy fen;
Left for a space by war, to mourn
Each sacred bond asunder torn.
Perchance they thought of many a scene
Departed, to return no more;
How, when the hunter's toil was o'er,
And dress'd his frugal meal had been,
His children cluster'd round his knee,
To hear the tales of former days,
And learn what men should strive to be,
While listening to the warrior's praise:
And she, thrice happy parent! sate,
Well pleased, beside her honour'd mate;
What time gray eve its welcome hue
O'er distant hills and forests threw:
Nor idle then, with dexterous hand,
She wrought the glittering wampum band;
Or loved the silken grass to braid;
Or through the deerskin, smooth and strong
Weaving the many-colour'd thong,
Her hunter's comely sandals made.

Thus they recall'd; and marvell'd they,
When bounteous earth is wide and free,
Why man, whose life is for a day,
So much in love with wo should be!

He slept, yet not the spirit slept;
Her feverish vigil memory kept;
In motley visions on her eye,
The phantom host of dreams pass'd by.
Tradition, meet for vulgar faith,
Has told of threats of coming skaith,
Spoke by the Evil One, who came,
This eve, his destined prey to claim,
In form, as when at noon of night,
He met him on the mountain's height:
O'er the gray rock the fiend outspread
His sable pinions as he fled,
And, ere the sounding air he cleft,
His foot gigantic impress left.
Such superstition's idle tale—
But let the minstrel's lore prevail.

He saw the world of souls; and there
Brave men and beauteous women were:
Fair forms to chiefs of godlike mien,
Reposing in their arbours green,
Supplied the spicy bowls they quaff'd,
And round them danced, and joyous laugh'd;
While aye the warriors smiled to see
Those lovely creatures in their glee;
And pledged them in the sparkling cup;
Or breathed their fragrant incense up;
Grateful and pure, 'twas seen to flow
From calumets like stainless snow.
Apart reclined in kingly state,
The ancient Massasoiet sate,
And earnest with Uncompeon old,
Speech grave, but pleasant, seem'd to hold;
Uncompoën, slain in recent fight,
Contending for his nephew's right.

Just from the woods, like hunter dight,
The gallant Ouamsutta came;
Bearing behind his plenteous game,
In order moved the warrior's train;
Joyous his bearing was, and free,
As if fatigue, and wounds, and pain,
In that bless'd world could never be;
His buskins trapp'd with glittering gold,
His floating mantle's graceful fold
 Clasp'd with a sparkling gem;
Dazzling his cincture's radiance gleam'd,
Woven from the heavenly bow it seem'd,
And like the sun-rays danced and stream'd
 His feathery diadem.
A spear with silver tipp'd he bore;
The gayly-tinkling rings before,
 The quiver rattling on his back,
His buoyant frame and kindling eye,
The thrilling pulse of transport high,
 The sense of power and pleasure spake.
And one and all the Sachem knew,
When near their blissful bower he drew;
And clapp'd their hands with joy to see
The hero join their company.
And strains of softest music round,
From flutes and tabors, with the sound
Of voices, sweet as sweetest bird,
To greet the entering guest were heard.
"Welcome," they sung, "thy toils are done,
Thy battles fought, thy rest is won;
And welcome to the world thou art,
Where kindred souls shall never part;
Honour on earth shall valour have,
And joy with us attends the brave."

That ravishing dream was rapt away,
Vanish'd the forms, the music died;
And changeful fancy's wayward sway
Visions of darker hue supplied.

O'er frozen plains he seem'd to go,
Mid driving sleet and blinding snow.
Then Assawomsett's lake he knew,
And dim descried, the tempest through,
Apostate Sausaman arise;
Stiff were his gory locks with ice,
  And mangled was his form;
It tower'd aloft to giant size;
Fierce shone the fury of his eyes,
  Like lightning through the storm.
He cried, "My spirit hath no home!
A weary, wandering ghost I roam.
This night the avengers lift the blade,
And my foul murder shall be paid!"

John Pierpont.

THE POWER OF MUSIC.

Hear yon poetic pilgrim* of the West
Chant Music's praise, and to her power attest;
Who now, in Florida's untrodden woods,
Bedecks, with vines of jessamine, her floods,
And flowery bridges o'er them loosely throws
Who hangs the canvass where Atala glows,
On the live oak, in floating drapery shrouded,
That like a mountain rises, lightly clouded:
Who, for the son of Outalissi, twines
Beneath the shade of ever-whispering pines
A funeral wreath, to bloom upon the moss
That Time already sprinkles on the cross
Raised o'er the grave where his young virgin sleeps,
And Superstition o'er her victim weeps;
Whom now the silence of the dead surrounds,
Among Scioto's monumental mounds;

* Chateaubriand.

Save that, at times, the musing pilgrim hears
A crumbling oak fall with the weight of years,
To swell the mass that Time and Ruin throw
O'er chalky bones that mouldering lie below,
By virtues unembalm'd, unstain'd by crimes,
Lost in those towering tombs of other times;
For, where no bard has cherished Virtue's flame,
No ashes sleep in the warm sun of Fame.
With sacred lore this traveller beguiles
His weary way, while o'er him Fancy smiles.
Whether he kneels in venerable groves,
Or through the wide and green savanna roves,
His heart leaps lightly on each breeze, that bears
The faintest breath of Iduméa's airs.

Now he recalls the lamentable wail
That pierced the shades of Rama's palmy vale,
When Murder struck, throned on an infant's bier,
A note for Satan's and for Herod's ear.
Now on a bank, o'erhung with waving wood,
Whose falling leaves flit o'er Ohio's flood,
The pilgrim stands; and o'er his memory rushes
The mingled tide of tears and blood, that gushes
Along the valleys where his childhood stray'd,
And round the temples where his fathers pray'd
How fondly then, from all but Hope exiled,
To Zion's wo recurs Religion's child!
He sees the tear of Judah's captive daughters
Mingle, in silent flow, with Babel's waters;
While Salem's harp, by patriot pride unstrung,
Wrapp'd in the mist that o'er the river hung,
Felt but the breeze that wanton'd o'er the billow,
And the long, sweeping fingers of the willow.

And could not Music sooth the captive's wo?
But should that harp be strung for Judah's foe?

While thus the enthusiast roams along the stream,
Balanced between a revery and a dream,

Backward he springs; and, through his bounding
heart,
The cold and curdling poison seems to dart.
For, in the leaves, beneath a quivering brake,
Spinning his death-note, lies a coiling snake,
Just in the act, with greenly venom'd fangs,
To strike the foot that heedless o'er him hangs.
Bloated with rage, on spiral folds he rides;
His rough scales shiver on his spreading sides;
Dusky and dim his glossy neck becomes,
And freezing poisons thicken on his gums;
His parch'd and hissing throat breathes hot and dry;
A spark of hell lies burning on his eye:
While, like a vapour, o'er his writhing rings,
Whirls his light tail, that threatens while it sings.

Soon as dumb Fear removes her icy fingers
From off the heart, where gazing wonder lingers,
The pilgrim, shrinking from a doubtful fight,
Aware of danger, too, in sudden flight,
From his soft flute throws Music's air around,
And meets his foe upon enchanted ground.
See! as the plaintive melody is flung,
The lightning flash fades on the serpent's tongue;
The uncoiling reptile o'er each shining fold
Throws changeful clouds of azure, green, and gold;
A softer lustre twinkles in his eye;
His neck is burnish'd with a glossier dye;
His slippery scales grow smoother to the sight,
And his relaxing circles roll in light.
Slowly the charm retires: with waving sides,
Along its track the graceful listener glides;
While Music throws her silver cloud around,
And bears her votary off in magic folds of sound

FOR A CELEBRATION OF THE MASSACHUSETTS MECHANICS' CHARITABLE ASSOCIATION.

Loud o'er thy savage child,
  Oh God, the night-wind roar'd,
As, houseless, in the wild
  He bow'd him and adored.
    Thou saw'st him there,
      As to the sky
      He raised his eye
    In fear and prayer.

Thine inspiration came!
  And, grateful for thine aid,
An altar to thy name
  He built beneath the shade,
    The limbs of larch
      That darken'd round,
      He bent and bound
    In many an arch;

Till in a sylvan fane
  Went up the voice of prayer,
And music's simple strain
  Arose in worship there.
    The arching boughs,
      The roof of leaves
      That summer weaves,
    O'erheard his vows.

Then beam'd a brighter day;
  And Salem's holy height
And Greece in glory lay
  Beneath the kindling light.
    Thy temple rose
      On Salem's hill,
      While Grecian skill
    Adorn'd thy foes.

Along those rocky shores,
Along those olive plains,
Where pilgrim Genius pores
O'er Art's sublime remains,
Long colonnades
Of snowy white
Look'd forth in light
Through classic shades.

Forth from the quarry stone
The marble goddess sprung;
And, loosely round her thrown,
Her marble vesture hung;
And forth from cold
And sunless mines
Came silver shrines
And gods of gold.

The Star of Bethlehem burn'd
And, where the Stoic trod,
The altar was o'erturn'd,
Raised "to an unknown God."
And now there are
No idol fanes
On all the plains
Beneath that star.

To honour thee, dread Power!
Our strength and skill combine;
And temple, tomb, and tower
Attest these gifts divine.
A swelling dome
For pride they gild,
For peace they build
An humbler home.

By these our fathers' host
Was led to victory first,
When on our guardless coast
The cloud of battle burst,

Through storm and spray,
By these controll'd,
Our navies hold
Their thundering way.

Great Source of every art!
Our homes, our pictured halls,
Our throng'd and busy mart,
That lifts its granite walls,
And shoots to heaven
Its glittering spires,
To catch the fires
Of morn and even;

These, and the breathing forms
The brush or chisel gives,
With this when marble warms,
With that when canvass lives;
These all combine
In countless ways
To swell thy praise,
For all are thine.

THE EXILE AT REST.

His falchion flash'd along the Nile;
His hosts he led through Alpine snows;
O'er Moscow's towers, that shook the while,
His eagle flag unroll'd—and froze.

Here sleeps he now alone: not one
Of all the kings whose crowns he gave,
Nor sire, nor brother, wife, nor son,
Hath ever seen or sought his grave.

Here sleeps he now alone: the star
That led him on from crown to crown
Hath sunk; the nations from afar
Gazed as it faded and went down.

He sleeps alone: the mountain cloud
  That night hangs round him, and the breath
Of morning scatters, is the shroud
  That wraps his martial form in death.

High is his couch: the ocean flood
  Far, far below by storms is curl'd,
As round him heaved, while high he stood,
  A stormy and inconstant world.

Hark! Comes there from the Pyramids,
  And from Siberia's wastes of snow,
And Europe's fields, a voice that bids
  The world he awed to mourn him? No:

The only, the perpetual dirge
  That's heard there is the seabird's cry,
The mournful murmur of the surge,
  The cloud's deep voice, the wind's low sigh.

HER CHOSEN SPOT.

While yet she lived, she walk'd alone
  Among these shades. A voice divine
Whisper'd, "This spot shall be thine own;
  Here shall thy wasting form recline,
  Beneath the shadow of this pine."

"Thy will be done!" the sufferer said.
  This spot was hallow'd from that hour;
And, in her eyes, the evening's shade
And morning's dew this green spot made
  More lovely than her bridal bower.

By the pale moon—herself more pale
  And spirit-like—these walks she trod;
And, while no voice, from swell or vale,
  Was heard, she knelt upon this sod
  And gave her spirit back to God.

That spirit, with an angel's wings,
Went up from the young mother's bed.
So, heavenward, soars the lark and sings;
She's lost to earth and earthly things;
But "weep not, for she is not dead,

She sleepeth!" Yea, she sleepeth here,
The first that in these grounds hath slept.
This grave, first water'd with the tear
That child or widow'd man hath wept,
Shall be by heavenly watchmen kept.

The babe that lay on her cold breast—
A rosebud dropp'd on drifted snow—
Its young hand in its father's press'd,
Shall learn that she, who first caress'd
Its infant cheek, now sleeps below.

And often shall he come alone,
When not a sound but evening's sigh
Is heard, and, bowing by the stone
That bears his mother's name, with none
But God and guardian angels nigh,

Shall say, "This was my mother's choice
For her own grave: oh, be it mine!
Even now, methinks, I hear her voice
Calling me hence, in the divine
And mournful whisper of this pine."

FOR THE CHARLESTOWN CENTENNIAL CELEBRATION.

Two hundred years! two hundred years!
How much of human power and pride,
What glorious hopes, what gloomy fears,
Have sunk beneath their noiseless tide!

The red man at his horrid rite,
  Seen by the stars at night's cold noon,
His bark canoe, its track of light
  Left on the wave beneath the moon;

His dance, his yell, his council-fire,
  The altar where his victim lay,
His death-song, and his funeral pyre,
  That still, strong tide hath borne away.

And that pale Pilgrim band is gone,
  That on this shore with trembling trod,
Ready to faint, yet bearing on
  The ark of freedom and of God.

And war—that since o'er ocean came,
  And thunder'd loud from yonder hill,
And wrapp'd its foot in sheets of flame,
  To blast that ark—its storm is still.

Chief, sachem, sage, bards, heroes, seers,
  That live in story and in song,
Time, for the last two hundred years,
  Has raised, and shown, and swept along.

'Tis like a dream when one awakes,
  This vision of the scenes of old;
'Tis like the moon when morning breaks,
  'Tis like a tale round watchfires told.

Then what are we? then what are we?
  Yes, when two hundred years have roll'd
O'er our green graves, our names shall be
  A morning dream, a tale that's told.

God of our fathers, in whose sight
  The thousand years that sweep away
Man and the traces of his might
  Are but the break and close of day,

Grant us that love of truth sublime,
That love of goodness and of thee,
That makes thy children, in all time,
To share thine own eternity.

George Hill.

FROM THE RUINS OF ATHENS.

The daylight fades o'er old Cyllene's hill,
And broad and dun the mountain shadows fall;
The stars are up and sparkling, as if still
Smiling upon their altars ; but the tall
Dark cypress, gently, as a mourner, bends—
Wet with the drops of evening as with tears—
Alike o'er shrine and worshipper, and blends,
All dim and lonely, with the wrecks of years,
As of a world gone by no coming morning cheers

There sits the queen of temples—gray and lone.
She, like the last of an imperial line,
Has seen her sister structures, one by one,
To time their gods and worshippers resign;
And the stars twinkle through the weeds that twine
Their roofless capitals ; and, through the night,
Heard the hoarse drum and the exploding mine,
The clash of arms and hymns of uncouth rite,
From their dismantled shrines, the guardian powers affright.

Go! thou from whose forsaken heart are reft
The ties of home; and, where a dwelling-place
Not Jove himself the elements have left,
The grass-grown, undefined arena pace! [hear
Look on its rent, though tower-like shafts, and
The loud winds thunder in their aged face;
Then slowly turn thine eye, where moulders near
A Cæsar's Arch, and the blue depth of space
Vaults like a sepulchre the wrecks of a past race.

Is it not better with the Eremite,
Where the weeds rustle o'er his airy cave,
Perch'd on their summit, through the long still night
To sit and watch their shadows slowly wave—
While oft some fragment, sapp'd by dull decay,
In thunder breaks the silence, and the fowl
Of Ruin hoots—and turn in scorn away
Of all man builds, time levels, and the cowl
Awards her moping sage in common with the owl?

Or, where the palm, at twilight's holy hour,
By Theseus' Fane her lonely vigil keeps:
Gone are her sisters of the leaf and flower,
With them the living crop earth sows and reaps.
But these revive not: the weed with them sleeps,
But clothes herself in beauty from their clay,
And leaves them to their slumber; o'er them weeps
Vainly the Spring her quickening dews away,
And Love as vainly mourns, and mourns, alas! for aye.

Or, more remote, on Nature's haunts intrude,
Where, since creation, she has slept on flowers,
Wet with the noonday forest-dew, and wooed
By untamed choristers in unpruned bowers:
By pathless thicket, rock that time-worn towers
O'er dells untrodden by the hunter, piled
Ere by its shadow measured were the hours
To human eye, the rampart of the wild,
Whose banner is the cloud, by carnage undefiled.

The weary spirit that forsaken plods
The world's wide wilderness, a home may find
Here, mid the dwellings of long banish'd gods
And thoughts they bring, the mourners of the mind;

The spectres that no spell has power to bind,
The loved, but lost, whose soul's life is in ours,
As incense in sepulchral urns, enshrined,
The sense of blighted or of wasted powers,
The hopes whose promised fruits have perish'd with
their flowers.

There is a small low cape—there, where the moon
Breaks o'er the shatter'd and now shapeless stone;
The waters, as a rude but fitting boon, [thrown
Weeds and small shells have, like a garland,
Upon it, and the wind's and wave's low moan,
And sighing grass, and cricket's plaint, are heard
To steal upon the stillness, like a tone
Remember'd. Here, by human foot unstirr'd,
Its seed the thistle sheds, and builds the ocean-bird.

Lurks the foul toad, the lizard basks secure
Within the sepulchre of him whose name
Had scatter'd navies like the whirlwind. Sure,
If aught ambition's fiery wing may tame,
'Tis here; the web the spider weaves where Fame
Planted her proud but sunken shaft, should be
To it a fetter, still it springs the same.
Glory's fool-worshipper! here bend thy knee!
The tomb thine altar-stone, thine idol Mockery:

A small gray elf, all sprinkled o'er with dust
Of crumbling catacomb, and mouldering shred
Of banner and embroider'd pall, and rust
Of arms, time-eaten monuments, that shed
A canker'd gleam on dim escutcheons, where
The groping antiquary pores to spy—
A what? a name—perchance ne'er graven there;
At whom the urchin with his mimic eye
Sits peering through a scull, and laughs continually.

THE MOUNTAIN GIRL.

THE clouds, that upward curling from
  Nevada's summit fly,
Melt into air: gone are the showers,
And, deck'd, as 'twere with bridal flowers,
  Earth seems to wed the sky.

All hearts are by the spirit that
  Breathes in the sunshine stirr'd;
And there's a girl that, up and down,
A merry vagrant, through the town
  Goes singing like a bird.

A thing all lightness, life, and glee;
  One of the shapes we seem
To meet in visions of the night;
And, should they greet our waking sight,
  Imagine that we dream.

With glossy ringlet, brow that is
  As falling snow-flake white,
Half hidden by its jetty braid,
And eye like dewdrop in the shade,
  At once both dark and bright:

And cheek whereon the sunny clime
  Its brown tint gently throws,
Gently, as it reluctant were
To leave its print on thing so fair—
  A shadow on a rose.

She stops, looks up—what does she see?
  A flower of crimson dye,
Whose vase, the work of Moorish hands,
A lady sprinkles, as it stands
  Upon a balcony:

High, leaning from a window forth,
  From curtains that half shroud
Her maiden form, with tress of gold,
And brow that mocks their snow-white fold,
  Like Dian from a cloud.

Nor flower, nor lady fair she sees—
  That mountain girl—but dumb
And motionless she stands, with eye
That seems communing with the sky:
  Her visions are of home.

That flower to her is as a tone
  Of some forgotten song,
One of a slumbering thousand, struck
From an old harp-string; but, once woke,
  It brings the rest along.

She sees beside the mountain brook,
  Beneath the old cork-tree
And toppling crag, a vine-thatch'd shed,
Perch'd, like the eagle, high o'erhead,
  The home of liberty;

The rivulet, the olive shade,
  The grassy plot, the flock;
Nor does her simple thought forget,
Haply, the little violet,
  That springs beneath the rock.

Sister and mate, they may not from
  Her dreaming eye depart;
And one, the source of gentler fears,
More dear than all, for whom she wears
  The token at her heart.

And hence her eye is dim, her cheek
  Has lost its livelier glow;
Her song has ceased, and motionless
She stands, an image of distress:
  Strange what a flower can do!

THE LOST PLEIAD.

There were Seven Sisters, and each wore
  A starry crown, as, hand in hand,
By Hesper woke, they led the hours—
  The minstrels of his virgin band.

And Love would come at eve, as they
  Were met their vesper hymn to sing,
And linger till it ceased, with eye
  Of raptured gaze and folded wing.

For ne'er on earth, in air, were heard
  More thrilling tones than, to the lyre
Of Heaven timed, rose nightly from
  The lips of that young virgin choir.

But they were coy, or seeming coy,
  Those minstrels of the twilight hour;
Nuns of the sky, as cold and shy,
  As blossoms of the woodland bower.

'Twas eve, and Hesper came to wake
  His starry troop, but wept—for one,
The brightest, fairest of the group,
  Where all were bright and fair, was gone.

They found within her bower the harp
  To which was tuned her vesper-hymn,
The star-gems of her coronet,
  And one was with a teardrop dim.

They told how Love had at the gate
  Of twilight linger'd, long before
The daylight set; but he was flown,
  And she, the lost one, seen no more.

AUTUMN NOON.

All was so still that I could almost count
The tinklings of the falling leaves. At times,
Perchance, a nut was heard to drop, and then—
As if it had slipp'd from him as he struck
The meat—a squirrel's short and fretful bark.
Anon, a troop of noisy, roving jays,
Whisking their gaudy topknots, would surprise
And seize upon the top of some tall tree,
Shrieking, as if on purpose to enjoy
The consternation of the noontide stillness.
Roused by the din, the squirrel from his hole,
Like some grave justice bent to keep the peace,
Thrust his gray pate, much wondering what it meant
And squatted near me on a stone, there bask'd
A fly of larger breed and o'ergrown bulk,
In the warm sunshine, vain of his green coat
Of variable velvet laced with gold,
That, ever and anon, would whisk about,
Vexing the stillness with his buzzing din,
As human fopling will do with his talk:
And o'er the mossy post of an old fence,
Lured from its crannies by the warmth, was spied
A swarm of gay motes waltzing to a tune
Of their own humming: quiet sounds, that [illegible]
More deeply to impress us with a sense
Of silent loneliness and trackless ways.

George W. Doane.

THERMOPYLÆ.

'Twas an hour of fearful issues,
When the bold three hundred stood
For their love of holy freedom,
By that old Thessalian flood:

When, lifting high each sword of flame,
They call'd on ev'ry sacred name,
And swore, beside those dashing waves,
They never, never would be slaves!

And oh! that oath was nobly kept,
From morn to setting sun,
Did desperation urge the fight
Which valour had begun;
Till, torrent-like, the stream of blood
Ran down and mingled with the flood,
And all, from mountain cliff to wave,
Was Freedom's, Valour's, Glory's grave.

Oh, yes, that oath was nobly kept,
Which nobly had been sworn,
And proudly did each gallant heart
The foeman's fetters spurn;
And firmly was the fight maintain'd,
And amply was the triumph gain'd;
They fought, fair Liberty, for thee:
They fell—TO DIE IS TO BE FREE.

THE WATERS OF MARAH.

"And Moses cried unto the LORD, and the LORD showed him a tree, which, when he had cast into the waters, the waters were made sweet."

BY Marah's stream of bitterness,
When Moses stood and cried,
JEHOVAH heard his fervent pray'r,
And instant help supplied:
The Prophet sought the precious tree
With prompt, obedient feet;
'Twas cast into the fount, and made
The bitter waters sweet.

Whene'er affliction o'er thee sheds
  Its influence malign,
Then, suff'rer, be the Prophet's pray'r,
  And prompt obedience, thine:
'Tis but a Marah's fount, ordain'd
  Thy faith in God to prove,
And pray'r and resignation shall
  Its bitterness remove

Lydia Huntley Sigourney.

INDIAN NAMES.

"How can the red men be forgotten, while so many of our states and territories, bays, lakes, and rivers, are indelibly stamped by names of their giving?"

Ye say they all have pass'd away,
  That noble race and brave,
That their light canoes have vanish'd
  From off the crested wave.
That, mid the forests where they roam'd,
  There rings no hunter's shout;
But their name is on your waters,
  Ye may not wash it out.

'Tis where Ontario's billow
  Like ocean's surge is curl'd,
Where strong Niagara's thunders wake
  The echo of the world,
Where red Missouri bringeth
  Rich tribute from the west,
And Rappahannock sweetly sleeps
  On green Virginia's breast.

Ye say their conelike cabins,
  That cluster'd o'er the vale,
Have disappear'd, as wither'd leaves
  Before the autumn's gale;

But their memory liveth on your hills,
  Their baptism on your shore,
Your everlasting rivers speak
  Their dialect of yore.

Old Massachusetts wears it
  Within her lordly crown,
And broad Ohio bears it
  Amid his young renown.
Connecticut hath wreath'd it
  Where her quiet foliage waves,
And bold Kentucky breathes it hoarse
  Through all her ancient caves.

Wachusett hides its lingering voice
  Within his rocky heart,
And Alleghany graves its tone
  Throughout his lofty chart.
Monadnock, on his forehead hoar,
  Doth seal the sacred trust,
Your mountains build their monument,
  Though ye destroy their dust.

CONTENTMENT.

Think'st thou the steed that restless roves
O'er rocks and mountains, fields and groves,
    With wild, unbridled bound,
Finds fresher pasture than the bee,
On thymy bank or vernal tree,
Intent to store her industry
    Within her waxen round?

Think'st thou the fountain forced to turn
Through marble vase or sculptured urn,
    Affords a sweeter draught
Than that which, in its native sphere,
Perennial, undisturb'd and clear,
Flows, the lone traveller's thirst to cheer,
    And wake his grateful thought?

Think'st thou the man whose mansions hold
The worldling's pomp and miser's gold,
    Obtains a richer prize
Than he who, in his cot at rest,
Finds heavenly peace, a willing guest,
And bears the promise in his breast
    Of treasure in the skies?

THE WESTERN EMIGRANT.

An ax rang sharply mid those forest shades
Which from creation towards the skies had tower'd
In unshorn beauty. There, with vigorous arm,
Wrought a bold emigrant, and by his side
His little son, with question and response,
Beguiled the toil.

"Boy, thou hast never seen
Such glorious trees. Hark, when their giant trunks
Fall, how the firm earth groans. Rememberest thou
The mighty river, on whose breast we sail'd,
So many days, on towards the setting sun?
Our own Connecticut, compared to that,
Was but a creeping stream."

"Father, the brook
That by our door went singing, where I launch'd
My tiny boat, with my young playmates round
When school was o'er, is dearer far to me
Than all these bold, broad waters. To my eye
They are as strangers. And those little trees
My mother nurtured in the garden bound
Of our first home, from whence the fragrant peach
Hung in its ripening gold, were fairer, sure,
Than this dark forest, shutting out the day."
"What, ho! my little girl," and with light step
A fairy creature hasted towards her sire,
And, setting down the basket that contain'd

His noon repast, look'd upward to his face
With sweet, confiding smile.

"See, dearest, see,
That bright-wing'd paroquet, and hear the song
Of yon gay redbird, echoing through the trees,
Making rich music. Didst thou ever hear,
In far New-England, such a mellow tone?"
"I had a robin that did take the crumbs
Each night and morning, and his chirping voice
Did make me joyful as I went to tend
My snowdrops. I was always laughing then
In that first home. I should be happier now,
Methinks, if I could find among these dells
The same fresh violets."

Slow night drew on,
And round the rude hut of the emigrant
The wrathful spirit of the rising storm
Spake bitter things. His weary children slept,
And he, with head declined, sat listening long
To the swoln waters of the Illinois,
Dashing against their shores.

Starting, he spake:
"Wife! did I see thee brush away a tear?
'Twas even so. Thy heart was with the halls
Of thy nativity. Their sparkling lights,
Carpets, and sofas, and admiring guests,
Befit thee better than these rugged walls
Of shapeless logs, and this lone, hermit home."
"No, no. All was so still around, methought
Upon mine ear that echoed hymn did steal,
Which, mid the church where erst we paid our vows,
So tuneful peal'd. But tenderly thy voice
Dissolved the illusion."

And the gentle smile
Lighting her brow, the fond caress that sooth'd
Her waking infant, reassured his soul
That, wheresoe'er our best affections dwell,

And strike a healthful root, is happiness.
Content and placid to his rest he sank;
But dreams, those wild magicians, that do play
Such pranks when reason slumbers, tireless wrought
Their will with him.

Up rose the thronging mart
Of his own native city; roof and spire,
All glittering bright, in fancy's frostwork ray.
The steed his boyhood nurtured proudly neigh'd;
The favourite dog came frisking round his feet,
With shrill and joyous bark; familiar doors
Flew open; greeting hands with his were link'd
In friendship's grasp; he heard the keen debate
From congregated haunts, where mind with mind
Doth blend and brighten; and till morning roved
Mid the loved scenery of his native land.

THE WIDOW'S CHARGE AT HER DAUGHTER'S BRIDAL.

Deal gently, thou, whose hand has won
The young bird from the nest away,
Where, careless 'neath a vernal sun,
She gayly caroll'd day by day:
The haunt is lone, the heart must grieve,
From whence her timid wing doth soar,
They pensive list, at hush of eve,
Yet hear her gushing song no more.

Deal gently with her: thou art dear
Beyond what vestal lips have told,
And like a lamb, from fountain clear,
She turns confiding to the fold;
She round thy sweet, domestic bower
The wreaths of changeless love shall twine,
Watch for thy step at vesper hour,
And blend her holiest prayer with thine.

Deal gently, thou, when far away,
  Mid stranger scenes her foot shall rove,
Nor let thy tender cares decay,
  The soul of woman lives in love;
And shouldst thou, wondering, mark a tear
  Unconscious from her eyelid break,
Be pitiful, and sooth the fear
  That man's strong heart can ne'er partake.

A mother yields her gem to thee,
  On thy true breast to sparkle rare;
She places 'neath thy household tree
  The idol of her fondest care;
And by thy trust to be forgiven,
  When judgment wakes in terror wild,
By all thy treasured hopes of Heaven,
  Deal gently with the widow's child.

Hannah F. Gould.

THE PEBBLE AND THE ACORN.

"I am a pebble! and yield to none!"
Were the swelling words of a tiny stone;
"Nor time nor seasons can alter me;
I am abiding, while ages flee.
The pelting hail and the drizzling rain
Have tried to soften me, long, in vain;
And the tender dew has sought to melt,
Or touch my heart, but it was not felt.
There's none that can tell about my birth,
For I'm as old as the big, round earth.
The children of men arise, and pass
Out of the world like the blades of grass;
And many a foot on me has trod,
That's gone from sight and under the sod!
I am a pebble! but who art thou,
Rattling along from the restless bough?"

The acorn was shock'd at this rude salute,
And lay for a moment abash'd and mute;
She never before had been so near
This gravelly ball, the mundane sphere;
And she felt for a time at a loss to know
How to answer a thing so coarse and low.
But to give reproof of a nobler sort
Than the angry look or the keen retort,
At length she said, in a gentle tone,
"Since it has happen'd that I am thrown
From the lighter element, where I grew,
Down to another so hard and new,
And beside a personage so august,
Abased, I will cover my head with dust,
And quickly retire from the sight of one
Whom time, nor season, nor storm, nor sun,
Nor the gentle dew, nor the grinding heel
Has ever subdued, or made to feel!"
And soon, in the earth, she sunk away
From the comfortless spot where the pebble lay.

But it was not long ere the soil was broke
By the peering head of an infant oak!
And, as it arose and its branches spread,
The pebble look'd up, and wondering said:
"A modest acorn! never to tell
What was enclosed in its simple shell;
That the pride of the forest was folded up
In the narrow space of its little cup!
And meekly to sink in the darksome earth,
Which proves that nothing could hide her worth!
And oh! how many will tread on me,
To come and admire the beautiful tree,
Whose head is towering towards the sky,
Above such a worthless thing as I!
Useless and vain, a cumberer here,
I have been idling from year to year.
But never, from this, shall a vaunting word
From the humbled pebble again be heard,

Till something without me or within,
Shall show the purpose for which I've been!"
The pebble its vow could not forget,
And it lies there wrapp'd in silence yet.

THE WATERFALL.

Ye mighty waters, that have join'd your forces,
Roaring and dashing with this awful sound,
Here are ye mingled; but the distant sources
Whence ye have issued, where shall they be found?

Who may retrace the ways that ye have taken,
Ye streams and drops? who separate you all,
And find the many places ye've forsaken,
To come and rush together down the fall?

Through thousand, thousand paths have ye been roaming,
In earth and air, who now each other urge
To the last point! and then, so madly foaming,
Leap down at once from this stupendous verge.

Some in the lowering cloud a while were centred,
That in the stream beheld its sable face,
And melted into tears, that, falling, enter'd
With sister waters on the sudden race.

Others, to light that beam'd upon the fountain,
Have from the vitals of the rock been freed,
In silver threads, that, shining down the mountain,
Twined off among the verdure of the mead.

And many a flower that bow'd beside the river,
In opening beauty, ere the dew was dried,
Stirr'd by the breeze, has been an early giver
Of her pure offering to the rolling tide.

Thus from the veins, through earth's dark bosom pouring,
Many have flow'd in tributary streams;
Some, in the bow that bent, the sun adoring,
Have shone in colours borrow'd from his beams.

But He who holds the ocean in the hollow
Of his strong hand can separate you all!
His searching eye the secret way will follow,
Of every drop that hurries to the fall!

We are, like you, in mighty torrents mingled,
And speeding downward to one common home;
Yet there's an eye that every drop hath singled,
And mark'd the winding ways through which we come.

Those who have here adored the Sun of heaven,
And shown the world their brightness drawn from him,
Again before him, though their hues be *seven*,
Shall blend their beauty, never to grow dim.

We bless the promise, as we thus are tending
Down to the tomb, that gives us hope to rise
Before the Power to whom we now are bending,
To stand his bow of glory in the skies!

THE DREAM.

I DREAM'D, and 'twas a lovely, blessed dream,
That I again my native hills had found,
The mossy rocks, the valley, and the stream
That used to hold me captive to its sound.

I was a child again: I roam'd anew
About my early haunts, and saw the whole
That fades, with waking memory, from the view
Of this mysterious thing we call the soul.

A very child, again beside the brook,
 I made my puny hand a cup to dip
Among the sparkling waters, where I took
 Its hollow full and brought it to my lip.

And oh! that cooling draught I still can taste,
 And feel it in the spirit and the flesh:
'Tis like a fount, that in the desert waste
 Leaps out, the weary pilgrim to refresh.

The spice of other days was borne along,
 From shrub and forest, on the balmy breeze;
I heard my warbling wild-bird's tender song
 Come sweet and thrilling through the rustling trees.

All was restored, as in the sunny day
 When I believed my little rural ground
The centre of the world, whose limits lay
 Just where the bright horizon hemm'd it round.

And she—who was my sister then, but now
 What she may be the pure immortals know,
Who round the throne of the Eternal bow,
 And bathe in glory, veil'd from all below—

Yes, she was there; who, with her riper years,
 Once walk'd, the guardian of my infant feet;
Drew from my hand the thorn, wiped off my tears,
 And brought fresh flowers to deck our grassy seat.

I saw her cheek with life's warm current flush'd;
 Clung to the fingers that I used to hold;
Heard the loved voice that is for ever hush'd,
 And felt the form that long ago was cold.

All I have been and known, in all the years
 Since I was sporting in that cherish'd spot,
My hopes, my joys, my wishes, and my tears,
 As only dreamings, were alike forgot.

'Twas this that made my dream so bless'd and
bright,
And me the careless thing that I was then:
Yet, Time, I would not now reverse thy flight,
And risk the running of my race again.

The fairest joys that struck their roots in earth,
I would not rear again to bloom and fade!
I've had them once in their ideal worth;
Their height I've measured, and their substance
weigh'd.

Nor those who sleep in peace would I awake,
To have their hearts with time's delusions fill'd;
The seal that God has set I would not break,
Nor call the voice to lips that he has still'd.

And yet I love my dream: 'twas very sweet
To be among my native hills again;
Where my light heart was borne by infant feet,
The careless, blissful creature I was then!

Whene'er I think of it, the warm tears roll,
Uncall'd and unforbidden, down my cheek;
But not for joy or sorrow. Oh, my soul,
Thy nature, power, or purpose, who can speak?

THE CHILD ON THE BEACH.

MARY, a beautiful, artless child,
Came down on the beach to me,
Where I sat, and a pensive hour beguiled
By watching the restless sea.

I never had seen her face before,
And mine was to her unknown;
But we each rejoiced on that peaceful shore
The other to meet alone.

Her cheek was the rose's opening bud,
  Her brow of an ivory white;
Her eyes were bright, as the stars that stud
  The sky of a cloudless night.

To reach my side as she gayly sped,
  With the step of a bounding fawn,
The pebbles scarce moved beneath her tread
  Ere the little light foot was gone.

With the love of a holier world than this,
  Her innocent heart seem'd warm;
While the glad young spirit look'd out with bliss
  From its shrine in her sylph-like form.

Her soul seem'd spreading the scene to span,
  That open'd before her view,
And longing for power to look the plan
  Of the universe fairly through.

She climb'd and stood on the rocky steep,
  Like a bird that would mount and fly
Far over the waves, where the broad, blue deep
  Roll'd up to the bending sky.

She placed her lips to the spiral shell,
  And breathed through every fold;
She look'd for the depth of its pearly cell,
  As a miser would look for gold.

Her small white fingers were spread to toss
  The foam, as it reach'd the strand:
She ran them along in the purple moss,
  And over the sparkling sand.

The green sea-egg, by its tenant left,
  And form'd to an ocean cup,
She held by its sides, of their spears bereft,
  To fill, as the waves roll'd up.

But the hour went round, and she knew the space
  Her mother's soft word assign'd;
While she seem'd to look with a saddening face
  On all she must leave behind.

She search'd mid the pebbles, and finding one
  Smooth, clear, and of amber dye,
She held it up to the morning sun,
  And over her own mild eye.

Then, " Here," said she, " I will give you this,
  That you may remember me !"
And she seal'd her gift with a parting kiss,
  And fled from beside the sea.

Mary, thy token is by me yet.
  To me 'tis a dearer gem
Than ever was brought from the mine, or set
  In the loftiest diadem.

It carries me back to the far-off deep,
  And places me on the shore,
Where the beauteous child, who bade me keep
  Her pebble, I meet once more.

And all that is lovely, pure, and bright,
  In a soul that is young, and free
From the stain of guile, and the deadly blight
  Of sorrow, I find in thee.

I wonder if ever thy tender heart
  In memory meets me there,
Where thy soft, quick sigh, as we had to part,
  Was caught by the ocean air.

Bless'd one ! over time's rude shore, on thee
  May an angel guard attend,
And " *a white stone bearing a new name*," be
  Thy passport when time shall end !

Prosper M. Wetmore.

"TWELVE YEARS HAVE FLOWN."

Twelve years have flown since last I saw
  My birthplace and my home of youth:
How oft its scenes would memory draw,
  Her tints the pencillings of truth:
Unto that spot I come once more,
  The dearest life hath ever known;
And still it wears the look it wore,
  Although twelve weary years have flown.

Again upon the soil I stand
  Where first my infant footsteps stray'd;
Again I view my "father-land,"
  And wander through its pleasant shade:
I gaze upon the hills, the skies,
  The verdant banks with flowers o'ergrown,
And while I look with glistening eyes,
  Almost forget twelve years are flown.

Twelve years are flown! those words are brief,
  Yet in their sound what fancies dwell:
The hours of bliss, the days of grief,
  The joys and woes remember'd well:
The hopes that fill'd the youthful breast,
  Alas! how many a one o'erthrown!
Deep thoughts, that long have been at rest,
  Wake at the words, twelve years have flown!

The past! the past! a saddening thought,
  A withering spell is in the sound!
It comes with memories deeply fraught
  Of youthful pleasure's giddy round;
Of forms that roved life's sunniest bowers,
  The cherish'd few for ever gone:
Of dreams that fill'd life's morning hours,
  Where are they now? Twelve years have flown!

A brief but eloquent reply!
  Where are youth's hopes—life's morning dream?
Seek for the flowers that floated by
  Upon the rushing mountain stream!
Yet gems beneath that wave may sleep,
  Till after years shall make them known
Thus golden thoughts the heart will keep,
  That perish not, though years have flown.

William C. Bryant.

THE PAST.

Thou unrelenting Past!
Strong are the barriers round thy dark domain,
  And fetters, sure and fast,
Hold all that enter thy unbreathing reign.

  Far in thy realm withdrawn
Old empires sit in sullenness and gloom,
  And glorious ages gone
Lie deep within the shadow of thy womb.

  Childhood, with all its mirth,
Youth, manhood, age, that draws us to the ground,
  And last, man's life on earth,
Glide to thy dim dominions, and are bound.

  Thou hast my better years,
Thou hast my earlier friends—the good—the kind,
  Yielded to thee with tears—
The venerable form—the exalted mind.

  My spirit yearns to bring
The lost ones back: yearns with desire intense,
  And struggles hard to wring
The bolts apart, and pluck thy captives thence.

In vain: thy gates deny
All passage save to those who hence depart;
Nor to the streaming eye
Thou giv'st them back, nor to the broken heart.

In thy abysses hide
Beauty and excellence unknown: to thee
Earth's wonder and her pride
Are gather'd, as the waters to the sea;

Labours of good to man,
Unpublish'd charity, unbroken faith:
Love, that midst grief began,
And grew with years, and falter'd not in death.

Full many a mighty name
Lurks in thy depths, unutter'd, unrevered;
With thee are silent fame,
Forgotten arts, and wisdom disappear'd.

Thine for a space are they:
Yet shalt thou yield thy treasures up at last;
Thy gates shall yet give way,
Thy bolts shall fall, inexorable Past!

All that of good and fair
Has gone into thy womb from earliest time,
Shall then come forth, to wear
The glory and the beauty of its prime.

They have not perish'd—no!
Kind words, remember'd voices once so sweet,
Smiles, radiant long ago,
And features, the great soul's apparent seat,

All shall come back; each tie
Of pure affection shall be knit again;
Alone shall Evil die,
And Sorrow dwell a prisoner in thy reign.

And then shall I behold
Him, by whose kind paternal side I sprung,
And her who, still and cold,
Fills the next grave—the beautiful and young.

THE PRAIRIES.

These are the gardens of the desert, these
The unshorn fields, boundless and beautiful,
For which the speech of England has no name—
The Prairies. I behold them for the first,
And my heart swells, while the dilated sight
Takes in the encircling vastness. Lo! they stretch
In airy undulations, far away,
As if the ocean, in his gentlest swell,
Stood still, with all his rounded billows fix'd,
And motionless for ever. Motionless?
No, they are all unchain'd again. The clouds
Sweep over with their shadows, and, beneath,
The surface rolls and fluctuates to the eye;
Dark hollows seem to glide along, and chase
The sunny ridges. Breezes of the South!
Who toss the golden and the flame-like flowers,
And pass the prairie-hawk, that, poised on high,
Flaps his broad wings, yet moves not—ye have play'd
Among the palms of Mexico and vines
Of Texas, and have crisp'd the limpid brooks
That from the fountains of Sonora glide
Into the calm Pacific—have ye fann'd
A nobler or a lovelier scene than this?
Man hath no part in all this glorious work:
The hand that built the firmament hath heaved
And smooth'd these verdant swells, and sown their slopes
With herbage, planted them with island groves,
And hedged them round with forests. Fitting floor
For this magnificent temple of the sky—

With flowers whose glory and whose multitude
Rival the constellations! The great heavens
Seem to stoop down upon the scene in love—
A nearer vault, and of a tenderer blue,
Than that which bends above the eastern hills.
As o'er the verdant waste I guide my steed,
Among the high, rank grass that sweeps his sides,
The hollow beating of his footstep seems
A sacrilegious sound. I think of those
Upon whose rest he tramples. Are they here—
The dead of other days? and did the dust
Of these fair solitudes once stir with life
And burn with passion? Let the mighty mounds
That overlook the rivers, or that rise
In the dim forest, crowded with old oaks,
Answer. A race, that long has pass'd away,
Built them; a disciplined and populous race
Heap'd, with long toil, the earth, while yet the Greek
Was hewing the Pentelicus to forms
Of symmetry, and rearing on its rock
The glittering Parthenon. These ample fields
Nourish'd their harvests, here their herds were fed,
When haply by their stalls the bison low'd,
And bow'd his maned shoulder to the yoke.
All day this desert murmur'd with their toils,
Till twilight blush'd, and lovers walk'd, and wooed
In a forgotten language, and old tunes,
From instruments of unremember'd form,
Gave the soft winds a voice. The red man came—
The roaming hunter tribes, warlike and fierce,
And the mound-builders vanish'd from the earth.
The solitude of centuries untold
Has settled where they dwelt. The prairie-wolf
Hunts in their meadows, and his fresh-dug den
Yawns by my path. The gopher mines the ground
Where stood their swarming cities. All is gone—
All—save the piles of earth that hold their bones—
The platforms where they worshipp'd unknown gods—

The barriers which they builded from the soil
To keep the foe at bay—till o'er the walls
The wild beleaguerers broke, and, one by one,
The strongholds of the plain were forced, and heap'd
With corpses. The brown vultures of the wood
Flock'd to those vast uncover'd sepulchres,
And sat, unscared and silent, at their feast.
Haply some solitary fugitive,
Lurking in marsh and forest, till the sense
Of desolation and of fear became
Bitterer than death, yielded himself to die.
Man's better nature triumph'd. Kindly words
Welcomed and sooth'd him; the rude conquerors
Seated the captive with their chiefs; he chose
A bride among their maidens, and at length
Seem'd to forget—yet ne'er forgot—the wife
Of his first love, and her sweet little ones
Butcher'd, amid their shrieks, with all his race.
  Thus change the forms of being. Thus arise
Races of living things, glorious in strength,
And perish, as the quickening breath of God
Fills them, or is withdrawn. The red man, too,
Has left the blooming wilds he ranged so long,
And, nearer to the Rocky Mountains, sought
A wider hunting-ground. The beaver builds
No longer by these streams, but far away,
On waters whose blue surface ne'er gave back
The white man's face; among Missouri's springs,
And pools whose issues swell the Oregon,
He rears his little Venice. In these plains
The bison feeds no more. Twice twenty leagues
Beyond remotest smoke of hunter's camp,
Roams the majestic brute, in herds that shake
The earth with thundering steps; yet here I meet
His ancient footprints stamp'd beside the pool.
  Still this great solitude is quick with life.
Myriads of insects, gaudy as the flowers
They flutter over, gentle quadrupeds,
And birds that scarce have learn'd the fear of man,

Are here, and sliding reptiles of the ground,
Startlingly beautiful. The graceful deer
Bounds to the wood at my approach. The bee,
A more adventurous colonist than man,
With whom he came across the eastern deep,
Fills the savannas with his murmurings,
And hides his sweets, as in the golden age,
Within the hollow oak. I listen long
To his domestic hum, and think I hear
The sound of that advancing multitude
Which soon shall fill the deserts. From the ground
Comes up the laugh of children, the soft voice
Of maidens, and the sweet and solemn hymn
Of Sabbath worshippers. The low of herds
Blends with the rustling of the heavy grain
Over the dark-brown furrows. All at once
A fresher wind sweeps by, and breaks my dream,
And I am in the wilderness alone.

THE RIVULET.

This little rill that, from the springs
Of yonder grove, its current brings,
Plays on the slope a while, and then
Goes prattling into groves again,
Oft to its warbling waters drew
My little feet, when life was new.
When woods in early green were dress'd,
And from the chambers of the west
The warmer breezes, travelling out,
Breathed the new scent of flowers about,
My truant steps from home would stray,
Upon its grassy side to play,
List the brown-thrasher's vernal hymn,
And crop the violet on its brim,
With blooming cheek and open brow,
As young and gay, sweet rill, as thou.

And when the days of boyhood came,
And I had grown in love with fame,
Duly I sought thy banks, and tried
My first rude numbers by thy side.
Words cannot tell how bright and gay
The scenes of life before me lay.
Then glorious hopes, that now to speak
Would bring the blood into my cheek,
Pass'd o'er me; and I wrote, on high,
A name I deem'd should never die.

Years change thee not. Upon yon hill
The tall old maples, verdant still,
Yet tell, in grandeur of decay,
How swift the years have pass'd away,
Since first, a child, and half afraid,
I wander'd in the forest shade.
Thou, ever joyous rivulet,
Dost dimple, leap, and prattle yet;
And sporting with the sands that pave
The windings of thy silver wave,
And dancing to thy own wild chime,
Thou laughest at the lapse of time.
The same sweet sounds are in my ear
My early childhood loved to hear;
As pure thy limpid waters run,
As bright they sparkle to the sun;
As fresh and thick the bending ranks
Of herbs that line thy oozy banks;
The violet there, in soft May dew,
Comes up, as modest and as blue;
As green amid thy current's stress
Floats the scarce-rooted watercress;
And the brown ground-bird, in thy glen,
Still chirps as merrily as then.

Thou changest not—but I am changed
Since first thy pleasant banks I ranged;
And the grave stranger, come to see
The play-place of his infancy,

Has scarce a single trace of him
Who sported once upon thy brim.
The visions of my youth are past—
Too bright, too beautiful to last.
I've tried the world: it wears no more
The colouring of romance it wore.
Yet well has Nature kept the truth
She promised to my earliest youth.
The radiant beauty, shed abroad
On all the glorious works of God,
Shows freshly, to my sober'd eye,
Each charm it wore in days gone by.

A few brief years shall pass away,
And I, all trembling, weak, and gray,
Bow'd to the earth, which waits to fold
My ashes in the embracing mould
(If haply the dark will of fate
Indulge my life so long a date),
May come for the last time to look
Upon my childhood's favourite brook.
Then dimly on my eye shall gleam
The sparkle of thy dancing stream;
And faintly on my ear shall fall
Thy prattling current's merry call;
Yet shalt thou flow as glad and bright
As when thou met'st my infant sight.

And I shall sleep: and on thy side,
As ages after ages glide,
Children their early sports shall try,
And pass to hoary age and die.
But thou, unchanged from year to year,
Gayly shalt play and glitter here;
Amid young flowers and tender grass
Thy endless infancy shalt pass;
And, singing down thy narrow glen,
Shalt mock the fading race of men.

"EARTH'S CHILDREN CLEAVE TO EARTH."

Earth's children cleave to earth: her frail,
  Decaying children dread decay.
Yon wreath of mist that leaves the vale,
  And lessens in the morning ray:
Look, how, by mountain rivulet,
  It lingers, as it upward creeps,
And clings to fern and copsewood set
  Along the green and dewy steps:
Clings to the fragrant kalmia, clings
  To precipices fringed with grass,
Dark maples where the wood-thrush sings,
  And bowers of fragrant sassafras.
Yet all in vain: it passes still
  From hold to hold; it cannot stay;
And in the very beams that fill
  The world with glory, wastes away.
Till, parting from the mountain's brow,
  It vanishes from human eye,
And that which sprung of earth is now
  A portion of the glorious sky.

James K. Paulding.

PASSAGE DOWN THE OHIO.

  As down Ohio's ever ebbing tide,
Oarless and sailless, silently they glide,
How still the scene, how lifeless, yet how fair,
Was the lone land that met the strangers there!
No smiling villages or curling smoke
The busy haunts of busy men bespoke;
No solitary hut the banks along,
Sent forth blithe Labour's homely, rustic song;
No urchin gamboll'd on the smooth white sand,
Or hurl'd the skipping-stone with playful hand,

While playmate dog plunged in the clear blue wave,
And swam, in vain, the sinking prize to save.
Where now are seen, along the river side,
Young busy towns, in buxom painted pride,
And fleets of gliding boats with riches crown'd,
To distant Orleans or St. Louis bound,
Nothing appear'd but nature unsubdued,
One endless, noiseless woodland solitude,
Or boundless prairie, that aye seem'd to be
As level and as lifeless as the sea;
They seem'd to breathe in this wide world alone,
Heirs of the Earth—the land was all their own!

'Twas evening now: the hour of toil was o'er,
Yet still they durst not seek the fearful shore,
Lest watchful Indian crew should silent creep,
And spring upon and murder them in sleep;
So through the livelong night they held their way,
And 'twas a night might shame the fairest day;
So still, so bright, so tranquil was its reign,
They cared not though the day ne'er came again.
The moon high wheel'd the distant hills above,
Silver'd the fleecy foliage of the grove,
That as the wooing zephyrs on it fell,
Whisper'd it loved the gentle visit well:
That fair-faced orb alone to move appear'd,
That zephyr was the only sound they heard.
No deep-mouth'd hound the hunter's haunt betray'd,
No lights upon the shore or waters play'd,
No loud laugh broke upon the silent air,
To tell the wand'rers man was nestling there.
All, all was still, on gliding bark and shore,
As if the earth now slept to wake no more.

John G. Whittier.

THE FEMALE MARTYR.

Mary G——, aged 18, a "Sister of Charity," died in one of our Atlantic cities, during the prevalence of the Indian Cholera, while in voluntary attendance upon the sick.

"Bring out your dead!" the midnight street
  Heard and gave back the hoarse, low call;
Harsh fell the tread of hasty feet;
Glanced through the dark the coarse white sheet;
  Her coffin and her pall.
"What! only one!" the brutal hackman said,
As, with an oath, he spurn'd away the dead.

How sunk the inmost hearts of all,
  As roll'd that dead-cart slowly by,
With creaking wheel and harsh hoof-fall!
The dying turn'd him to the wall,
  To hear it and to die!
Onward it roll'd; while oft its driver stay'd,
And hoarsely clamour'd, "Ho! bring out your dead."

It paused beside the burial-place:
  "Toss in your load!" and it was done.
With quick hand and averted face,
Hastily to the grave's embrace
  They cast them, one by one—
Stranger and friend—the evil and the just,
Together trodden in the churchyard dust!

And thou, young martyr! thou wast there:
  No white-robed sisters round thee trod,
Nor holy hymn, nor funeral prayer
Rose through the damp and noisome air,
  Giving thee to thy God;
Nor flower, nor cross, nor hallow'd taper gave
Grace to the dead, and beauty to the grave!

Yet, gentle sufferer! there shall be,
  In every heart of kindly feeling,
A rite as holy paid to thee
As if beneath the convent-tree
  Thy sisterhood were kneeling,
At vesper hours, like sorrowing angels, keeping
Their tearful watch around thy place of sleeping.

For thou wast one in whom the light
  Of Heaven's own love was kindled well,
Enduring with a martyr's might,
Through weary day and wakeful night,
  Far more than words may tell:
Gentle, and meek, and lowly, and unknown,
Thy mercies measured by thy God alone!

Where manly hearts were failing—where
  The throngful street grew foul with death,
Oh high soul'd martyr! thou wast there,
Inhaling from the loathsome air
  Poison with every breath.
Yet shrinking not from offices of dread
For the wrung dying and the unconscious dead.

And, where the sickly taper shed
  Its light through vapours, damp, confined,
Hush'd as a seraph's fell thy tread,
A new Electra by the bed
  Of suffering human-kind!
Pointing the spirit, in its dark dismay,
To that pure hope which fadeth not away.

Innocent teacher of the high
  And holy mysteries of Heaven!
How turn'd to thee each glazing eye,
In mute and awful sympathy,
  As thy low prayers were given;
And the o'erhovering spoiler wore, the while,
An angel's features, a deliverer's smile!

A blessed task! and worthy one
  Who, turning from the world, as thou,
Ere being's pathway had begun
To leave its spring-time flower and sun,
  Had seal'd her early vow,
Giving to God her beauty and her youth,
Her pure affections and her guileless truth.

Earth may not claim thee. Nothing here
  Could be for thee a meet reward;
Thine is a treasure far more dear:
Eye hath not seen it, nor the ear
  Of living mortal heard,
The joys prepared, the promised bliss above,
The holy presence of Eternal Love!

Sleep on in peace. The earth has not
  A nobler name than thine shall be.
The deeds by martial manhood wrought,
The lofty energies of thought,
  The fire of poesy—
These have but frail and fading honours; thine
Shall Time unto Eternity consign.

Yea: and when thrones shall crumble down,
  And human pride and grandeur fall—
The herald's pride of long renown,
The mitre and the kingly crown—
  Perishing glories all!
The pure devotion of thy generous heart
Shall live in Heaven, of which it was a part!

THE WORSHIP OF NATURE.

"It hath beene as it were especially rendered unto mee, and made plaine and legible to my understandynge, that a great worshipp is going on among the thyngs of God."—*Gralt.*

The Ocean looketh up to Heaven
  As 'twere a living thing,
The homage of its waves is given
  In ceaseless worshipping.

They kneel upon the sloping sand,
As bends the human knee,
A beautiful and tireless band,
The Priesthood of the Sea!

They pour the glittering treasures out
Which in the deep have birth,
And chant their awful hymns about
The watching hills of earth.

The green earth sends its incense up
From every mountain shrine,
From every flower and dewy cup
That greeteth the sunshine.

The mists are lifted from the rills
Like the white wing of prayer,
They lean above the ancient hills
As doing homage there.

The forest tops are lowly cast
O'er breezy hill and glen,
As if a prayerful spirit pass'd
On Nature as on men.

The clouds weep o'er the fallen world,
E'en as repentant love;
Ere to the blessed breeze unfurl'd,
They fade in light above.

The sky is as a temple's arch,
The blue and wavy air
Is glorious with the spirit-march
Of messengers of prayer.

The gentle moon, the kindling sun,
The many stars are given,
As shrines to burn earth's incense on—
The altar-fires of Heaven!

PENTUCKET.

The village of Haverhill, on the Merrimack, called by the Indians Pentucket, was for nearly seventy years a frontier town, and during thirty years endured all the horrors of savage warfare. In the year 1708, a combined body of French and Indians, under the command of De Challions, and Hertel de Rouville, the infamous and bloody sacker of Deerfield, made an attack upon the village, which at that time contained only thirty houses. Sixteen of the villagers were massacred, and a still larger number made prisoners. About thirty of the enemy also fell, and among them Hertel de Rouville. The minister of the place, Benjamin Rolfe, was killed by a shot through his own door.

How sweetly on the wood-girt town
The mellow light of sunset shone!
Each small bright lake, whose waters still
Mirror the forest and the hill,
Reflected from its waveless breast
The beauty of a cloudless west,
Glorious as if a glimpse were given
Within the western gates of Heaven,
Left, by the spirit of the star
Of sunset's holy hour, ajar!

Beside the river's tranquil flood
The dark and low-wall'd dwellings stood,
Where many a rood of open land
Stretch'd up and down on either hand,
With corn-leaves waving freshly green
The thick and blacken'd stumps between;
Behind, unbroken, deep and dread,
The wild, untravell'd forest spread,
Back to those mountains, white and cold,
Of which the Indian trapper told,
Upon whose summits never yet
Was mortal foot in safety set.

Quiet and calm, without a fear
Of danger darkly lurking near,
The weary labourer left his plough,
The milkmaid caroll'd by her cow;

From cottage door and household hearth
Rose songs of praise or tones of mirth.
At length the murmur died away,
And silence on that village lay:
So slept Pompeii, tower and hall,
Ere the quick earthquake swallow'd all,
Undreaming of the fiery fate
Which made its dwellings desolate!

Hours pass'd away. By moonlight sped
The Merrimack along his bed.
Bathed in the pallid lustre stood
Dark cottage-wall, and rock, and wood,
Silent, beneath that tranquil beam,
As the hush'd grouping of a dream.
Yet on the still air crept a sound—
No bark of fox, no rabbit's bound,
No stir of wings, nor waters flowing,
Nor leaves in midnight breezes blowing.

Was that the tread of many feet,
Which downward from the hillside beat?
What forms were those which darkly stood
Just on the margin of the wood?
Charr'd tree-stumps in the moonlight dim,
Or paling rude, or leafless limb?
No: through the trees fierce eyeballs glow'd,
Dark human forms in moonshine show'd,
Wild from their native wilderness,
With painted limbs and battle-dress!

A yell, the dead might wake to hear,
Swell'd on the night-air far and clear:
Then smote the Indian tomahawk
On crashing door and shattering lock;
Then rang the rifle-shot; and then
The shrill death-scream of stricken men;
Sunk the red axe in woman's brain,
And childhood's cry arose in vain;

Bursting through roof and window came,
Red, fast and fierce, the kindled flame;
And blended fire and moonlight glared
Over dead corse and weapons bared.

The morning sun look'd brightly through
The river willows, wet with dew.
No sound of combat fill'd the air,
No shout was heard, nor gunshot there:
Yet still the thick and sullen smoke
From smouldering ruins slowly broke;
And on the greensward many a stain,
And, here and there, the mangled slain,
Told how that midnight bolt had sped,
Pentucket, on thy fated head!

Even now the villager can tell
Where Rolfe beside his hearthstone fell;
Still show the door of wasting oak,
Through which the fatal death-shot broke,
And point the curious stranger where
De Rouville's corse lay grim and bare;
Whose hideous head, in death still fear'd,
Bore not a trace of hair or beard;
And still, within the churchyard ground,
Heaves darkly up the ancient mound,
Beneath whose grass-grown surface lies
The victims of that sacrifice.

Jonathan Lawrence.

LOOK ALOFT.

In the tempest of life, when the wave and the gale
Are around and above, if thy footing should fail,
If thine eye should grow dim, and thy caution depart,
"Look aloft!" and be firm, and be fearless of heart.

If the friend who embraced in prosperity's glow,
With a smile for each joy and a tear for each wo,

Should betray thee when sorrows like clouds are
array'd,
"Look aloft" to the friendship which never shall
fade.

Should the visions which hope spreads in light to
thine eye,
Like the tints of the rainbow, but brighten to fly,
Then turn, and through tears of repentant regret,
"Look aloft" to the Sun that is never to set.

Should they who are dearest, the son of thy heart,
The wife of thy bosom in sorrow depart,
"Look aloft" from the darkness and dust of the tomb,
To that soil where affection is ever in bloom.

And oh! when death comes in his terrors, to cast
His fears on the future, his pall on the past,
In that moment of darkness, with hope in thy heart
And a smile in thine eye, "look aloft" and depart.

TO —— ON THE DEATH OF A FAVOURITE BIRD.

Alas! sweet cousin, how can I,
In harsh, discordant rhyme, rehearse
His sweet, sweet song, whose melody
Had charms beyond the reach of verse?

Ah! I should need his tuneful art,
His tone with more than music rife,
In fitting numbers to impart
The tale of his harmonious life.

And yet that tale how shortly told,
One feast of flowers, one ceaseless strain;
At morn to plume, at eve to fold
His wings, to feed and sleep again.

A simple life of joyance his,
  A life of song, no care had he,
Except, perchance, thy glance to miss,
  And in sad silence pine for thee.

Bless'd in thy smile of sunshine given,
  His pinions sought no softer sky:
Happy to find his loveliest heaven
  In the blue beauty of thine eye.

And, basking in that smile so bright,
  He had no wish his wings to free;
Found in its beam his full delight,
  And loved his sweet captivity.

But ah! that eye, that joyous voice
  No more his dreamy sleep shall break;
No more his little heart rejoice,
  Nor songs of warbling welcome wake.

In vain spring woos with balmy breath,
  And bears sweet music on her wings;
The fine, quick ear is dull in death,
  The answering throat no longer sings.

His lonely mate has lost her cheer;
  Or, if to song her bosom stir,
Fixes her tiny head to hear
  The note that ne'er shall answer her.

That note which hail'd thee to the last,
  And call'd thee to his cage to see
That he was happy, thus to cast
  His last, last lingering look on thee.

Then, since for ever hush'd his strain,
  Lay him in fitting grave to sleep,
Where spring's soft dews and summer's rain,
  With gentle tears his death may weep.

There let the first soft sunbeam fling
  A fresher green o'er all the ground;
There the first lonely wild flower spring,
  And shed its sweetest fragrance round.

Thither let each fond bird repair,
  At music's grave its vows to pay;
Or, doom'd to die, seek refuge there,
  And, swan-like, sing its soul away.

Oliver Wendell Holmes.

THE CAMBRIDGE CHURCHYARD.

Our ancient church! its lowly tower,
    Beneath the loftier spire,
Is shadow'd when the sunset hour
    Clothes the tall shaft in fire;
It sinks beyond the distant eye,
    Long ere the glittering vane,
High wheeling in the western sky,
    Has faded o'er the plain.

Like sentinel and nun, they keep
    Their vigil on the green;
One seems to guard, and one to weep,
    The dead that lie between;
And both roll out, so full and near,
    Their music's mingling waves,
They shake the grass, whose pennon'd spear
    Leans on the narrow graves.

The stranger parts the flaunting weeds,
    Whose seeds the winds have strown
So thick beneath the line he reads,
    They shade the sculptured stone;
The child unveils his cluster'd brow,
    And ponders for a while
The graven willow's pendent bough,
    Or rudest cherub's smile.

But what to them the dirge, the knell?
    These were the mourner's share;
The sullen clang, whose heavy swell
    Throbb'd through the beating air;
The rattling cord, the rolling stone,
    The shelving sand that slid,
And, far beneath, with hollow tone,
    Rung on the coffin's lid.

The slumberer's mound grows fresh and green,
    Then slowly disappears;
The mosses creep, the gray stones lean,
    Earth hides his date and years;
But long before the once-loved name
    Is sunk or worn away,
No lip the silent dust may claim,
    That press'd the breathing clay.

Go where the ancient pathway guides,
    See where our sires laid down
Their smiling babes, their cherish'd brides,
    The patriarchs of the town;
Hast thou a tear for buried love?
    A sigh for transient power?
All that a century left above,
    Go, read it in an hour!

The Indian's shaft, the Briton's ball,
    The sabre's thirsting edge,
The hot shell, shattering in its fall,
    The bayonet's rending wedge,
Here scatter'd death; yet seek the spot,
    No trace thine eye can see,
No altar; and they need it not
    Who leave their children free!

Look where the turbid rain-drops stand
    In many a chiselled square,
The knightly crest, the shield, the brand
    Of honour'd names were there;

Alas! for every tear is dried
    Those blazon'd tablets knew,
Save when the icy marble's side
    Drips with the evening dew.

Or gaze upon yon pillar'd stone,
    The empty urn of pride;
There stands the goblet and the sun,
    What need of more beside?
Where lives the memory of the dead,
    Who made their tomb a toy?
Whose ashes press that nameless bed?
    Go, ask the village boy!

Lean o'er the slender western wall,
    Ye ever-roaming girls;
The breath that bids the blossom fall
    May lift your floating curls,
To sweep the simple lines that tell
    An exile's date and doom;
And sigh, for where his daughters dwell,
    They wreathe the stranger's tomb.

And one amid these shades was born,
    Beneath this turf who lies,
Once beaming as the summer's morn,
    That closed her gentle eyes;
If sinless angels love as we,
    Who stood thy grave beside,
Three seraph welcomes waited thee,
    The daughter, sister, bride!

I wander'd to thy buried mound
    When earth was hid, below
The level of the glaring ground,
    Choked to its gates with snow,
And when with summer's flowery waves
    The lake of verdure roll'd,
As if a sultan's white-robed slaves
    Had scatter'd pearls and gold.

Nay, the soft pinions of the air,
That lift this trembling tone,
Its breath of love may almost bear
To kiss thy funeral stone;
And, now thy smiles have pass'd away,
For all the joy they gave,
May sweetest dews and warmest ray
Lie on thine early grave!

When damps beneath, and storms above,
Have bow'd these fragile towers,
Still o'er the graves yon locust-grove
Shall swing its orient flowers;
And I would ask no mouldering bust,
If e'er this humble line,
Which breathed a sigh o'er others' dust,
Might call a tear on mine.

OLD IRONSIDES.

Ay, tear her tatter'd ensign down!
Long has it waved on high,
And many an eye has danced to see
That banner in the sky;
Beneath it rung the battle shout,
And burst the cannon's roar;
The meteor of the ocean air
Shall sweep the clouds no more!

Her deck—once red with heroes' blood,
Where knelt the vanquish'd foe,
When winds were hurrying o'er the flood,
And waves were white below—
No more shall feel the victor's tread,
Or know the conquer'd knee;
The harpies of the shore shall pluck
The eagle of the sea!

Oh! better that her shatter'd hulk
Should sink beneath the wave;
Her thunders shook the mighty deep,
And there should be her grave;
Nail to the mast her holy flag,
Set every threadbare sail,
And give her to the god of storms,
The lightning and the gale!

THE TREADMILL SONG.

The stars are rolling in the sky,
The earth rolls on below,
And we can feel the rattling wheel
Revolving as we go.
Then tread away, my gallant boys,
And make the axle fly;
Why should not wheels go round about,
Like planets in the sky?

Wake up, wake up, my duck-legg'd man,
And stir your solid pegs;
Arouse, arouse, my gawky friend,
And shake your spider-legs;
What though you're awkward at the trade
There's time enough to learn,
So lean upon the rail, my lad,
And take another turn.

They've built us up a noble wall
To keep the vulgar out;
We've nothing in the world to do
But just to walk about:
So faster, now, you middle men,
And try to beat the ends;
It's pleasant work to ramble round
Among one's honest friends.

Here! tread upon the long man's toes;
He sha'n't be lazy here:
And punch the little fellow's ribs,
And tweak that lubber's ear—
He's lost them both: don't pull his hair,
Because he wears a scratch,
But poke him in the farther eye,
That isn't in the patch.

Hark! fellows, there's the supper-bell,
And so our work is done;
It's pretty sport—suppose we take
A round or two for fun!
If ever they should turn me out
When I have better grown,
Now hang me, but I mean to have
A treadmill of my own!

John H. Bryant.

"And I went and washed, and I received sight."—John ix., 11.

When the great Master spoke,
He touch'd his wither'd eyes,
And at one gleam upon him broke
The glad earth and the skies.

And he saw the city's walls,
And kings' and prophets' tomb,
And mighty arches and vaulted halls,
And the temple's lofty dome.

He look'd on the river's flood,
And the flash of mountain rills,
And the gentle wave of the palms that stood
Upon Judea's hills.

He saw on heights and plains
Creatures ef every race,
But a mighty thrill run through his veins
When he met the human face.

And his virgin sight beheld
  The ruddy glow of even,
And the thousand shining orbs that fill'd
  The azure depths of heaven.

And woman's voice before
  Had cheer'd his gloomy night,
But to see the angel form she wore
  Made deeper the delight.

And his heart at daylight's close,
  For the bright world where he trod,
And when the yellow morning rose,
  Gave speechless thanks to God.

MY NATIVE VILLAGE.

THERE lies a village in a peaceful vale,
  With sloping hills and waving woods around,
Fenced from the blasts. There never ruder gale
  Bows the tall grass that covers all the ground;
And planted shrubs are there, and cherish'd flowers,
And a bright verdure born of gentle showers.

'Twas there my young existence was begun,
  My earliest sports were on its flowery green,
And often, when my schoolboy task was done,
  I climbed its hills to view the pleasant scene,
And stood and gazed till the sun's setting ray
Shone on the height—the sweetest of the day.

There, when that hour of mellow light was come,
  And mountain shadows cool'd the ripen'd grain,
I watch'd the weary yeoman plodding home,
  In the lone path that winds across the plain,
To rest his limbs, and watch his child at play,
And tell him o'er the labours of the day.

And when the woods put on their autumn glow,
  And the bright sun came in among the trees,
And leaves were gathering in the glen below,
  Swept softly from the mountains by the breeze,
I wander'd till the starlight on the stream
At length awoke me from my fairy dream.

Ah! happy days, too happy to return,
  Fled on the wings of youth's departed years,
A bitter lesson has been mine to learn,
  The truth of life, its labours, pains, and fears;
Yet does the memory of my boyhood stay,
A twilight of the brightness pass'd away.

My thoughts steal back to that sweet village still;
Its flowers and peaceful shades before me rise;
The play-place and the prospect from the hill,
  Its summer verdure, and autumnal dyes;
The present brings its storms; but, while they last,
I shelter me in the delightful past.

Elizabeth F. Ellet.

LAKE ONTARIO.

Deep thoughts o'ershade my spirit while I gaze
  Upon the blue depths of thy mighty breast:
Thy glassy face is bright with sunset rays,
  And thy far-stretching waters are at rest,
Save the small wave that on thy margin plays,
  Lifting to summer airs its flashing crest;
While the fleet hues across thy surface driven,
Mingle afar in the embrace of heaven.

Thy smile is glorious when the morning's spring
  Gives half its glowing beauty to the deep;
When the dusk swallow dips his drooping wing,
  And the gay winds that o'er thy bosom sweep,
Tribute from dewy woods and violets bring,
  Thy restless billows in their gifts to steep.

Thou'rt beautiful when evening moonbeams shine,
And the soft hour of night and stars is thine.

Thou hast thy tempests, too; the lightning's home
Is near thee, though unseen; thy peaceful shore,
When storms have lash'd these waters into foam,
Echoes full oft the pealing thunder's roar.
Thou hast dark trophies: the unhonour'd tomb
Of those now sought and wept on earth no more:
Full many a goodly form, the loved and brave,
Lies whelm'd and still beneath thy sullen wave.

The world was young with thee; this swelling flood
As proudly swell'd, as purely met the sky,
When sound of life roused not the ancient wood,
Save the wild eagle's scream, or panther's cry.
Here on this verdant bank the savage stood,
And shook his dart and battle-axe on high,
While hues of slaughter tinged thy billows blue,
As deeper and more close the conflict grew.

Here, too, at early morn, the hunter's song
Was heard from wooded isle and grassy glade;
And here at eve, these cluster'd bowers among,
The low, sweet carol of the Indian maid,
Chiding the slumbering breeze and shadows long,
That kept her lingering lover from the shade:
While, scarcely seen, thy willing waters o'er,
Sped the light bark that bore him to the shore.

Those scenes are past. The spirit of changing years
Has breathed on all around save thee alone.
More faintly the receding woodland hears
Thy voice, once full and joyous as its own.
Nations have gone from earth, nor trace appears
To tell their tale—forgotten or unknown.
Yet here, unchanged, untamed, thy waters lie,
Azure, and clear, and boundless as the sky.

THE VANITY OF THE VULGAR GREAT.

Stay, thou ambitious rill,
Ignoble offering of some fount impure!
Beneath the rugged hill,
Gloomy with shade, thou hadst thy birth obscure
With faint steps issuing slow,
In scanty waves among the rocks to flow.

Fling not abroad thy spray,
Nor fiercely lash the green turf at thy side!
What though indulgent May
With liquid snows hath swoln thy foaming tide?
August will follow soon,
To still thy boastings with his scorching noon.

Lo! calmly through the vale
The Po, the king of rivers, sweeps along;
Yet many a mighty sail
Bears on his breast—proud vessels, swift and strong
Nor from the meadow's side
'Neath summer's sun recedes his lessen'd tide.

Thou, threatening all around,
Dost foam and roar along thy troubled path;
In grandeur newly found,
Stunning the gazer with thy noisy wrath!
Yet, foolish stream! not one
Of all thy boasted glories is thine own.

The smile of yonder sky
Is brief, and change the fleeting seasons know;
On barren sands and dry,
Soon to their death thy brawling waves shall flow.
O'er thee, in summer's heat,
Shall pass the traveller with unmoisten'd feet.

TO THE WHIPPORWILL.

Bird of the lone and joyless night,
Whence is thy sad and solemn lay?
Attendant on the pale moon's light,
Why shun the gairish blaze of day?

When darkness fills the dewy air,
Nor sounds the song of happier bird,
Alone, amid the silence there,
Thy wild and plaintive note is heard.

Thyself unseen, thy pensive moan
Pour'd in no living comrade's ear,
The forest's shaded depths alone
Thy mournful melody can hear.

Beside what still and secret spring,
In what dark wood the livelong day,
Sett'st thou with dusk and folded wing,
To while the hours of light away.

Sad minstrel! thou hast learn'd, like me,
That life's deceitful gleam is vain;
And well the lesson profits thee,
Who will not trust its charm again.

Thou, unbeguiled, thy plaint dost trill
To listening night, when mirth is o'er:
I, heedless of the warning, still
Believe, to be deceived once more.

Grenville Mellen.

MOUNT WASHINGTON.

Mount of the clouds, on whose Olympian height
The tall rocks brighten in the ether air,
And spirits from the skies come down at night,
To chant immortal songs to freedom there!

Thine is the rock of other regions; where
The world of life, which blooms so far below,
Sweeps a wide waste: no gladdening scenes appear,
Save where, with silvery flash, the waters flow
Beneath the far off mountain, distant, calm, and slow.

Thine is the summit where the clouds repose,
Or eddying wildly round thy cliffs are borne;
When Tempest mounts his rushing car, and throws
His billowy mist amid the thunder's home!
Far down the deep ravines the whirlwinds come,
And bow the forests as they sweep along;
While, roaring deeply from their rocky womb,
The storms come forth, and, hurrying darkly on,
Amid the echoing peaks the revelry prolong!

And when the tumult of the air is fled,
And quench'd in silence all the tempest flame,
There come the dim forms of the mighty dead,
Around the steep which bears the hero's name,
The stars look down upon them; and the same
Pale orb that glistens o'er his distant grave,
Gleams on the summit that enshrines his fame,
And lights the cold tear of the glorious brave,
The richest, purest tear that memory ever gave!

Mount of the clouds! when winter round thee throws
The hoary mantle of the dying year,
Sublime amid thy canopy of snows,
Thy towers in bright magnificence appear!
'Tis then we view thee with a chilling fear,
Till summer robes thee in her tints of blue;
When, lo! in soften'd grandeur far yet clear,
Thy battlements stand clothed in Heaven's own hue,
To swell as Freedom's home on man's unbounded view!

James G. Brooks.

JOY AND SORROW.

Joy kneels, at morning's rosy prime,
  In worship to the rising sun;
But Sorrow loves the calmer time,
  When the day-god his course hath run:
When Night is in her shadowy car,
  Pale Sorrow wakes while Joy doth sleep;
And, guided by the evening star,
  She wanders forth to muse and weep.

Joy loves to cull the summer flower,
  And wreath it round his happy brow;
But when the dark autumnal hour
  Hath laid the leaf and blossom low;
When the frail bud hath lost its worth,
  And Joy hath dash'd it from his crest,
Then Sorrow takes it from the earth,
  To wither on her wither'd breast.

Anna Maria Wells.

THE WHITE HARE.

It was the Sabbath eve: we went,
My little girl and I, intent
  The twilight hour to pass,
Where we might hear the waters flow,
And scent the freighted winds that blow
  Athwart the vernal grass.

In darker grandeur, as the day
Stole scarce perceptibly away,
  The purple mountain stood,
Wearing the young moon as a crest:
The sun, half sunk in the far west,
  Seem'd mingling with the flood.

The cooling dews their balm distill'd;
A holy joy our bosoms thrill'd;
  Our thoughts were free as air;
And by one impulse moved, did we
Together pour, instinctively,
  Our songs of gladness there.

The green-wood waved its shade hard by,
While thus we wove our harmony:
  Lured by the mystic strain,
A snow-white hare, that long had been
Peering from forth her covert green,
  Came bounding o'er the plain.

Her beauty 'twas a joy to note;
The pureness of her downy coat,
  Her wild, yet gentle eye;
The pleasure that, despite her fear,
Had led the timid thing so near,
  To list our minstrelsy!

All motionless, with head inclined,
She stood, as if her heart divined
  The impulses of ours,
Till the last note had died, and then
Turn'd half reluctantly again
  Back to her green-wood bowers.

Once more the magic sounds we tried;
Again the hare was seen to glide
  From out her sylvan shade;
Again, as joy had given her wings,
Fleet as a bird she forward springs
  Along the dewy glade.

Go, happy thing! disport at will;
Take thy delight o'er vale and hill,
  Or rest in leafy bower:
The harrier may beset thy way,
The cruel snare thy feet betray!
  Enjoy thy little hour!

We know not, and we ne'er may know,
The hidden springs of joy and wo
  That deep within thee lie:
The silent workings of thy heart,
They almost seem to have a part
  With our humanity!

TO A YOUNG MOTHER.

Belinda! the young blossom that doth lie
So lightly on thy bosom, clasp it there:
For on her brow an empress doth not wear,
Nor in her jewell'd zone, a gem more fair,
Or that doth deck her more becomingly.
Forget not, then, that deep within thy flower
The germes lie hid of lovelier, holier things:
Filial affection, that spontaneous springs;
High *truth* and maiden *purity*; the *power*
That comes of *gentleness*; ay, and more,
Piety, nourish'd in the bosom's core:
These, if so cherish'd, shall thy blossom bear,
And with the dews of heavenly love impearl'd,
It shall adorn thee in another world.

Caroline Gilman.

TO ——.

Oh, pure and gentle ones, within your ark
    Securely rest!
Blue be the sky above; your quiet bark
    By soft winds bless'd!

Still toil in duty and commune with Heaven,
    World-wean'd and free:
God to his humblest creatures room has given,
    And space to be.

Space for the eagle in the vaulted sky
To plume his wing;
Space for the ringdove by her young to lie,
And softly sing.

Space for the sunflower, bright with yellow glow,
To court the sky;
Space for the violet, where the wild woods grow,
To live and die.

Space for the ocean, in its giant might,
To swell and rave;
Space for the river, tinged with rosy light,
Where green banks wave.

Space for the sun, to tread his path in might
And golden pride;
Space for the glow-worm, calling, by her light,
Love to her side.

Then, pure and gentle ones, within *your* ark
Securely rest!
Blue be the skies above, and your still bark
By kind winds bless'd.

Sarah J. Hale.

THE ROSE-TREE AT THE BIRTHPLACE OF WASHINGTON.

Bright rose! what dost thou here, amid
These sad mementoes of the past?
The crumbling stones thy roots have hid,
The bramble's shade is o'er thee cast,
Yet still thy glowing beauty seems
Fair as young childhood's happy dreams.

The sunbeam on the heaving surf
Proclaims the tempest's rage is o'er;
The violet, on the frozen turf,
Breathes of the smiling spring once more;

But, rose, thy mission to the heart,
In things that alter, hath no part.

The mossgrown ruins round are spread,
  Scarce rescued from earth's trodden mass,
And time-scathed trees, whose branches dead
  Lie cumbering o'er the matted grass:
These tell the tale of life's brief day,
Hope, toil, enjoyment, death, decay!

The common record this of man,
  We read, regret, and pass it by,
And rear the towers that deck our span,
  Above the grave where nations lie;
And heroes, who like meteors shone,
Are, like that meteor's flashings, gone.

But, radiant rose, thy beauty breaks
  Like eve's first star upon the sight;
A holier hue the vision takes,
  The ruins shine with heaven's clear light;
His *name*, who placed thy root in earth,
Doth consecrate thy place of birth.

Yet 'tis not here his wreath we twine,
  Nor here that Freedom's chief we praise;
The stars at rising softer shine,
  Than when o'er night's dark vault they blaze
Not here, with Washington's great name,
Blend his achievements or his fame.

But brighter, holier is the ray
  Which rests on this devoted ground;
Here pass'd his childhood's happy day,
  Here glory's bud meet culture found:
Maternal smiles, and tears, and prayer,
These were its light, its dew, its air.

Bright rose! for this thy flower hath sprung,
  The mother's steadfast love to show;
Thy odour on the gale is flung,
  As pours that love its lavish flow:

The mother's lot with hope to cheer,
Type of her heart, thou bloomest here.

Charles F. Hoffman.

INDIAN SUMMER.

Light as love's smiles, the silvery mist at morn
  Floats in loose flakes along the limpid river;
The bluebird's notes, upon the soft breeze borne,
  As high in air she carols, faintly quiver;
The weeping birch, like banners idly waving,
Bends to the stream, its spicy branches laving;
  Beaded with dew the witch elm's tassels shiver,
The timid rabbit from the furze is peeping, [ing.
And from the springy spray the squirrel's gayly leap-

I love thee, Autumn, for thy scenery, ere
  The blasts of winter chase the varied dyes
That gayly deck the slow-declining year;
  I love the splendour of thy sunset skies,
The gorgeous hues that tinge each falling leaf,
Lovely as Beauty's cheek, as woman's love too brief;
  I love the note of each wild bird that flies,
As on the wind she pours her parting lay, [away.
And wings her loitering flight to summer climes

Oh, Nature! still I fondly turn to thee
  With feelings fresh as e'er my childhood's were;
Though wild and passion-toss'd my youth may be,
  Towards thee I still the same devotion bear;
To thee—to thee—though health and hope no more
Life's wasted verdure may to me restore—
  I still can, childlike, come as when in prayer
I bow'd my head upon a mother's knee,
And deem'd the world, like her, all truth and purity

Park Benjamin.

SONNET.

Time! thou destroy'st the relics of the past,
And hidest all the footprints of thy march
On shatter'd column and on crumbled arch,
By moss and ivy growing green and fast.
Hurl'd into fragments by the tempest-blast,
The Rhodian monster lies: the obelisk,
That with sharp line divided the broad disc
Of Egypt's sun, down to the sands was cast:
And where these stood, no remnant-trophy stands,
And even the art is lost by which they rose:
Thus, with the monuments of other lands,
The place that knew them now no longer knows
Yet triumph not, oh Time; strong towers decay,
But a great name shall never pass away!

SONNET.

To see a fellow of a summer's morning,
With a large foxhound of a slumberous eye
And a slim gun, go slowly lounging by,
About to give the feather'd bipeds warning,
That probably they may be shot hereafter,
Excites in me a quiet kind of laughter;
For, though I am no lover of the sport
Of harmless murder, yet it is to me
Almost the funniest thing on earth to see
A corpulent person, breathing with a snort,
Go on a shooting frolic all alone;
For well I know that when he's out of town,
He and his dog and gun will all lie down,
And undestructive sleep till game and light are flown.

William B. Tappan.

THE TWENTY THOUSAND CHILDREN OF THE SABBATH SCHOOLS IN NEW-YORK, CELEBRATING TOGETHER THE FOURTH OF JULY, 1839.

Oh, sight sublime! oh, sight of fear!
The shadowing of infinity!
Numbers! whose murmur rises here
Like whisperings of the mighty sea.

Ye bring strange vision to my gaze;
Earth's-dreamer, heaven before me swims;
The sea of glass, the throne of days,
Crowns, harps, and the melodious hymns.

Ye rend the air with grateful songs
For freedom by old warriors won:
Oh, for the battle which your throngs
May wage and win through David's Son!

Wealth of young beauty! that now blooms
Before me like a world of flowers;
High expectation! that assumes
The hue of life's serenest hours,

Are ye *decaying?* Must these forms,
So agile, fair, and brightly gay,
Hidden in dust, be given to worms
And everlasting night the prey?

Are ye *immortal?* Will this mass
Of life, be life, undying still,
When all these sentient thousands pass
To where corruption works its will?

Thought! that takes hold of heaven and hell,
Be in each teacher's heart to-day!
So shall Eternity be well
With these, when Time has fled away.

George Lunt.

AUTUMN MUSINGS.

Come thou with me! If thou hast worn away
All this most glorious summer in the crowd,
Amid the dust of cities, and the din,
While birds were carolling on every spray;
If, from gray dawn to solemn night's approach,
Thy soul hath wasted all its better thoughts,
Toiling and panting for a little gold;
Drudging amid the very lees of life
For this accursed slave that makes men slaves;
Come thou with me into the pleasant fields,
Let Nature breathe on us and make us free!

For thou shalt hold communion, pure and high,
With the great Spirit of the Universe;
It shall pervade thy soul; it shall renew
The fancies of thy boyhood: thou shalt know
Tears, most unwonted tears dimming thine eyes;
Thou shalt forget, under the old brown oak,
That the good south-wind and the liberal west
Have other tidings than the songs of birds,
Or the soft news wafted from fragrant flowers.
Look out on Nature's face, and what hath she
In common with thy feelings? That brown hill,
Upon whose sides, from the gray mountain ash,
We gather'd crimson berries, look'd as brown
When the leaves fell twelve autumn suns ago;
This pleasant stream, with the well-shaded verge,
On whose fair surface have our buoyant limbs
So often play'd, caressing and caress'd;
Its verdant banks are green as then they were,
So went its bubbling murmur down the tide.
Yes, and the very trees, those ancient oaks,
The crimson-crested maple, feathery elm,
And fair, smooth ash, with leaves of graceful gold,
Look like familiar faces of old friends.

From their broad branches drop the wither'd leaves,
Drop, one by one, without a single breath,
Save when some eddying curl round the old roots
Twirls them about in merry sport a while.
They are not changed; their office is not done;
The first soft breeze of spring shall see them fresh
With sprouting twigs bursting from every branch,
As should fresh feelings from our wither'd hearts.
Scorn not the moral; for, while these have warm'd
To annual beauty, gladdening the fields
With new and ever-glorious garniture,
Thou hast grown worn and wasted, almost gray
Even in thy very summer. 'Tis for this
We have neglected nature! Wearing out
Our hearts and all life's dearest charities
In the perpetual turmoil, when we need
To strengthen and to purify our minds
Amid the venerable woods; to hold
Chaste converse with the fountains and the winds!
So should we elevate our souls; so be
Ready to stand and act a nobler part
In the hard, heartless struggles of the world.

Day wanes; 'tis autumn eventide again;
And, sinking on the blue hills' breast, the sun
Spreads the large bounty of his level blaze,
Lengthening the shades of mountains and tall trees,
And throwing blacker shadows o'er the sheet
Of this dark stream, in whose unruffled tide
Waver the bank-shrub and the graceful elm,
As the gay branches and their trembling leaves
Catch the soft whisper of the coming air:
So doth it mirror every passing cloud,
And those which fill the chambers of the west
With such strange beauty, fairer than all thrones,
Blazon'd with orient gems and barbarous gold.
I see thy full heart gathering in thine eyes;
I see those eyes swelling with precious tears;
But, if thou couldst have look'd upon this scene

With a cold brow, and then turn'd back to thoughts
Of traffic in thy fellow's wretchedness,
Thou wert not fit to gaze upon the face
Of Nature's naked beauty; most unfit
To look on fairer things, the loveliness
Of earth's most lovely daughters, whose glad forms
And glancing eyes do kindle the great souls
Of better men to emulate pure thoughts,
And, in high action, all ennobling deeds.

But lo! the harvest moon! She climbs as fair
Among the cluster'd jewels of the sky,
As, mid the rosy bowers of paradise,
Her soft light, trembling upon leaf and flower,
Smiled o'er the slumbers of the first-born man.
And, while her beauty is upon our hearts,
Now let us seek our quiet home, that sleep
May come without bad dreams; may come as light
As to that yellow-headed cottage-boy,
Whose serious musings, as he homeward drives
His sober herd, are of the frosty dawn,
And the ripe nuts which his own hand shall pluck.
Then, when the bird, high-courier of the morn,
Looks from his airy vantage o'er the world,
And, by the music of his mounting flight,
Tells many blessed things of gushing gold,
Coming in floods o'er the eastern wave,
Will we arise, and our pure orisons
Shall keep us in the trials of the day.

Epes Sargent.

A WISH.

That I were in some forest's green retreat,
  Beneath a towering arch of proud old elms,
Where a clear streamlet gurgled at my feet,
  Its wavelets glittering in their tiny helms!

Thick, clustering vines, in many a rich festoon,
  From the high, rustling branches should depend,
Weaving a net through which the sultry noon
  Might stoop in vain its fiery darts to send.
There, prostrate on some rock's gray sloping side,
  Upon whose tinted moss the dew yet lay,
Would I catch glimpses of the clouds that ride
  Athwart the sky, and dream the hours away;
While, through the alleys of the sunless wood,
The fanning breeze might steal, with wild flowers' breath imbued.

John Neal.

THE SOLDIER'S VISIT TO HIS FAMILY.

And there the stranger stays: beneath that oak,
Whose shatter'd majesty hath felt the stroke
Of heaven's own thunder—yet it proudly heaves,
A giant sceptre wreathed with blasted leaves—
As though it dared the elements, and stood
The guardian of that cot, the monarch of that wood
  Beneath its venerable vault he stands:
And one might think, who saw his outstretch'd hands
That something more than soldiers e'er may feel,
Had touch'd him with its holy, calm appeal:
That yonder wave—the heaven—the earth—the ai
Had call'd upon his spirit for her prayer.
His eye goes dimly o'er the midnight scene;
The oak—the cot—the wood—the faded green—
The moon—the sky—the distant moving light—
All! all are gathering on his dampen'd sight.
His warrior helm and plume, his fresh-dyed blade,
Beneath a window on the turf are laid;
The panes are ruddy through the clambering vines
And blushing leaves, that Summer intertwines
In warmer tints than e'er luxuriant Spring,
O'er flower-imbosom'd roof led wandering.

His pulses quicken: for a rude old door
Is open'd by the wind: he sees the floor,
Strew'd with white sand, on which he used to trace
His boyhood's battles, and assign a place
To charging hosts, and give the Indian yell,
And shout to hear his hoary grandsire tell
How he had fought with savages, whose breath
He felt upon his cheek like mildew till his death.
  Hark! that sweet song, how full of tenderness!
Oh! who would breathe in this voluptuous press
Of lulling thoughts! so soothing and so low,
Like singing fountains in their faintest flow:
It is as if some holy, lovely thing,
Within our very hearts were murmuring.
The soldier listens, and his arms are press'd
In thankfulness, and trembling on his breast:
Now, on the very window where he stands
Are seen a clambering infant's rosy hands:
And now—ah Heaven! blessings on that smile!
Stay, soldier, stay! oh linger yet a while!
An airy vision now appears, with eyes
As tender as the blue of weeping skies:
Yet sunny in their radiance, as that blue
When sunset glitters on its falling dew:
With form—all joy and dance—as bright and free
As youthful nymph of mountain liberty,
Or naked angels dream'd by poesy:
A blooming infant to her heart is press'd,
And ah! a mother's song is lulling it to rest.
  A single bound! our chief is standing by,
Trembling from head to foot with ecstasy; [love!
"Bless thee!" at length he murmur'd, "bless thee,
My wife! my boy!" Their eyes are raised above.
His soldier's tread of sounding strength is gone,
A choking transport drowns his manly tone.
He sees the closing of that mild blue eye,
His bosom echoes to a faint low cry:
His glorious boy springs freshly from his sleep;
Shakes his thin sun-curls, while his eyebeams leap

As half in fear, along the stranger's dress,
Then, half advancing, yields to his caress:
Then peers beneath his locks, and seeks his eye
With the clear look of radiant infancy,
The cherub smile of love, the azure of the sky.
  The stranger now is kneeling by the side
Of that young mother, watching for the tide
Of her returning life: it comes: a glow
Goes faintly, slowly o'er her cheek and brow:
A rising of the gauze that lightly shrouds
A snowy breast, like twilight's melting clouds,
In nature's pure, still eloquence, betrays
The feelings of the heart that reels beneath his gaze

Robert M. Charlton.

TO THE RIVER OGEECHEE.

Oh wave that glidest swiftly
  On thy bright and happy way,
From the morning until evening,
  And from twilight until day,
Why leapest thou so joyously,
  While coldly on thy shore
Sleeps the noble and the gallant heart,
  For aye and evermore?

Or dost thou weep, oh river,
  And is this bounding wave,
But the tear thy bosom sheddeth
  As a tribute o'er his grave?
And when, in midnight's darkness,
  The winds above thee moan,
Are they mourning for our sorrows,
  Do they sigh for him that's gone?

Keep back thy tears, then, river,
  Or, if they must be shed,
Let them flow but for the living,
  They're needless for the dead.

His soul shall dwell in glory,
  Where bounds a brighter wave,
But our pleasures, with his troubles,
  Are buried in the grave.

Jones Very.

TO THE CANARY-BIRD.

I cannot hear thy voice with others' ears,
Who make of thy lost liberty a gain;
And in thy tale of blighted hopes and fears
Feel not that every note is born with pain.
Alas! that with thy music's gentle swell
Past days of joy should through thy memory throng,
And each to thee their words of sorrow tell,
While ravish'd sense forgets thee in thy song.
The heart that on the past and future feeds,
And pours in human words its thoughts divine,
Though at each birth the spirit inly bleeds,
Its song may charm the listening ear like thine,
And men with gilded cage and praise will try
To make the bard, like thee, forget his native sky.

THE TREE.

I love thee when thy swelling buds appear,
And one by one their tender leaves unfold,
As if they knew that warmer suns were near,
Nor longer sought to hide from winter's cold;
And when with darker growth thy leaves are seen
To veil from view the early robin's nest,
I love to lie beneath thy waving screen
With limbs by summer's heat and toil oppress'd;

And when the autumn winds have stripp'd thee bare,
And round thee lies the smooth untrodden snow,
When naught is thine that made thee once so fair,
I love to watch thy shadowy form below,
And through thy leafless arms to look above
On stars that brighter beam when most we need their love.

THE WIND-FLOWER.

Thou lookest up with meek, confiding eye
Upon the clouded smile of April's face,
Unharm'd, though Winter stands uncertain by,
Eying with jealous glance each opening grace.
Thou trustest wisely! in thy faith array'd,
More glorious thou than Israel's wisest king;
Such faith was his whom men to death betray'd,
As thine who hear'st the timid voice of Spring,
While other flowers still hide them from her call,
Along the river's brink and meadow bare.
Thee will I seek beside the stony wall,
And in thy trust with childlike heart would share,
O'erjoyed that in thy early leaves I find
A lesson taught by him who loved all human kind.

THE SON.

Father, I wait thy word. The sun doth stand
Beneath the mingling line of night and day,
A listening servant, waiting thy command
To roll rejoicing on its silent way;
The tongue of Time abides the appointed hour,
Till on our ear its solemn warnings fall;
The heavy cloud withholds the pelting shower,
Then every drop speeds onward at thy call;

The bird reposes on the yielding bough,
With breast unswollen by the tide of song,
So does my spirit wait thy presence now
To pour thy praise in quickening life along,
Chiding with voice divine man's lengthen'd sleep
While round the Unutter'd Word and Love thei
vigils keep.

ENOCH.

I LOOK'D to find a man who walk'd with God,
Like the translated patriarch of old;
Though gladden'd millions on his footstool trod,
Yet none with him did such sweet converse hold;
I heard the wind in low complaint go by,
That none its melodies like him could hear;
Day unto day spoke wisdom from on high,
Yet none, like David, turn'd a willing ear;
God walk'd alone unhonour'd through the earth;
For him no heart-built temple open stood;
The soul, forgetful of her nobler birth,
Had hewn him lofty shrines of stone and wood,
And left unfinish'd and in ruins still
The only temple he delights to fill.

THE LIVING GOD.

THERE is no death with Thee! Each plant and tree
In living haste their stems push onward still;
The pointed blade, each rooted trunk we see,
In various movement all attest thy will.
The vine must die when its long race is run,
The tree must fall when it no more can rise;
The worm has at its root his task bugun,
And hour by hour his steady labour plies;

Nor man can pause, but in thy will must grow,
And, as his roots within more deep extend,
He shall o'er sons of sons his branches throw,
And to the latest born his shadows lend;
Nor know in thee disease nor length of days,
But lift his head for ever in thy praise.

Frances Sargent Osgood.

THE MORNING WALK, OR THE STOLEN BLUSH.

Never tell me that cheek is not painted, false maid!
'Tis a fib, though your pretty lip parts while I say [it;
And if the cheat were not already betray'd,
Those exquisite blushes themselves would betray it.

But listen! This morning you rose ere the dawn,
To keep an appointment, perhaps—with Apollo;
And, finding a fairy footprint on the lawn
Which I could not mistake, I determined to follow.

To the hillside I track'd it, and, tripping above me,
Her sun-ringlets flying and jewell'd with dew,
A maiden I saw! Now the truth, if you love me—
But why should I question—I'm sure it was you.

And you cannot deny you were met in ascending—
I, meanwhile, pursuing my truant by stealth—
By a blooming young seraph, who turn'd, and, attending
Your steps, said her name was the Spirit of Health.

Meantime, through the mist of transparent vermilion
That suddenly flooded the brow of the hill,
All fretted with gold rose Aurora's pavilion,
Illumining meadow, and mountain, and rill.

And Health, floating up through the luminous air,
  Dipp'd her fingers of snow in those clouds growing bright;
Then turn'd, and dash'd down o'er her votary fair
  A handful of rose-beams that bathed her in light.

Even yet they're at play here and there in your form,
  Through your fingers they steal to your white taper tips,
Now rush to that cheek its soft dimples to warm,
  Now deepen the crimson that lives in your lips.

Will you tell me again, with that scorn-lighted eye,
  That you do not use paint, while such tinting is there?
While the glow still affirms what the glance would deny?
  No, in future disclaim the sweet theft, if you dare!

ANDREWS NORTON.

SCENE AFTER A SUMMER SHOWER.

THE rain is o'er. How dense and bright
  Yon pearly clouds reposing lie!
Cloud above cloud, a glorious sight,
  Contrasting with the dark blue sky!

In grateful silence, earth receives
  The general blessing; fresh and fair,
Each flower expands its little leaves,
  As glad the common joy to share.

The soften'd sunbeams pour around
  A fairy light, uncertain, pale;
The wind flows cool; the scented ground
  Is breathing odours on the gale.

Mid yon rich clouds' voluptuous pile,
  Methinks some spirit of the air
Might rest, to gaze below a while,
  Then turn to bathe and revel there.

The sun breaks forth ; from off the scene
  Its floating veil of mist is flung;
And all the wilderness of green
  With trembling drops of light is hung.

Now gaze on Nature—yet the same—
  Glowing with life, by breezes fann'd,
Luxuriant, lovely, as she came,
  Fresh in her youth, from God's own hand.

Hear the rich music of that voice,
  Which sounds from all below, above ;
She calls her children to rejoice,
  And round them throws her arms of love.

Drink in her influence ; lowborn Care,
  And all the train of mean Desire,
Refuse to breathe this holy air,
  And mid this living light expire.

W. O. P. Peabody.

HYMN OF NATURE.

God of the earth's extended plains !
  The dark green fields contented lie :
The mountains rise like holy towers,
  Where man might commune with the sky
The tall cliff challenges the storm
  That lowers upon the vale below,
Where shaded fountains send their streams,
  With joyous music in their flow.

God of the dark and heavy deep!
  The waves lie sleeping on the sands,
Till the fierce trumpet of the storm
  Hath summon'd up their thundering bands;
Then the white sails are dash'd like foam,
  Or hurry, trembling, o'er the seas,
Till, calm'd by thee, the sinking gale
  Serenely breathes, Depart in peace.

God of the forest's solemn shade!
  The grandeur of the lonely tree,
That wrestles singly with the gale,
  Lifts up admiring eyes to thee;
But more majestic far they stand,
  When, side by side, their ranks they form,
To wave on high their plumes of green,
  And fight their battles with the storm.

God of the light and viewless air!
  Where summer breezes sweetly flow,
Or, gathering in their airy might,
  The fierce and wintry tempests blow;
All—from the evening's plaintive sigh,
  That hardly lifts the drooping flower,
To the wild whirlwind's midnight cry—
  Breathe forth the language of thy power.

God of the fair and open sky!
  How gloriously above us springs
The tented dome, of heavenly blue,
  Suspended on the rainbow's rings!
Each brilliant star that sparkles through,
  Each gilded cloud that wanders free
In evening's purple radiance, gives
  The beauty of its praise to thee.

God of the rolling orbs above!
  Thy name is written clearly bright
In the warm day's unvarying blaze,
  Or evening's golden shower of light.

For every fire that fronts the sun,
And every spark that walks alone
Around the utmost verge of heaven,
Were kindled at thy burning throne.

God of the world! the hour must come,
And Nature's self to dust return;
Her crumbling altars must decay;
Her incense fires shall cease to burn;
But still her grand and lovely scenes
Have made man's warmest praises flow,
For hearts grow holier as they trace
The beauty of the world below.

THE AUTUMN EVENING.

Behold the western evening light!
It melts in deepening gloom;
So calmly Christians sink away,
Descending to the tomb.

The wind breathes low; the withering leaf
Scarce whispers from the tree;
So gently flows the parting breath,
When good men cease to be.

How beautiful on all the hills
The crimson light is shed!
'Tis like the peace the Christian gives
To mourners round his bed.

How mildly on the wandering cloud
The sunset beam is cast!
'Tis like the memory left behind
When loved ones breathe their last.

And now, above the dews of night,
The yellow star appears;
So faith springs in the heart of those
Whose eyes are bathed in tears.

But soon the morning's happier light
Its glory shall restore,
And eyelids that are seal'd in death
Shall wake to close no more.

Elizabeth Townsend.

INCOMPREHENSIBILITY OF GOD.

Where art thou? Thou! Source and Support of
That is or seen or felt; Thyself unseen, [all
Unfelt, unknown—alas! unknowable!
I look abroad among thy works: the sky,
Vast, distant, glorious with its world of suns,
Life-giving earth, and ever-moving main,
And speaking winds, and ask if these are Thee!
The stars that twinkle on, the eternal hills,
The restless tide's outgoing and return,
The omnipresent and deep-breathing air—
Though hailed as gods of old, and only less—
Are not the Power I seek; are thine, not Thee!
I ask Thee from the past; if in the years,
Since first Intelligence could search its source,
Or in some former, unremember'd being
(If such, perchance, were mine), did they behold
And next interrogate Futurity— [Thee?
So fondly tenanted with better things
Than e'er experience own'd—but both are mute;
And past and future, vocal on all else,
So full of memories and phantasies,
Are deaf and speechless here! Fatigued, I turn
From all vain parley with the elements;
And close mine eyes, and bid the thought turn in-
From each material thing its anxious guest, [ward.
If, in the stillness of the waiting soul,
He may vouchsafe himself, Spirit to spirit!
Oh Thou, at once most dreaded and desired,
Pavilion'd still in darkness, wilt thou hide thee?

What though the rash request be fraught with fate,
Nor human eye may look on thine and live?
Welcome the penalty! let that come now
Which soon or late must come. For light like this
Who would not dare to die?
Peace, my proud aim,
And hush the wish that knows not what it asks.
Await his will, who hath appointed this
With every other trial. Be that will
Done now as ever. For thy curious search,
And unprepared solicitude to gaze
On Him—the Unreveal'd—learn hence, instead,
To temper highest hope with humbleness.
Pass thy novitiate in these outer courts,
Till rent the veil, no longer separating
The holiest of all; as erst disclosing
A brighter dispensation; whose results
Ineffable, interminable, tend
E'en to the perfecting thyself, thy kind,
Till meet for that sublime beatitude,
By the firm promise of a voice from heaven
Pledged to the pure in heart!

Henry Ware, Jr.

TO THE URSA MAJOR.

With what a stately and majestic step
That glorious constellation of the north
Treads its eternal circle! going forth
Its princely way among the stars in slow
And silent brightness. Mighty one, all hail!
I joy to see thee on thy glowing path
Walk, like some stout and girded giant; stern,
Unwearied, resolute, whose toiling foot
Disdains to loiter on its destined way.
The other tribes forsake their midnight track,

And rest their weary orbs beneath the wave ;
But thou dost never close thy burning eye,
Nor stay thy steadfast step. But on, still on,
While systems change, and suns retire, and worlds
Slumber and wake, thy ceaseless march proceeds.
The near horizon tempts to rest in vain.
Thou, faithful sentinel, dost never quit
Thy long appointed watch ; but, sleepless still,
Dost guard the fix'd light of the universe,
And bid the north for ever know its place.
  Ages have witness'd thy devoted trust,
Unchanged, unchanging. When the sons of God
Sent forth that shout of joy which rang through
    heaven,
And echoed from the outer spheres that bound
The illimitable universe, thy voice
Join'd the high chorus ; from thy radiant orbs
The glad cry sounded, swelling to His praise,
Who thus had cast another sparkling gem,
Little, but beautiful, amid the crowd
Of splendours that enrich his firmament.
As thou art now, so wast thou then the same.
Ages have roll'd their course, and time grown gray;
The earth has gather'd to her womb again,
And, yet again, the myriads that were born
Of her uncounted, unremember'd tribes.
The seas have changed their beds ; the eternal hills
Have stoop'd with age ; the solid continents
Have left their banks ; and man's imperial works—
The toil, pride, strength of kingdoms, which had flung
Their haughty honours in the face of Heaven,
As if immortal—have been swept away :
Shatter'd and mouldering, buried and forgot.
But time has shed no dimness on thy front,
Nor touch'd the firmness of thy tread; youth,
    strength,
And beauty still are thine ; as clear, as bright,
As when the Almighty Former sent thee forth,
Beautiful offspring of his curious skill,

To watch earth's northern beacon, and proclaim
The eternal chorus of eternal Love.
  I wonder as I gaze. That stream of light,
Undimm'd, unquench'd—just as I see it now—
Has issued from those dazzling points through years
That go back far into eternity.
Exhaustless flood! for ever spent, renew'd
For ever! Yea, and those refulgent drops,
Which now descend upon my lifted eye,
Left their far fountain twice three years ago.
While those winged particles, whose speed outstrips
The flight of thought, were on their way, the earth
Compass'd its tedious circuit round and round,
And, in the extremes of annual change, beheld
Six autumns fade, six springs renew their bloom.
So far from earth those mighty orbs revolve!
So vast the void through which their beams descend!
  Yes, glorious lamp of God! He may have quench'd
Your ancient flames, and bid eternal night
Rest on your spheres; and yet no tidings reach
This distant planet. Messengers still come
Laden with your far fire, and we may seem
To see your lights still burning; while their blaze
But hides the black wreck of extinguish'd realms,
Where anarchy and darkness long have reign'd.
  Yet what is this, which to the astonish'd mind
Seems measureless, and which the baffled thought
Confounds? A span, a point, in those domains
Which the keen eye can traverse. Seven stars
Dwell in that brilliant cluster, and the sight
Embraces all at once; yet each from each
Recedes as far as each of them from earth.
And every star from every other burns
No less remote. From the profound of heaven,
Untravell'd even in thought, keen, piercing rays
Dart through the void, revealing to the sense
Systems and worlds unnumber'd. Take the glass
And search the skies. The opening skies pour down
Upon your gaze thick showers of sparkling fire;

Stars, crowded, throng'd, in regions so remote,
That their swift beams—the swiftest things that be—
Have travell'd centuries on their flight to earth.
Earth, sun, and nearer constellations! what
Are ye amid this infinite extent
And multitude of God's most infinite works!
And these are suns! vast, central, living fires,
Lords of dependant systems, kings of worlds
That wait as satellites upon their power,
And flourish in their smile. Awake, my soul,
And meditate the wonder! Countless suns
Blaze round thee, leading forth their countless worlds!
Worlds in whose bosoms living things rejoice,
And drink the bliss of being from the fount
Of all-pervading Love. What mind can know,
What tongue can utter, all their multitudes!
Thus numberless in numberless abodes!
Known but to thee, bless'd Father! Thine they are,
Thy children, and thy care; and none o'erlook'd
Of thee! No, not the humblest soul that dwells
Upon the humblest globe, which wheels its course
Amid the giant glories of the sky,
Like the mean mote that dances in the beam
Among the mirror'd lamps, which fling
Their wasteful splendour from the palace wall,
None, none escape the kindness of thy care;
All compass'd underneath thy spacious wing,
Each fed and guided by thy powerful hand.
Tell me, ye splendid orbs! as from your throne
Ye mark the rolling provinces that own
Your sway, what beings fill those bright abodes?
How form'd, how gifted? what their powers, their state,
Their happiness, their wisdom? Do they bear
The stamp of human nature? Or has God
Peopled those purer realms with lovelier forms
And more celestial minds? Does Innocence
Still wear her native and untainted bloom?
Or has Sin breathed his deadly blight abroad,

And sow'd corruption in those fairy bowers?
Has War trod o'er them with his foot of fire?
And Slavery forged his chains; and Wrath, and Hate,
And sordid Selfishness, and cruel Lust,
Leagued their base bands to tread out light and truth,
And scatter'd wo where Heaven had planted joy?
Or are they yet all paradise, unfallen
And uncorrupt; existence one long joy,
Without disease upon the frame, or sin
Upon the heart, or weariness of life;
Hope never quench'd, and age unknown,
And death unfear'd; while fresh and fadeless youth
Glows in the light from God's near throne of love?
   Open your lips, ye wonderful and fair!
Speak, speak! the mysteries of those living worlds
Unfold! No language? Everlasting light
And everlasting silence? Yet the eye
May read and understand. The hand of God
Has written legibly what man may know,
THE GLORY OF THE MAKER. There it shines,
Ineffable, unchangeable; and man,
Bound to the surface of this pigmy globe,
May know and ask no more. In other days,
When death shall give the encumber'd spirit wings,
Its range shall be extended; it shall roam,
Perchance, among those vast mysterious spheres,
Shall pass from orb to orb, and dwell in each,
Familiar with its children; learn their laws,
And share their state, and study and adore
The infinite varieties of bliss
And beauty, by the hand of Power divine
Lavish'd on all its works. Eternity
Shall thus roll on with ever fresh delight;
No pause of pleasure or improvement; world
On world still opening to the instructed mind
An unexhausted universe, and time
But adding to its glories. While the soul,
Advancing ever to the Source of light
And all perfection, lives, adores, and reigns
In cloudless knowledge, purity, and bliss

THE VISION OF LIBERTY.

The evening heavens were calm and bright;
No dimness rested on the glittering light, [high;
That sparkled from that wilderness of worlds on
Those distant suns burn'd on in quiet ray;
The placid planets held their modest way; [sky.
And silence reign'd profound o'er earth, and sea, and

Oh what an hour for lofty thought!
My spirit burn'd within; I caught
A holy inspiration from the hour.
Around me man and nature slept;
Alone my solemn watch I kept,
Till morning dawn'd, and sleep resumed her power.

A vision pass'd upon my soul.
I still was gazing up to heaven,
As in the early hours of even;
I still beheld the planets roll,
And all those countless sons of light [less night.
Flame from the broad blue arch, and guide the moon-

When lo, upon the plain,
Just where it skirts the swelling main,
A massive castle, far and high,
In towering grandeur broke upon my eye.
Proud in its strength and years, the pond'rous pile
Flung up its time-defying towers;
Its lofty gates seem'd scornfully to smile
At vain assault of human powers,
And threats and arms deride.
Its gorgeous carvings of heraldic pride
In giant masses graced the walls above,
And dungeons yawn'd below.
Yet ivy there and moss their garlands wove,
Grave, silent chroniclers of time's protracted flow.

Bursting on my steadfast gaze,
See, within, a sudden blaze!

So small at first, the zephyr's slightest swell,
That scarcely stirs the pine-tree top,
Nor makes the wither'd leaf to drop,
The feeble fluttering of that flame would quell.

But soon it spread—
Waving, rushing, fierce, and red—
From wall to wall, from tower to tower,
Raging with resistless power;
Till every fervent pillar glow'd,
And every stone seem'd burning coal,
Instinct with living heat, that flow'd
Like streaming radiance from the kindled pole.

Beautiful, fearful, grand,
Silent as death, I saw the fabric stand.
At length a crackling sound began;
From side to side, throughout the pile it ran;
And louder yet and louder grew,
Till now in rattling thunder-peals it grew;
Huge shiver'd fragments from the pillars broke,
Like fiery sparkles from the anvil's stroke.
The shatter'd walls were rent and riven,
And piecemeal driven
Like blazing comets through the troubled sky.
'Tis done; what centuries had rear'd,
In quick explosion disappear'd,
Nor even its ruins met my wondering eye.

But in their place—
Bright with more than human grace,
Robed in more than mortal seeming,
Radiant glory in her face,
And eyes with heaven's own brightness beaming—
Rose a fair majestic form,
As the mild rainbow from the storm.
I mark'd her smile, I knew her eye;
And when, with gesture of command,
She waved aloft the cap-crown'd wand,
My slumbers fled mid shouts of "Liberty!"

Read ye the dream? and know ye not
  How truly it unlock'd the world of fate?
Went not the flame from this illustrious spot,
  And spreads it not, and burns in every state?
And when their old and cumbrous walls,
  Fill'd with this spirit, glow intense,
  Vainly they rear'd their impotent defence:
The fabric falls!
That fervent energy must spread,
  Till despotism's towers be overthrown;
And in their stead,
  Liberty stands alone!

Hasten the day, just Heaven!
  Accomplish thy design;
And let the blessings thou hast freely given,
  Freely on all men shine;
Till equal rights be equally enjoy'd,
And human power for human good employ'd;
Till law, not, the sovereign rule sustain,
And peace and virtue undisputed reign.

W. E. Gallaudet.

LINES TO THE WESTERN MUMMY.

Oh, stranger, whose repose profound
  These latter ages dare to break,
And call thee from beneath the ground
  Ere nature did thy slumber shake!

What wonders of the secret earth
  Thy lip, too silent, might reveal!
Of tribes round whose mysterious birth
  A thousand envious ages wheel!

X

Thy race, by savage war o'errun,
  Sunk down, their very name forgot;
But, ere those fearful times begun,
Perhaps, in this sequester'd spot,

By Friendship's hand thine eyelids closed,
  By Friendship's hand the turf was laid;
And Friendship here, perhaps, reposed,
  With moonlight vigils in the shade.

The stars have run their nightly round,
  The sun look'd out and pass'd his way,
And many a season o'er the ground
  Has trod where thou so softly lay.

And wilt thou not one moment raise
  Thy weary head, a while to see
The later sports of earthly days,
  How like what once enchanted thee?

Thy name, thy date, thy life declare;
  Perhaps a queen, whose feathery band
A thousand maids have sigh'd to wear,
  The brightest in thy beauteous land;

Perhaps a Helen, from whose eye
  Love kindled up the flames of war:
Ah, me! do thus thy graces lie
  A faded phantom, and no more?

Oh, not like thee would I remain,
  But o'er the earth my ashes strew,
And in some rising bud regain
  The freshness that my childhood knew

But has thy soul, oh maid! so long
  Around this mournful relic dwelt?
Or burst away, with pinion strong,
  And at the foot of Mercy knelt?

Or has it, in some distant clime,
  With curious eye, unsated, stray'd,
And, down the winding stream of time,
  On every changeful current play'd?

Or, lock'd in everlasting sleep,
  Must we thy heart extinct deplore,
Thy fancy lost in darkness weep,
  And sigh for her who feels no more?

Or, exiled to some humbler sphere,
  In yonder wood-dove dost thou dwell,
And, murmuring in the stranger's ear,
  Thy tender melancholy tell?

Whoe'er thou be, thy sad remains
  Shall from the Muse a tear demand,
Who, wandering on these distant plains,
  Looks fondly to a distant land.

I. M'Lellan, Jr.

THE NOTES OF THE BIRDS.

Well do I love those various harmonies
That ring so gayly in Spring's budding woods,
And in the thickets, and green, quiet haunts,
And lonely copses of the Summer-time,
And in red Autumn's ancient solitudes.

If thou art pain'd with the world's noisy stir,
Or crazed with its mad tumults, and weigh'd down
With any of the ills of human life;
If thou art sick and weak, or mournest at the loss
Of brethren gone to that far-distant land
To which we all do pass, gentle and poor,
The gayest and the gravest, all alike,

Then turn into the peaceful woods, and hear
The thrilling music of the forest birds.

How rich the varied choir! The unquiet finch
Calls from the distant hollows, and the wren
Uttereth her sweet and mellow plaint at times,
And the thrush mourneth where the kalmia hangs
Its crimson-spotted cups, or chirps, half hid
Amid the lowly dogwood's snowy flowers,
And the blue jay flits by, from tree to tree,
And, spreading its rich pinions, fills the ear
With its shrill-sounding and unsteady cry.

With the sweet airs of Spring, the robin comes,
And in her simple song there seems to gush
A strain of sorrow when she visiteth
Her last year's wither'd nest. But when the gloom
Of the deep twilight falls, she takes her perch
Upon the red stemm'd hazel's slender twig,
That overhangs the brook, and suits her song
To the slow rivulet's inconstant chime.

In the last days of Autumn, when the corn
Lies sweet and yellow in the harvest field,
And the gay company of reapers bind
The bearded wheat in sheaves, then peals abroad
The blackbird's merry chant. I love to hear,
Bold plunderer, thy mellow burst of song
Float from thy watchplace on the mossy tree
Close at the cornfield edge.

Lone whipporwill,
There is much sweetness in thy fitful hymn,
Heard in the drowsy watches of the night.
Ofttimes, when all the village lights are out,
And the wide air is still, I hear thee chant
Thy hollow dirge, like some recluse who takes
His lodging in the wilderness of woods,
And lifts his anthem when the world is still:
And the dim, solemn night, that brings to man
And to the herds deep slumbers, and sweet dews

To the red roses and the herbs, doth find
No eye, save thine, a watcher in her halls.
I hear thee oft at midnight, when the thrush
And the green, roving linnet are at rest,
And the blithe, twittering swallows have long ceased
Their noisy note, and folded up their wings.

Far up some brook's still course, whose current mines
The forest's blacken'd roots, and whose green marge
Is seldom visited by human foot,
The lonely heron sits, and harshly breaks
The Sabbath silence of the wilderness:
And you may find her by some reedy pool,
Or brooding gloomily on the time-stain'd rock,
Beside some misty and far-reaching lake.

Most awful is thy deep and heavy boom,
Gray watcher of the waters! Thou art king
Of the blue lake; and all the wing'd kind
Do fear the echo of thine angry cry.
How bright thy savage eye! Thou lookest down,
And seest the shining fishes as they glide;
And, poising thy gray wing, thy glossy beak
Swift as an arrow strikes its roving prey.
Ofttimes I see thee, through the curling mist,
Dart like a spectre of the night, and hear
Thy strange, bewildering call, like the wild scream
Of one whose life is perishing in the sea.

And now, wouldst thou, oh man! delight the ear
With earth's delicious sounds, or charm the eye
With beautiful creations? Then pass forth,
And find them mid those many-colour'd birds
That fill the glowing woods. The richest hues
Lie in their splendid plumage, and their tones
Are sweeter than the music of the lute,
Or the harp's melody, or the notes that gush
So thrillingly from Beauty's ruby lip.

Micah P. Flint.

LINES ON PASSING THE GRAVE OF MY SISTER

On yonder shore, on yonder shore,
  Now verdant with the depth of shade,
Beneath the white-arm'd sycamore,
  There is a little infant laid.
Forgive this tear. A brother weeps.
'Tis there the faded floweret sleeps.

She sleeps alone, she sleeps alone,
  And summer's forests o'er her wave;
And sighing winds at autumn moan
  Around the little stranger's grave,
As though they murmur'd at the fate
Of one so lone and desolate.

In sounds that seem like Sorrow's own,
  Their funeral dirges faintly creep;
Then, deep'ning to an organ tone,
  In all their solemn cadence sweep,
And pour, unheard, along the wild,
Their desert anthem o'er a child.

She came and pass'd. Can I forget
  How we, whose hearts had hail'd her birth,
Ere three autumnal suns had set,
  Consign'd her to her mother Earth!
Joys and their memories pass away;
But griefs are deeper traced than they.

We laid her in her narrow cell,
  We heap'd the soft mould on her breast,
And parting tears, like raindrops, fell
  Upon her lonely place of rest.
May angels guard it; may they bless
Her slumbers in the wilderness.

She sleeps alone, she sleeps alone ;
 For, all unheard, on yonder shore,
The sweeping flood, with torrent moan,
 At evening lifts its solemn roar,
As, in one broad, eternal tide,
Its rolling waters onward glide.

There is no marble monument,
 There is no stone, with graven lie,
To tell of love and virtue blent
 In one almost too good to die.
We needed no such useless trace
To point us to her resting-place.

She sleeps alone, she sleeps alone;
 But, mid the tears of April showers,
The genius of the wild hath strown
 His germes of fruits, his fairest flowers,
And cast his robe of vernal bloom,
In guardian fondness, o'er her tomb.

She sleeps alone, she sleeps alone ;
 But yearly is her grave-turf dress'd,
And still the summer-vines are thrown,
 In annual wreaths, across her breast.
And still the sighing autumn grieves,
And strews the hallow'd spot with leaves.

George H. Calvert.

WASHINGTON. FROM ARNOLD AND ANDRE, A DRAMATIC FRAGMENT.

Old Officer. My general, I know this people well;
And all the virtues which Old England claims,
As the foundations of her happiness
And greatness—such as reverence of law
And custom, prudence, female chastity,
And with them, independence, fortitude.

Courage, and sturdiness of purpose—have
Been here transplanted from their native soil,
And flourish undegenerate. From these—
Sources exhaustible but with the life
That feeds them—their severe intents take birth,
And draw the lusty sustenance to mould
The limbs and body of their own fulfilment,
So that performance lag not after purpose.
They are our countrymen. They are, as well
In manly resolution as in blood,
The children of our fathers. Washington
Doth know no other language than the one
We speak: and never did an English tongue
Give voice unto a larger, wiser mind.
You'll task your judgment vainly to point out,
Through all this desp'rate conflict, in his plans
A flaw, or fault in execution. He
In spirit is unconquerable, as
In genius perfect. Side by side I fought
With him in that disastrous enterprise
Where rash young Braddock fell; and there I mark'd
The vet'ran's skill contend for mastery
With youthful courage in his wondrous deeds.
Well might the bloody Indian warrior pause,
Amid his massacre confounded, and
His baffled rifle's aim, till then unerring,
Turn from "that tall young man," and deem in awe
That the Great Spirit hover'd over him;
For he, of all our mounted officers,
Alone came out unscathed from that dread carnage,
To guard our shatter'd army's swift retreat.
For years did his majestic form hold place
Upon my mind, stamp'd in that perilous hour,
In th' image of a strong-arm'd friend, until
I met him next as a resistless foe.
'Twas at the fight near Princeton. In quick march,
Victorious o'er his van, onward we press'd;
When, moving with firm pace, led by the chief
Himself, the central force encounter'd us.
One moment paused th' opposing hosts, and then

The rattling volley hid the death it bore :
Another, and the sudden cloud, uproll'd,
Display'd, midway between the adverse lines,
His drawn sword gleaming high, the chief, as though
That crash of deadly music, and the burst
Of sulphurous vapour, had from out the earth
Summon'd the god of war. Doubly exposed,
He stood unharm'd. Like eagles tempest-borne
Rush'd to his side his men ; and had our souls
And arms with twofold strength been braced, we yet
Had not withstood that onset. Thus does he
Keep ever with occasion even step ;
Now warily before our eager speed
Retreating, tempting us with battle's promise
Only to toil us with a vain pursuit ;
Now wheeling rapidly about our flanks,
Startling our ears with sudden peal of war,
And fronting in the thickest of the fight
The common soldier's death, stirring the blood
Of faintest hearts to deeds of bravery
By his great presence.

Alfred B. Street.

A FOREST WALK.

> " Why should we crave a hallowed spot ?
> An altar is in each man's cot,
> A church in every grove that spreads
> Its living roof above our heads."
> Wordsworth's " *God in Natur* "

A lovely sky, a cloudless sun,
  A wind that breathes of leaves and flowers,
O'er hill, through dale, my steps have won,
  To the cool forest's shadowy bowers ;
One of the paths all round that wind,
  Traced by the browsing herds, I choose,
And sights and sounds of human kind,
  In nature's lone recesses lose ;

The beech displays its marbled bark,
  The spruce its green tent stretches wide,
While scowls the hemlock, grim and dark,
  The maple's scallop'd dome beside:
All weave on high a verdant roof,
That keeps the very sun aloof,
Making a twilight scft and green,
Within the column'd, vaulted scene.

Sweet forest odours have their birth
From the clothed boughs and teeming earth;
Where pinecones dropp'd, leaves piled and dead,
  Long tufts of grass, and stars of fern,
  With many a wild flower's fairy urn,
A thick, elastic carpet spread;
Here, with its mossy pall, the trunk,
Resolving into soil, is sunk;
There, wrench'd but lately from its throne,
  By some fierce whirlwind circling past,
Its huge roots mass'd with earth and stone,
  One of the woodland kings is cast.

Above, the forest tops are bright
With the broad blaze of sunny light:
But now, a fitful airgust parts
  The screening branches, and a glow
Of dazzling, startling radiance darts
  Down the dark stems, and breaks below;
The mingled shadows off are roll'd,
The sylvan floor is bathed in gold:
Low sprouts and herbs, before unseen,
Display their shades of brown and green;
Tints brighten o'er the velvet moss,
Gleams twinkle on the laurel's gloss;
The robin, brooding in her nest,
Chirps as the quick ray strikes her breast,
And as my shadow prints the ground,
I see the rabbit upward bound,
With pointed ears an instant look,
Then scamper to the darkest nook,

Where, with crouch'd limb and staring eye,
He watches while I saunter by.

A narrow vista, carpeted
With rich green grass, invites my tread;
Here showers the light in golden dots,
There sleeps the shade in ebon spots;
So blended, that the very air
Seems network as I enter there.
The partridge, whose deep-rolling drum
  Afar has sounded on my ear,
Ceasing his beatings as I come,
  Whirrs to the sheltering branches near;
The little milksnake glides away,
The brindled marmot dives from day;
And now, between the boughs, a space
Of the blue laughing sky I trace;
On each side shrinks the bowery shade;
Before me spreads an emerald glade;
The sunshine steeps its grass and moss,
That couch my footsteps as I cross;
Merrily hums the tawny bee,
The glittering humming-bird I see;
Floats the bright butterfly along,
The insect choir is loud in song:
A spot of light and life, it seems
A fairy haunt for fancy dreams.

Here stretch'd, the pleasant turf I press,
In luxury of idleness;
Sun-streaks, and glancing wings, and sky,
Spotted with cloud-shapes, charm my eye;
While murmuring grass, and waving trees,
Their leaf-harps sounding to the breeze,
And water-tones that tinkle near,
Blend their sweet music to my ear;
And by the changing shades alone,
The passage of the hours are known.

AN AMERICAN FOREST SPRING.

Now fluttering breeze, now stormy blast,
  Mild rain, then blustering snow:
Winter's stern, fettering cold is pass'd,
  But, sweet Spring! where art thou?
The white cloud floats mid smiling blue,
The broad bright sunshine's golden hue
  Bathes the still frozen earth:
'Tis changed! above, black vapours roll:
We turn from our expected stroll,
  And seek the blazing hearth.

Hark! that sweet carol! with delight
  We leave the stifling room!
The little bluebird greets our sight,
  Spring, glorious Spring has come!
The south wind's balm is in the air,
The melting snow-wreathes everywhere
  Are leaping off in showers;
And Nature, in her brightening looks,
Tells that her flowers, and leaves, and brooks,
  And birds will soon be ours.

A few soft, sunny days have shone,
  The air has lost its chill,
A bright green tinge succeeds the brown
  Upon the southern hill.
Off to the woods! a pleasant scene!
Here sprouts the fresh young wintergreen,
  There swells a mossy mound;
Though in the hollows drifts are piled,
The wandering wind is sweet and mild,
  And buds are bursting round.

Where its long rings uncurls the fern,
  The violet, nestling low,
Casts back the white lid of its urn,
  Its purple streaks to show:

Beautiful blossom! first to rise
And smile beneath Spring's wakening skies.
  The courier of the band
Of coming flowers, what feelings sweet
Gush, as the silvery gem we meet
  Upon its slender wand.

A sudden roar—a shade is cast—
  We look up with a start,
And, sounding like a transient blast,
  O'erhead the pigeons dart;
Scarce their blue glancing shapes the eye
Can trace, ere, dotted on the sky,
  They wheel in distant flight.
A chirp! and swift the squirrel scours
Along the prostrate trunk, and cowers
  Within its clefts from sight.

Amid the creeping vine, which spreads
  Its thick and verdant wreath,
The scaurberry's downy spangle sheds
  Its rich, delicious breath.
The bee-swarm murmurs by, and now
It clusters black on yonder bough:
  The robin's mottled breast
Glances that sunny spot across,
As round it seeks the twig and moss
  To frame its summer nest.

Warmer is each successive sky,
  More soft the breezes pass,
The maple's gems of crimson lie
  Upon the thick green grass.
The dogwood sheds its clusters white,
The birch has dropp'd its tassels slight.
  Cowslips are round the rill;
The thresher whistles in the glen,
Flutters around the warbling wren,
  And swamps have voices shrill.

A simultaneous burst of leaves
   Has clothed the forest now,
A single day's bright sunshine weaves
   This vivid, gorgcous show.
Masses of shade are cast beneath,
The flowers are spread in varied wreath,
   Night brings its soft, sweet moon;
Morn wakes in mist, and twilight gray
Weeps its bright dew, and smiling May
   Melts into blooming June!

J. K. Mitchell.

SONG OF THE PRAIRIE.

Oh! fly to the prairie, sweet maiden, with me,
As green, and as wide, and as wild as the sea!
Its bosom of velvet the summer winds ride,
And rank grass is waving in billowy pride.

The city's a prison too narrow for thee—
Then away to the prairies so boundless and free!
Where the sight is not check'd till the prairie and skies,
In harmony blending, commingle their dyes.

The fawns in the meadow-fields fearlessly play—
Away to the chase, lovely maiden, away!
Bound, bound to thy courser, the bison is near!
And list to the tramp of the light-footed deer.

Let England exult in her dogs and her chase—
Oh! what's a king's park to this limitless space?
No fences to leap and no thickets to turn,
No owners to injure, no furrows to spurn.

But, softly as thine on the carpeted hall,
Is heard the light foot of the courser to fall;
And close matted grass no impression receives,
As ironless hoofs bound aloft from the leaves.

Oh, fly to the prairie! the eagle is there:
He gracefully wheels in the cloud-speckled air;
And timidly hiding her delicate young,
The prairie-hen hushes her beautiful song.

Oh, fly to the prairie, sweet maiden, with me!
The vine and the prairie-rose blossom for thee;
And, hailing the moon in the prairie-propp'd sky,
The mocking-bird echoes the katydid's cry.

Let Mexicans boast of their herds and their steeds,
The free prairie-hunter no shepherd-boy needs;
The bison, like clouds, overshadow the place,
And the wild spotted coursers invite to the chase.

The citizen picks at his turtle and fowls,
And stomachless over his fricassee growls:
We track the wild turkey; the rifle supplies
The food for the board and the stomach to prize.

The farmer may boast of his grass and his grain—
He sows them in labour, and reaps them in pain;
But here the deep soil no exertion requires,
Enrich'd by the ashes, and clear'd by the fires.

Then fly to the prairie in wonder, and gaze,
As sweeps o'er the grass the magnificent blaze;
The world cannot boast more romantic a sight—
A continent flaming, and oceans of light!

The woodman delights in his trees and his shade—
But see! there's no sun on the cheek of his maid;
His flowers are faded, his blossoms are pale,
And mildew is riding his vapoury gale.

Then fly to the prairie! no bush to obscure,
No marsh to exhale, and no ague to cure.
Translucent and fresh comes the grass-scented breeze,
Unchill'd by the mountain, unbroken by trees.

Sublime from the north he descends in his wrath,
And scatters the reeds in his snow-cover'd path;
Or, loaded with incense, steals in from the west,
As bees from the prairie-rose fly to their nest.

Oh, fly to the prairie! for freedom is there!
Love lights not that home with the torch of despair!
No wretch to entreat, and no lord to deny,
No gossips to slander, no neighbour to pry.

But struggling not there the heart's impulse to hide,
Love leaps like the fount from the crystal-rock side,
And strong as its adamant, pure as its spring,
Waves wildly in sunbeams his rose-colour'd wing

Edward Sanford.

ADDRESS TO BLACK HAWK.

There's beauty on thy brow, old chief! the high
And manly beauty of the Roman mould,
And the keen flashing of thy full dark eye
Speaks of a heart that years have not made cold;
Of passions scathed not by the blight of time;
Ambition, that survives the battle route.
The man within thee scorns to play the mime
To gaping crowds that compass thee about.
Thou walkest, with thy warriors by thy side,
Wrapp'd in fierce hate, and high, unconquer'd pride.

Chief of a hundred warriors! dost thou yet—
Vanquish'd and captive—dost thou deem that here,
The glowing daystar of thy glory set—
Dull night has closed upon thy bright career?
Old forest lion, caught and caged at last,
Dost pant to roam again thy native wild?
To gloat upon the lifeblood flowing fast
Of thy crush'd victims; and to slay the child,
To dabble in the gore of wives and mothers,
And kill, old Turk! thy harmless, pale-faced brothers?

For it was cruel, Black Hawk, thus to flutter
  The dovecotes of the peaceful pioneers,
To let thy tribe commit such fierce and utter
  Slaughter among the folks of the frontiers.
Though thine be old, hereditary hate,
  Begot in wrongs, and nursed in blood, until
It had become a madness, 'tis too late
  To crush the hordes who have the power and will
To rob thee of thy hunting-grounds and fountains,
And drive thee backward to the Rocky Mountains.

Spite of thy looks of cold indifference, [wonder;
  There's much thou'st seen that must excite thy
Wakes not upon thy quick and startled sense
  The cannon's harsh and pealing voice of thunder?
Our big canoes, with white and widespread wings,
  That sweep the waters as birds sweep the sky;
Our steamboats, with their iron lungs, like things
  Of breathing life, that dash and hurry by?
Or, if thou scorn'st the wonders of the ocean,
What think'st thou of our railroad locomotion?

Thou'st seen our museums, beheld the dummies
  That grin in darkness in their coffin cases;
What think'st thou of the art of making mummies,
  So that the worms shrink from their dry embraces?
Thou'st seen the mimic tyrants of the stage
  Strutting, in paint and feathers, for an hour;
Thou'st heard the bellowing of their tragic rage,
  Seen their eyes glisten, and their dark brows lower.
Anon, thou'st seen them, when their wrath cool'd
Pass in a moment from a king—to clown. [down,

Thou see'st these things unmoved! say'st so, old fellow?
  Then tell us, have the white man's glowing daughters
Set thy cold blood in motion? Has't been mellow
  By a sly cup or so of our fire-waters?

They are thy people's deadliest poison. They
First make them cowards, and then white men's
And sloth, and penury, and passion's prey, [slaves;
And lives of misery, and early graves.
For, by their power, believe me, not a day goes
But kills some Foxes, Sacs, and Winnebagoes.

Say, does thy wandering heart stray far away,
To the deep bosom of thy forest-home?
The hillside, where thy young pappooses play,
And ask, amid their sports, when thou wilt come?
Come not the wailings of thy gentle squaws
For their lost warrior loud upon thine ear,
Piercing athwart the thunder of huzzas,
That, yell'd at every corner, meet thee here?
The wife who made that shell-deck'd wampum belt
Thy rugged heart must think of her—and melt.

Chafes not thy heart, as chafes the panting breast
Of the caged bird against his prison bars,
That thou, the crown'd warrior of the West,
The victor of a hundred forest wars,
Shouldst in thy age become a raree show,
Led, like a walking bear, about the town,
A new-caught monster, who is all the go,
And stared at, gratis, by the gaping clown?
Boils not thy blood while thus thou'rt led about,
The sport and mockery of the rabble rout?

Whence came thy cold philosophy? whence came
Thou tearless, stern, and uncomplaining one,
The power that taught thee thus to veil the flame
Of thy fierce passions? Thou despisest fun,
And thy proud spirit scorns the white men's glee,
Save thy fierce sport, when at the funeral-pile
Of a bound warrior in his agony,
Who meets thy horrid laugh with dying smile.
Thy face, in length, reminds one of a Quaker's,
Thy dances, too, are solemn as a Shaker's.

Proud scion of a noble stem! thy tree
  Is blanch'd, and bare, and sear'd, and leafless now.
I'll not insult its fallen majesty,
  Nor drive, with careless hand, the ruthless plough
Over its roots. Torn from its parent mould,
  Rich, warm, and deep, its fresh, free, balmy air,
No second verdure quickens in our cold,
  New, barren earth; no life sustains it there.
But, even though prostrate, 'tis a noble thing,
Though crownless, powerless, "every inch a king."

Give us thy hand, old nobleman of nature,
  Proud ruler of the forest aristocracy;
The best of blood glows in thy every feature,
  And thy curl'd lip speaks scorn for our democracy.
Thou wear'st thy titles on that godlike brow;
  Let him who doubts them meet thine eagle eye,
He'll quail beneath its glance, and disavow
  All question of thy noble family;
For thou may'st here become, with strict propriety,
A leader in our city good society.

J. B. Van Schaick.

JOSHUA COMMANDING THE SUN AND MOON TO STAND STILL.

The day rose clear on Gibeon. Her high towers
Flash'd the red sunbeams gloriously back,
And the wind-driven banners, and the steel
Of her ten thousand spears caught dazzlingly
The sun, and on the fortresses of rock
Play'd a soft glow, that as a mockery seem'd
To the stern men who girded by its light.
Beth-Horon in the distance slept, and breath
Was pleasant in the vale of Ajalon,
Where armed heels trod carelessly the sweet
Wild spices, and the trees of gum were shot

By the rude armour on their branches hung.
Suddenly in the camp without the walls
Rose a deep murmur, and the men of war
Gather'd around their kings, and "Joshua!
From Gilgal, Joshua!" was whisper'd low,
As with a secret fear, and then, at once,
With the abruptness of a dream, he stood
Upon the rock before them. Calmly then
Raised he his helm, and with his temples bare,
And hands uplifted to the sky, he pray'd:
"God of this people, hear! and let the sun
Stand upon Gibeon, still; and let the moon
Rest in the vale of Ajalon!" He ceased:
And lo! the moon sits motionless, and earth
Stands on her axis indolent. The sun
Pours the unmoving column of his rays
In undiminish'd heat; the hours stand still;
The shade hath stopp'd upon the dial's face;
The clouds and vapours that at night are wont
To gather and enshroud the lower earth,
Are struggling with strange rays, breaking them up,
Scattering the misty phalanx like a wand,
Glancing o'er mountain tops, and shining down
In broken masses on the astonish'd plains.
The fever'd cattle group in wondering herds;
The weary birds go to their leafy nests,
But find no darkness there, and wander forth
On feeble, fluttering wing to find a rest;
The parch'd, baked earth, undamp'd by usual dews,
Has gaped and crack'd, and heat, dry, midday heat,
Comes like a drunkard's breath upon the heart.
On with thy armies, Joshua! The Lord
God of Sabaoth is the avenger now!
His voice is in the thunder, and his wrath
Poureth the beams of the retarded sun,
With the keen strength of arrows, on their sight
The unwearied sun rides in the zenith sky;
Nature, obedient to her Maker's voice,
Stops in full course all her mysterious wheels.

On! till avenging swords have drunk the blood
Of all Jehovah's enemies, and till
Thy banners in returning triumph wave;
Then yonder orb shall set mid golden clouds,
And, while a dewy rain falls soft on earth,
Show in the heavens the glorious bow of God,
Shining, the rainbow-banner of the skies.

Clement C. Moore.

A VISIT FROM ST. NICHOLAS.

'Twas the night before Christmas, when all through the house
Not a creature was stirring, not even a mouse;
The stockings were hung by the chimney with care,
In hopes that St. Nicholas soon would be there;
The children were nestled all snug in their beds,
While visions of sugarplums danced through their heads;
And mamma in her 'kerchief, and I in my cap,
Had just settled our brains for a long winter's nap;
When out on the lawn there arose such a clatter,
I sprang from the bed to see what was the matter:
Away to the window I flew like a flash,
Tore open the shutters and threw up the sash.
Thc moon, on the breast of the new-fallen snow,
Gave the lustre of midday to objects below.
When, what to my wondering eyes should appear,
But a miniature sleigh and eight tiny reindeer,
With a little old driver, so lively and quick,
I knew in a moment it must be St. Nick.
More rapid than eagles his coursers they came,
And he whistled, and shouted, and called them by name;
"Now, Dasher! now, Dancer! now, Prancer! now, Vixen!
On! Comet, on! Cupid, on! Donder and Blixon—

To the top of the porch! to the top of the wall!
Now, dash away, dash away, dash away all!"
As leaves that before the wild hurricane fly,
When they meet with an obstacle, mount to the sky
So up to the house-top the coursers they flew,
With the sleigh full of toys—and St. Nicholas too
And then in a twinkling I heard on the roof
The prancing and pawing of each little hoof.
As I drew in my head, and was turning around,
Down the chimney St. Nicholas came with a bound.
He was dress'd all in fur, from his head to his foot,
And his clothes were all tarnish'd with ashes and soot;
A bundle of toys he had flung on his back,
And he look'd like a pedler just opening his pack.
His eyes, how they twinkled! his dimples, how merry!
His cheeks were like roses, his nose like a cherry;
His droll little mouth was drawn up like a bow,
And the beard on his chin was as white as the snow.
The stump of a pipe he held tight in his teeth,
And the smoke it encircled his head like a wreath.
He had a broad face, and a little round belly,
That shook, when he laugh'd, like a bowl full of jelly.
He was chubby and plump; a right jolly old elf;
And I laugh'd, when I saw him, in spite of myself.
A wink of his eye, and a twist of his head,
Soon gave me to know I had nothing to dread.
He spoke not a word, but went straight to his work,
And fill'd all the stockings; then turn'd with a jerk,
And, laying his finger aside of his nose,
And giving a nod, up the chimney he rose.
He sprang to his sleigh, to his team gave a whistle,
And away they all flew like the down of a thistle;
But I heard him exclaim, ere he drove out of sight,
"Happy Christmas to all, and to all a good-night!"

Lucy Hooper.

THE DAUGHTER OF HERODIAS.

Lines written after seeing among a collection of beautiful paintings—copies from the old masters, recently sent to New-York from Italy—one representing the daughter of Herodias bearing the head of John the Baptist in a charger, and wearing upon her countenance an expression, not of triumph, as one might suppose, but rather of soft and sorrowful remorse, as she looks upon the calm and beautiful features of her victim.

Mother! I bring thy gift;
Take from my hand the dreaded boon; I pray,
Take it; the still, pale sorrow of the face
Hath left upon my soul its living trace,
Never to pass away,
Since from these lips one word of idle breath
Blanch'd that calm face. Oh, mother! this is death!

What is it that I see
From all the pure and settled features gleaming?
Reproach! reproach! My dreams are strange and wild.
Mother! hadst thou no pity on thy child?
Lo! a celestial smile seems softly beaming
On thy hush'd lips; my mother! canst thou brook
Longer upon thy victim's face to look?

Alas! at yester morn
My heart was light, and to the viol's sound
I gayly danced, while crown'd with summer flowers,
And swiftly by me sped the flying hours;
And all was joy around,
Not death! Oh, mother! could I say thee nay?
Take from thy daughter's hand thy boon away!

Take it! my heart is sad;
And the pure forehead hath an icy chill.
I dare not touch it, for avenging Heaven
Hath shuddering visions to my fancy given;
And the pale face appals me, cold and still,
With the closed lips. Oh, tell me! could I know
That the pale features of the dead were so?

I may not turn away
From the charm'd brow; and I have heard his
Even as a prophet by his people spoken; [name
And that high brow in death bears seal and token
Of one whose words were flame.
Oh, holy teacher! couldst thou rise and live,
Would not those hush'd lips whisper, "I forgive?"

Away with lute and harp,
With the glad heart for ever, and the dance!
Never again shall tabret sound for me!
Oh, fearful mother! I have brought to thee
The silent dead, with his rebuking glance,
And the crush'd heart of one to whom is given
Wild dreams of judgment and offended Heaven!

Thomas C. Upham.

THE MILLENNIAL DAY.

"They shall not hurt nor destroy in all my holy mountain: for the earth shall be full of the knowledge of the Lord, as the waters that cover the sea."—Isa. xi., 9.

Upon God's holy mountain all is peace.
Of clanging arms, and cries, and wail, no sound
Goes up to mingle with the gentle breeze,
That bears its perfumed whispers all around.
Beneath its trees, that spread their blooming light,
The spotted leopard walks; the ox is there;
The yellow lion stands in conscious might,
Breathing the dewy and illumined air.
A little child doth take him by the mane,
And leads him forth, and plays beneath his breast
Naught breaks the quiet of that bless'd domain,
Naught mars its harmony and heavenly rest:
Picture divine and emblem of that day, [sway.
When peace on earth and truth shall hold unbroken

GOD WORSHIPPED IN HIS WORKS.

"The heavens declare the glory of God: and the firmament showeth his handiwork. Day unto day uttereth speech, and night unto night showeth knowledge. There is no speech nor language where their voice is not heard."—Ps. xix., 1, 2, 3.

MEN use a different speech in different climes,
But Nature hath one voice, and only one.
Her wandering moon, her stars, her golden sun,
Her woods and waters, in all lands and times,
In one deep song proclaim the wondrous story
They tell it to each other in the sky,
Upon the winds they send it sounding high,
Jehovah's wisdom, goodness, power, and glory.
I hear it come from mountain, cliff, and tree,
Ten thousand voices in one voice united;
On every side the song encircles me,
The whole round world reveres and is delighted.
Ah! why, when heaven and earth lift up their voice,
Ah! why should man alone nor worship nor rejoice?

ELIZA FOLLEN.

NAHANT.

HAIL, boundless Ocean! mighty rolling deep!
Thou ever restless, still rejoicing sea!
Now slowly heaving in thine awful sleep,
Now wildly roaring in glad revelry.

The stars look glorious in their silent place;
The fixed hills in tranquil grandeur stand;
The moon renews her gentle, smiling face;
The sun proclaims his Maker's bounteous hand—

"In solemn silence all;" while thy glad voice
Went forth at first in its eternal roar,
And billow after billow cries, Rejoice!
In ceaseless murmurs on the sounding shore.

I love to stand upon the giant rock
  That thrusts his scowling front against the wave,
And feel the trembling from the mighty shock,
  And hear it roaring through each hollow cave;

Then mark the billows gathering up their force,
  Tossing their foam back like a lion's mane;
And, rushing on in their exulting course,
  In idle murmurs swift recoil again.

And, while the baffled waters seem to sleep,
  Far off they gather mightier than before;
Onward they move, with slow, majestic sweep,
  And break in thunder round the rocky shore.

There is a power within me that awakes
  Mid this wild conflict of the stormy sea;
And moves, and swells, and its stern thraldom breaks,
  And heaves and pants for immortality.

This wind must die away ere long, and thou,
  Old Ocean, must recall thy truant waves;
Dress thee with smiles, and smooth thy furrow'd brow,
  And calmly rest thee in thy silent caves:

While, restless, by no earthly shores confined,
  The sea of Thought nor ebb nor limit knows,
Fed from the fountains of Creative Mind,
  Through realms, through worlds unknown for ever flows.

W. J. Snelling.

THE BIRTH OF THUNDER.—A DAHCOTAH LEGEND.

Twenty-eight miles from the Big Stone Lake, near the sources of the St. Peter's River, is a cluster of small lakes or ponds, lying much below the level of the surrounding prairie, and ornamented with an oak wood. The Dahcotahs call this place The Nest of Thunder, and say that here Thunder was born. As soon as the infant spirit could go alone, he set out to see the world, and, at the first step, placed his foot upon a hill twenty five miles distant; a rock on the top of which actually seems to bear the print of a gigantic human foot. The Indians call the hill THUNDER'S TRACKS. The Nest of Thunder is, to this day, visited by the being whose birth it witnessed. He comes clad in a mantle of storms, and lightnings play round his head.

LOOK, white man, well on all around,
  These hoary oaks, those boundless plains;
Tread lightly; this is holy ground:
  Here Thunder, awful spirit! reigns.
Look on those waters far below,
  So deep beneath the prairie sleeping,
The summer sun's meridian glow
  Scarce warms the sands their waves are heaping;
And scarce the bitter blast can blow
  In winter on their icy cover;
The Wind Sprite may not stoop so low,
  But bows his head and passes over.
Perch'd on the top of yonder pine,
  The heron's billow-searching eye
  Can scarce his finny prey descry,
Glad leaping where their colours shine.
Those lakes, whose shores but now we trod,
  Scars deeply on Earth's bosom dinted,
Are the strong impress of a god,
  By Thunder's giant foot imprinted.
Nay, stranger, as I live 'tis truth!
  The lips of those who never lied
Repeat it daily to our youth.
  Famed heroes, erst my nation's pride,
Beheld the wonder; and our sages
Gave down the tale to after ages.
Dost not believe? though blooming fair
  The flowerets court the breezes coy,
Though now the sweet-grass scents the air,
And sunny nature basks in joy,
  It is not ever so.
Come when the lightning flashes,
Come when the forest crashes,
  When shrieks of pain and wo,

Break on thine ear-drum thick and fast,
From ghosts that shiver in the blast;
Then shalt thou know, and bend the knee
Before the angry deity.

But now attend, while I unfold
  The lore my brave forefathers taught:
As yet the storm, the heat, the cold,
  The changing seasons had not brought.
Famine was not; each tree and grot
  Grew greener for the rain;
The wanton doe, the buffalo,
  Blithe bounded on the plain.
In mirth did man the hours employ
  Of that eternal spring;
With song and dance, and shouts of joy,
  Did hill and valley ring.
No death-shot peal'd upon the ear,
No painted warrior poised the spear,
No stake-doom'd captive shook for fear;
  No arrow left the string,
Save when the wolf to earth was borne;
From foeman's head no scalp was torn;
Nor did the pangs of hate and scorn
  The red man's bosom wring.
Then waving fields of yellow corn
Did our bless'd villages adorn.

Alas! that man will never learn
His good from evil to discern.
At length, by furious passions driven,
  The Indian left his babes and wife,
And every blessing God has given,
  To mingle in the deadly strife.
Fierce Wrath and haggard Envy soon
Achieved the work that War begun;
He left, unsought, the beast of chase,
And prey'd upon his kindred race.
But He who rules the earth and skies,
Who watches every bolt that flies;

From whom all gifts, all blessings flow,
With grief beheld the scene below.
He wept; and, as the balmy shower
Refreshing to the ground descended,
Each drop gave being to a flower,
And all the hills in homage bended.
"Alas!" the good Great Spirit said,
"Man merits not the climes I gave;
Where'er a hillock rears its head,
He digs his brother's timeless grave:
To every crystal rill of water,
He gives the crimson stain of slaughter.
No more for him my brow shall wear
A constant, glad, approving smile;
Ah, no! my eyes must withering glare
On bloody hands and deeds of guile.
Henceforth shall my lost children know
The piercing wind, the blinding snow;
The storm shall drench, the sun shall burn,
The winter freeze them, each in turn.
Henceforth their feeble frames shall feel
A climate like their hearts of steel."

The moon that night withheld her light.
By fits, instead, a lurid glare
Illumed the skies; while mortal eyes
Were closed, and voices rose in prayer.
While the revolving sun
Three times his course might run,
The dreadful darkness lasted.
And all that time the red man's eye
A sleeping spirit might espy,
Upon a tree-top cradled high,
Whose trunk his breath had blasted.
So long he slept, he grew so fast,
Beneath his weight the gnarled oak
Snapp'd, as the tempest snaps the mast.
It fell, and Thunder woke!

The world to its foundation shook,
The grisly bear his prey forsook,
The scowling heaven an aspect bore
That man had never seen before;
The wolf in terror fled away,
And shone at last the light of day.

'Twas here he stood; these lakes attest
Where first Waw-kee-an's footsteps press'd.
About his burning brow a cloud,
  Black as the raven's wing, he wore;
Thick tempests wrapp'd him like a shroud,
  Red lightnings in his hand he bore;
Like two bright suns his eyeballs shone,
His voice was like the cannon's tone;
And, where he breathed, the land became,
Prairie and wood, one sheet of flame.
Not long upon this mountain height
  The first and worst of storms abode,
For, moving in his fearful might,
  Abroad the God-begotten strode.
Afar, on yonder faint blue mound,
In the horizon's utmost bound,
At the first stride his foot he set;
  The jarring world confess'd the shock.
Stranger! the track of Thunder yet
  Remains upon the living rock.
The second step, he gain'd the sand
On far Superior's storm-beat strand:
Then with his shout the concave rung,
As up to heaven the giant sprung
  On high, beside his sire to dwell;
But still, of all the spots on earth,
He loves the woods that gave him birth.—
  Such is the tale our fathers tell.

Willis Gaylord Clark.

THE BURIAL-PLACE AT LAUREL HILL.

Here the lamented dead in dust shall lie,
  Life's lingering languors o'er, its labours done;
Where waving boughs, betwixt the earth and sky,
  Admit the farewell radiance of the sun.

Here the long concourse from the murmuring town,
  With funeral pace and slow, shall enter in;
To lay the loved in tranquil silence down,
  No more to suffer, and no more to sin.

And in this hallow'd spot, where Nature showers
  Her summer smiles from fair and stainless skies,
Affection's hand may strew her dewy flowers,
  Whose fragrant incense from the grave shall rise.

And here the impressive stone, engraved with words
  Which grief sententious gives to marble pale,
Shall teach the heart; while waters, leaves, and birds
  Make cheerful music in the passing gale.

Say, wherefore should we weep, and wherefore pour
  On scented airs the unavailing sigh—
While sun-bright waves are quivering to the shore,
  And landscapes blooming—that the loved must die?

There is an emblem in this peaceful scene:
  Soon rainbow colours on the woods will fall;
And autumn gusts bereave the hills of green,
  As sinks the year to meet its cloudy pall.

Then, cold and pale, in distant vistas round,
  Disrobed and tuneless, all the woods will stand;
While the chain'd streams are silent as the ground,
  As Death had numb'd them with his icy hand.

Yet when the warm, soft winds shall rise in spring,
  Like struggling daybeams o'er a blasted heath,
The bird return'd shall poise her golden wing,
  And liberal Nature break the spell of Death

So, when the tomb's dull silence finds an end,
  The blessed dead to endless youth shall rise;
And hear th' archangel's thrilling summons blend
  Its tone with anthems from the upper skies.

There shall the good of earth be found at last,
  Where dazzling streams and vernal fields expand
Where Love her crown attains—her trials past—
  And, fill'd with rapture, hails the "better land!"

THE EARLY DEAD.

"Why mourn for the young? Better that the light cloud should fade away in the morning's breath, than travel through the weary day, to gather in darkness, and end in storm."—Bulwer.

If it be sad to mark the bow'd with age
  Sink in the halls of the remorseless tomb,
Closing the changes of life's pilgrimage
  In the still darkness of its mouldering gloom;
Oh! what a shadow o'er the heart is flung,
When peals the requiem of the loved and young!

They to whose bosoms, like the dawn of spring
  To the unfolding bud and scented rose,
Comes the pure freshness age can never bring,
  And fills the spirit with a rich repose,
How shall we lay them in their final rest?
How pile the clods upon their wasting breast?

Life openeth brightly to their ardent gaze;
  A glorious pomp sits on the gorgeous sky;
O'er the broad world Hope's smile incessant plays,
  And scenes of beauty win the enchanted eye:
How sad to break the vision, and to fold
Each lifeless form in earth's embracing mould!

Yet this is life! To mark from day to day,
  Youth, in the freshness of its morning prime,
Pass, like the anthem of a breeze away,
  Sinking in waves of Death ere chill'd by Time!

Ere yet dark years on the warm cheek had shed
Autumnal mildew o'er its roselike red!

And yet what mourner, though the pensive eye
  Be dimly thoughtful in its burning tears,
But should with rapture gaze upon the sky, [reers?
  Through whose far depths the spirit's wing ca-
There gleams eternal o'er their ways are flung,
Who fade from earth while yet their years are young!

DEATH OF THE FIRSTBORN.

"Ah! welaway! most angel-like of face,
A childe, young in his pure innocence,
Tender of limbes, God wrote, full guilteless,
The goodly faire that lieth here speecheless.
  A mouth he has, but words hath he none;
Cannot complain, alas! for none outrage,
  Nor grutcheth not, but lies here, all alone,
Still as a lambe, most meke of his visage:
What hearte of stele could do to him damage,
Or suffer him die, beholding the manere,
And looke benigne of his tweine eyen clere?"

LYDGATE.

  YOUNG mother, he is gone!
His dimpled cheek no more will touch thy breast;
  No more the music-tone
Float from his lips, to thine all fondly press'd;
His smile and happy laugh are lost to thee:
Earth must his mother and his pillow be.

  His was the morning hour;
And he hath pass'd in beauty from the day,
  A bud, not yet a flower,
Torn, in its sweetness, from the parent spray:
The death-wind swept him to his soft repose,
As frost, in springtime, blights the early rose.

  Never on earth again
Will his rich accents charm thy listening ear,
  Like some Æolian strain,
Breathing at eventide serene and clear;

His voice is choked in dust, and on his eyes
The unbroken seal of peace and silence lies.

And from thy yearning heart,
Whose inmost core was warm with love for him,
A gladness must depart,
And those kind eyes with many tears be dim;
While lonely memories, an unceasing train,
Will turn the raptures of the past to pain.

Yet, mourner! while the day
Rolls like the darkness of a funeral by,
And Hope forbids one ray
To stream athwart the grief-discolour'd sky;
There breaks upon thy sorrow's evening gloom,
A trembling lustre from beyond the tomb.

'Tis from the Better Land!
There, bathed in radiance that around them springs,
Thy loved one's wings expand;
As with the choiring cherubim he sings,
And all the glory of that God can see,
Who said, on earth, to children, " Come to me."

Mother, thy child is bless'd:
And though his presence may be lost to thee,
And vacant leave thy breast,
And miss'd, a sweet load from thy parent knee;
Though tones familiar from thine ear have pass'd,
Thou'lt meet thy firstborn with his Lord at last.

Albert Pike.

TO SPRING.

Oh thou delicious Spring!
Nursed in the lap of thin and subtle showers,
Which fall from clouds that lift their snowy wing
From odorous beds of light-infolded flowers,
And from enmass'd bowers,
That over grassy walks their greenness fling,
Come, gentle Spring!

Thou lover of young wind,
That cometh from the invisible upper sea [bind,
Beneath the sky, which clouds, its white foam,
And, settling in the trees deliciously,
Makes young leaves dance with glee,
Even in the teeth of that old sober hind,
Winter unkind,

Come to us; for thou art
Like the fine love of children, gentle Spring!
Touching the sacred feeling of the heart,
Or like a virgin's pleasant welcoming;
And thou dost ever bring
A tide of gentle but resistless art
Upon the heart.

Red Autumn from the south
Contends with thee; alas! what may he show?
What are his purple-stain'd and rosy mouth,
And browned cheeks, to thy soft feet of snow,
And timid, pleasant glow,
Giving earth-piercing flowers their primal growth,
And greenest youth?

Gay Summer conquers thee;
And yet he has no beauty such as thine:
What is his ever-streaming, fiery sea,
To the pure glory that with thee doth shine?
Thou season most divine,
What may his dull and lifeless minstrelsy
Compare with thee?

Come, sit upon the hills,
And bid the waking streams leap down their side,
And green the vales with their slight-sounding rills;
And when the stars upon the sky shall glide,
And crescent Dian ride,
I too will breathe of thy delicious thrills,
On grassy hills.

Alas! bright Spring, not long
Shall I enjoy thy pleasant influence;
For thou shalt die the summer heat among,
Sublimed to vapour in his fire intense,
And, gone for ever hence,
Exist no more: no more to earth belong,
Except in song.

So I who sing shall die:
Worn unto death, perchance, by care and sorrow
And, fainting thus with an unconscious sigh,
Bid unto this poor body a good-morrow,
Which now sometimes I borrow,
And breathe of joyance keener and more high
Ceasing to sigh!

H. T. Tuckerman.

TRI-MOUNTAIN.

Through Time's dim atmosphere, behold
Those ancient hills again,
Rising to Fancy's eager view
In solitude, as when
Beneath the summer firmament,
So silently of yore,
The shadow of each passing cloud
Their rugged bosoms bore!

They sloped in pathless grandeur then
Down to the murmuring sea,
And rose upon the woodland plain
In lonely majesty.
The breeze, at noontide, whisper'd soft
Their emerald knolls among,
And midnight's wind, amid their heights,
Its wildest dirges sung.

As on their brow the forest king
  Paused in his weary way,
From far below his quick ear caught
  The moaning of the bay.
The dry leaves, fann'd by Autumn's breath,
  Along their ridges crept;
And snow-wreaths, like storm-whiten'd waves,
  Around them rudely swept.

For ages, o'er their swelling sides,
  Grew the wild flowers of Spring,
And stars smiled down, and dew-founts pour'd
  Their gentle offering.
The moonbeams play'd upon their peaks,
  And at their feet the tide;
And thus, like altar-mounts they stood,
  By nature sanctified.

Now, when to mark their beacon forms
  The seaman turns his gaze,
It quails, as roof, and spire, and dome
  Flash in the sun's bright rays.
On those wild hills a thousand homes
  Are rear'd in proud array,
And argosies float safely o'er
  That lone and isle-gemm'd bay.

Those shadowy mounds, so long untrod,
  By countless feet are press'd;
And hosts of loved ones meekly sleep
  Below their teeming breast.
A world's unnumber'd voices float
  Within their narrow bound:
Love's gentle tone, and traffic's hum,
  And music's thrilling sound.

There Liberty first found a tongue
  Beneath New-England's sky,
And there her earliest martyrs stood,
  And nerved themselves to die.

And long upon these ancient hills,
  By glory's light enshrined,
May rise the dwellings of the free,
  The city of the mind.

Seba Smith.

THE MOTHER PERISHING IN A SNOWSTORM.

"In the year 1821, a Mrs. Blake perished in a snowstorm in the nighttime, while travelling over a spur of the Green Mountains in Vermont. She had an infant with her, which was found alive and well in the morning, being carefully wrapped in the mother's clothing."

The cold winds swept the mountain's height,
  And pathless was the dreary wild,
And mid the cheerless hours of night
  A mother wander'd with her child:
As through the drifting snow she press'd,
The babe was sleeping on her breast.

And colder still the winds did blow,
  And darker hours of night came on,
And deeper grew the drifting snow:
  Her limbs were chill'd, her strength was gone:
"Oh, God!" she cried, in accents wild,
"If I must perish, save my child!"

She stripp'd her mantle from her breast,
  And bared her bosom to the storm,
And round the child she wrapp'd the vest,
  And smiled to think her babe was warm.
With one cold kiss one tear she shed,
And sunk upon her snowy bed.

At dawn a traveller passed by,
  And saw her 'neath a snowy veil;
The frost of death was in her eye,
  Her cheek was cold, and hard, and pale;
He moved the robe from off the child,
The babe look'd up and sweetly smiled!

Nehemiah Cleaveland.

AN AIR-CHATEAU.

How beauteous in the glowing west,
  Those thousand-tinted isles that float;
On the broad sea of light they rest,
  Or pass to lovelier realms remote.

Methinks it were a bliss to roam
  Where those far fields in beauty lie;
Methinks there were a welcome home
  In the soft clime of yonder sky.

On some bright, sunny cloud, I'd build
  My palace in the verge of heaven;
On marble fix it firm, and gild
  Its cornices with gold of even.

From amethystine beds I'd draw
  My blocks to shape its swelling dome;
Here should you trace the old Doric law,
  There the Corinthian grace of Rome.

In avenues of enchanting sweep,
  Broad oaks and towering elms should stand;
Blue lakes in placid stillness sleep,
  And currents roll o'er silver sand.

Perchance, to animate the scene,
  Beyond the reach of art and gold,
Some spirit, whose seraphic mien
  Should wear no trace of earthly mould,

Crowning each hope, might cheer my eyes
  With beauty, and with love my heart,
And to my sky-hung Paradise
  Its last and loveliest charm impart.

The day, with her, more calm, more bright,
  Would flit on silken wing away;
With her, the dark and drowsy night
  Seem soft and cheerful as the day.

Pensive we'd rove where scarce a ray
  Pierces the dun o'erhanging shade,
Or, arm in arm, delighted stray
  Through flowery lawn and emerald glade.

The joys of high, soul-kindling thought;
  Sweet converse at the twilight hour;
The pleasures of a life, untaught
  To pant for wealth or sigh for power;

The calm delights of letter'd ease;
  Of virtuous toil the peaceful rest:
Who finds his bliss in such as these,
  How truly wise, how deeply bless'd!

Of joy, on earth or in the skies,
  But one perennial spring is found;
Deep in the soul that fountain lies,
  And flowers of Eden fringe it round.

WILLIAM D. GALLAHER.

AUGUST.

> "The quiet August noon has come;
>   A slumberous silence fills the sky;
> The winds are still, the trees are dumb,
>   In glassy sleep the waters lie." BRYANT.

Dust on thy mantle! dust,
Bright Summer, on thy livery of green!
A tarnish, as of rust,
Dimmeth thy brilliant sheen:
And the young glories—leaf, and bud, and flower,
Change cometh o'er them with every hour.

These hath the August sun
Look'd on with hot, and fierce, and brassy face:
And still and lazily run,
Scarce whispering in their pace,

The half-dried rivulets, that lately sent
A shout of gladness up, as on they went.

Flame-like, the long midday,
With not so much of sweet air as hath stirr'd
The down upon the spray,
Where rests the panting bird,
Dozing away the hot and tedious noon,
With fitful twitter, sadly out of tune.

Seeds in the sultry air,
And gossamer webwork on the sleeping trees!
E'en the tall pines, that rear
Their plumes to catch the breeze,
The slightest breeze from the unfruitful West,
Partake the general languor and deep rest.

Happy, as man may be,
Stretch'd on his back, in homely beanvine bower,
While the voluptuous bee
Robs each surrounding flower,
And prattling childhood clambers o'er his breast,
The husbandman enjoys his noonday rest.

Against the mazy sky,
Motionless rests the thin and fleecy cloud,
Lee, such have met thine eye,
And such thy canvass crowd!
And, painter, ere it from thy easel goes,
With the sky's light, and shade, and warmth it glows.

Thy pencil, too, can give
Form to the glowing images that throng
The poet's brain, and live
For ever in his song.
Glory awaits thee, gifted one! and Fame
High in Art's temple shall inscribe thy name.

Soberly, in the shade,
Repose the patient cow and toilworn ox;
Or in the shoal stream wade,
Shelter'd by jutting rocks:

The fleecy flock, fly-scourged and restless, rush
Madly from fence to fence, from bush to bush.

Slow, now, along the plain,
Creeps the cool shade, and on the meadow's edge:
The kine are forth again,
The bird flits in the hedge;
Now in the molten west sinks the hot sun.
Welcome, mild eve! the sultry day is done.

Pleasantly comest thou,
Dew of the evening, to the crisp'd-up grass;
And the curled cornblades bow
As the light breezes pass,
That their parch'd lips may feel thee, and expand,
Thou sweet reviver of the fever'd land.

So to the thirsting soul
Cometh the dew of the Almighty's love;
And the scathed heart, made whole,
Turneth in joy above,
To where the spirit freely may expand,
And rove untrammell'd in that "better land."

Elizabeth Park.

SCENE FROM "MIRIAM."

[*Euphas, a young Roman and a Christian, appears before Piso, a persecutor of the Christians at Rome, to demand the liberation of his father Thraseno, who is in prison on account of his faith. He informs him that Paulus, the son of Piso, who had become enamoured of Miriam, the sister of Euphas, is in the hands of the Christians, and proposes to give him up in exchange for Thraseno. The dialogue thus proceeds:*

Euphas. Let me but die
First of thy victims—

Piso. Would that among them—
Where is the sorceress? I fain would see
The beauty that hath witch'd Rome's noblest youth.
Euphas. Hers is a face thou never wilt behold.
Piso. I will.
On her—on her shall fall my worst revenge;
And I will know what foul and magic arts—
[*Miriam glides in. A pause.*
Beautiful shadow! in this hour of wrath,
What dost thou here? In life thou wert too meek,
Too gentle for a lover stern as I.
And, since I saw thee last, my days have been
Deep steep'd in sin and blood! What seekest thou?
I have grown old in strife, and hast thou come,
With thy dark eyes and their soul-searching glance,
To look me into peace? It cannot be.
Go back, fair spirit, to thine own dim realms!
He whose young love thou didst reject on earth,
May tremble at this visitation strange,
But never can know peace or virtue more!
Thou wert a Christian, and a Christian dog
Did win thy precious love. I have good cause
To hate and scorn the whole detested race;
And till I meet that man, whom most of all
My soul abhors, will I go on and slay!
Fade, vanish, shadow bright! In vain that look!
That sweet, sad look! My lot is cast in blood!
Miriam. Oh, say not so!
Piso. The voice that won me first!
Oh, what a tide of recollections rush
Upon my drowning soul! my own wild love—
Thy scorn—the long, long days of blood and guilt
That since have left their footprints on my fate!
The dark, dark nights of fever'd agony,
When, mid the strife and struggling of my dreams,
The gods sent thee at times to hover round,
Bringing the mem'ry of those peaceful days
When I beheld thee first! But never yet
Before my waking eyes hast thou appear'd

Distinct and visible as now! Spirit!
What wouldst thou have?
Miriam. Oh, man of guilt and wo!
Thine own dark phantasies are busy now,
Lending unearthly seeming to a thing
Of earth, as thou art!
Piso. How! Art thou not *she?*
I know that face! I never yet beheld
One like to it among earth's loveliest.
Why dost thou wear *that* semblance, if thou art
A thing of mortal mould? Oh, better meet
The wailing ghosts of those whose blood doth clog
My midnight dreams, than that half-pitying eye!
Miriam. Thou art a wretched man! and I do feel
Pity ev'n for the suff'ring guilt hath brought.
But from the quiet grave I have not come,
Nor from the shadowy confines of the world
Where spirits dwell, to haunt thy midnight hour.
The disimbodied should be passionless,
And wear not eyes that swim in earth-born tears,
As mine do now! Look up, thou conscience-struck!
Piso. Off! off! She touch'd me with her damp, cold hand!
But 'twas a hand of flesh and blood! Away!
Come thou not near me till I study thee.
Miriam. Why are thine eyes so fix'd and wild? thy lips
Convulsed and ghastly white? Thine own dark sins,
Vexing thy soul, have clad me in a form
Thou dar'st not look upon—I know not why.
But I must speak to thee. Mid thy remorse,
And the unwonted terrors of thy soul,
I must be heard, for God hath sent me here.
Piso. Who, who hath sent thee here?
Miriam. The Christian's God,
The God thou knowest not.
Piso. Thou art of earth!
I see the rose-tint on thy pallid cheek,
Which was not there at first; it kindles fast!

Say on. Although I dare not meet that eye,
I hear thee.
Miriam. *He* hath given me strength,
And led me safely through the broad lone streets,
Ev'n at the midnight hour! My heart sunk not;
My noiseless foot paced on unfaltering
Through the long colonnades, where stood aloft
Pale gods and goddesses on either hand,
Bending their sightless eyes on me! by cool founts,
Waking with ceaseless plash the midnight air!
Through moonlit squares, where, ever and anon,
Flash'd from some dusky nook the red torchlight,
Flung on my path by passing reveller.
And *He* hath brought me here before thy face;
And it was *He* who smote thee even now
With a strange, nameless fear.
Piso. Girl! name it not.
I deem'd I look'd on one whose bright young face
First glanced upon me mid the shining leaves
Of a green bower in sunny Palestine,
In my youth's prime! I knew the dust,
The grave's corroding dust, had soil'd
That spotless brow long since. A shadow fell
Upon the soul that never yet knew fear.
But it is past. Earth holds not what I dread;
And what the gods did make me am I now.
What seekest thou?
Euphas. Miriam! go thou hence.
Why shouldst thou die?
Miriam. Brother!
Piso. Ha! is this so!
Now, by the gods!—Bar, bar the gates, ye slaves!
If they escape me now—Why this is good!
I had not dream'd of hap so glorious.
His sister! she that beguiled my son!
Miriam. Peace!
Name not with tongue unhallow'd love like ours.
Piso. Thou art *her* image; and the mystery
Confounds my purposes. Take other form,
Foul sorceress, and I will baffle thee!

Miriam. I have no other form than this God gave;
And he already hath stretch'd forth his hand,
And touch'd it for the grave.

Piso. It is most strange.
Is not the air around her full of spells?
Give me the son thou hast seduced!

Miriam. Piso!
Thy son hath seen me, loved me, and hath won
A heart too prone to worship noble things,
Although of earth; and he, alas! *was* earth's!
I strove, I pray'd in vain! In all things else
I might have stirr'd his soul's best purposes.
But for the pure and cheering faith of Christ,
There was no entrance in that iron soul.
And I—amid such hopes, despair arose,
And laid a with'ring hand upon my heart.
I feel it yet! We parted! Ay, this night
We met to meet no more.

Euphas. Sister! my tears—
They choke my words—else—

Miriam. Euphas, thou wert wroth
When there was little cause; I loved thee more.
Thy very frowns in such a holy cause
Were beautiful. The scorn of virtuous youth,
Looking on fancied sin, is noble.

Piso. Maid!
Hath then my son withstood thy witchery,
And on this ground ye parted?

Miriam. It is so.
Alas! that I rejoice to say it.

Piso. Nay,
Well thou mayst, for it hath wrought his pardon.
That he *had* loved thee would have been a sin
Too full of degradation—infamy,
Had not these cold and aged eyes themselves
Beheld thee in thy loveliness! And yet, bold girl!
Think not thy Jewish beauty is the spell
That works on one grown old in deeds of blood.
I have look'd calmly on when eyes as bright

Were drown'd in tears of bitter agony,
When forms as full of grace and pride, perchance,
Were writhing in the sharpness of their pain,
And cheeks as fair were mangled—
Euphas. Tyrant! cease
Wert thou a fiend, such brutal boasts as these
Were not for ears like hers!
Miriam. I tremble not.
He spake of pardon for his guiltless son,
And that includeth life for those I love.
What need I more?
Euphas. Let us go hence. Piso!
Bid thou thy myrmidons unbar the gates,
That shut our friends from light and air.
Piso. Not yet,
My haughty boy, for we have much to say
Ere you two pretty birds go free. Chafe not!
Ye are caged close, and can but flutter here
Till I am satisfied.
Miriam. How! hast thou changed—
Piso. Nay; but I must detain ye till I ask—
Miriam. Detain us if thou wilt. But look—
Piso. At what?
Miriam. There, through yon western arch! the moon sinks low.
The mists already tinge her orb with blood.
Methinks I feel the breeze of morn ev'n now.
Know'st thou the hour?
Piso. I do: but one thing more
I fain would know; for, after this wild night,
Let me no more behold you. Why didst thou,
Bold, dark-hair'd boy, wear in those pleading eyes,
When thou didst name thy boon, an earnest look
That fell familiar on my soul? And thou,
The lofty, calm, and oh! most beautiful!
Why are not only that soul-searching glance,
But ev'n thy features and thy silver voice
So like to hers I loved long years ago,
Beneath Judea's palms? Whence do ye come?

Miriam. For me, I bear my own dear mother's
Her eye, her form, her very voice are mine. [brow;
So, in his tears, my father oft hath said.
We lived beneath Judea's shady palms
Until that saintlike mother faded, droop'd,
And died. Then hither came we o'er the waves,
And till this night have worshipp'd faithfully
The one, true, living God, in secret peace.
Piso. Thou art her child! I could not harm thee
Oh, wonderful! that things so long forgot— [now.
A love I thought so crush'd and trodden down,
Ev'n by the iron tread of passion wild—
Ambition, pride, and, worst of all, revenge—
Revenge, that hath shed seas of Christian blood!
To think this heart was once so waxen soft,
And then congeal'd so hard, that naught of all
Which hath been since could ever have the pow'r
To wear away the image of that girl—
That fair young Christian girl! 'Twas a wild love!
But I was young, a soldier in strange lands,
And she, in very gentleness, said nay
So timidly, I hoped—until, ye gods!
She loved another! Yet I slew him not!
I fled! Oh, had I met him since!
Euphas. Sister!
The hours wear on.
Piso. Ye shall go forth in joy—
And take with you yon pris'ners. Send my son,
Him whom *she* did not bear—home to these arms,
And go ye out of Rome with all your train.
I will shed blood no more; for I have known
What sort of peace deep-glutted vengeance brings.
My son is brave, but of a gentler mind
Than I have been. His eyes shall never more
Be grieved with sight of sinless blood pour'd forth
From tortured veins. Go forth, ye gentle two!
Children of her who might perhaps have pour'd
Her own meek spirit o'er my nature stern,
Since the bare image of her buried charms,

Soft gleaming from your youthful brows. hath pow'r
To stir my spirit thus! But go ye forth!
Ye leave an alter'd and a milder man
Than him ye sought. Tell Paulus this,
To quicken his young steps.
Miriam. Now may the peace
That follows just and worthy deeds be thine!
And may deep truths be born, mid thy remorse,
In the recesses of thy soul, to make
That soul ev'n yet a shrine of holiness.
Euphas. Piso! how shall we pass yon steelclad
Keeping stern vigil round the dungeon gate? [men,
Piso. Take ye my well-known ring—and here—the list—
Ay, this is it, methinks: show these—Great gods!
Euphas. What is there on yon scroll which shakes him thus?
Miriam. A name, at which he points with stiff'ning
And eyeballs full of wrath! Alas! alas! [hand,
I guess too well. My brother, droop thou not.
Piso. Your *father*, did ye say? Was it *his* life
Ye came to beg?
Miriam. *His* life: but not alone
The life so dear to us; for he hath friends
Sharing his fetters and his final doom.
Piso. Little reck I of *them*. Tell me his name!
[*A pause.*
Speak, boy! or I will tear thee piecemeal!
Miriam. Stay!
Stern son of violence! the name thou askest
Is—Thraseno!
Piso. Did I not know it, girl?
Now, by the gods! had I not been entranced,
I sooner had conjectured this. Foul name!
Thus do I tear thee out—and even thus
Rend with my teeth. Oh rage! she wedded him,
And ever since that hated name hath been
The voice of serpents in mine ear! But now—
Why go ye not? Here is your list! and all,

Ay, every one whose name is here set down
Will my good guard release to you!
Miriam. Piso!
In mercy mock us not! children of her
Whom thou didst love—
Piso. Ay, maid! but ye are *his*
Whom I do hate! That chord is broken now—
Its music hush'd! Is *she* not in her grave,
And *he* within my grasp?
Miriam. Where is thy peace,
Thy penitence?
Piso. Fled all; a moonbeam brief
Upon a stormy sea. That magic name
Hath roused the wild, loud winds again. Begone!
Save whom ye may.
Miriam. Piso! I go not hence
Until my father's name be on this scroll.
Piso. Take root, then, where thou art! for, by dark [Styx,
I swear—
Miriam. Nay, swear thou not till I am heard.
Hast thou forgot thy son?
Piso. No! let him die,
So that I have my long-deferr'd revenge!
Thy lip grows pale! Art thou not answer'd now?
Miriam. Deep horrors fall upon me! Can it be
Such demon spirits dwell on earth?
Piso. Maiden!
While thou art safe, go hence; for, in his might,
The tiger wakes within me!
Miriam. Be it so.
He can but rend me where I stand. And here,
Living or dying, will I raise my voice
In a firm hope! The God that brought me here
Is round me in the silent air. On me
Falleth the influence of an unseen Eye!
And, in the strength of secret, earnest pray'r,
This awful consciousness doth nerve my frame.
Thou man of evil and ungovern'd soul!
My father thou *mayst* slay! Flames will not fall

From heaven to scorch and wither thee! The earth
Will ope not underneath thy feet! and peace,
Mock, hollow, *seeming* peace, may shadow still
Thy home and hearth! But deep within thy breast
A fierce, consuming fire shall ever dwell.
Each night shall ope a gulf of horrid dreams
To swallow up thy soul. The livelong day
That soul shall yearn for peace and quietness,
As the hart panteth for the water brooks,
And know that even in *death* is no repose!
And this shall be thy life! Then a dark hour
Will surely come—

Piso. Maiden, be warn'd! All this
I know. It moves me not.

Miriam. Nay, one thing more
Thou knowest not. There is on all this earth—
Full as it is of young and gentle hearts—
One man alone that loves a wretch like thee:
And he, thou sayst, must die! All other eyes
Do greet thee with a cold or wrathful look,
Or, in the baseness of their fear, shun thine;
And he whose loving glance alone spake peace,
Thou sayst must die in youth! Thou know'st not [yet
The deep and bitter sense of loneliness,
The throes and achings of a childless heart,
Which yet will all be thine! Thou know'st not yet
What 'tis to wander mid thy spacious halls,
And find them desolate! wildly to start
From thy deep musings at the distant sound
Of voice or step like his, and sink back sick—
Ay! sick at heart—with dark remembrances!
When, in his bright and joyous infancy,
His laughing eyes amid thick curls sought thine,
And his soft arms were twined around thy neck,
And his twin rosebud lips just lisp'd thy name—
Yet feel in agony 'tis but a dream!
Thou know'st not yet what 'tis to lead the van
Of armies hurrying on to victory,
Yet, in the pomp and glory of that hour,

Sadly to miss the well-known snowy plume,
Whereon thine eyes were ever proudly fix'd
In battle-field! to sit, at deep midnight,
Alone within thy tent, all shuddering,
When, as the curtain'd door lets in the breeze,
Thy fancy conjures up the gleaming arms
And bright young hero-face of him who once
Had been most welcome there! and, worst of all—

Piso. It is enough! The gift of prophecy
Is on thee, maid! A pow'r that is not thine
Looks out from that dilated, awful form—
Those eyes, deep-flashing with unearthly light—
And stills my soul. My Paulus must not die!
And yet, to give up thus the boon—

Miriam. What boon?
A boon of blood? To him, the good old man,
Death is not terrible, but only seems
A dark, short passage to a land of light,
Where, mid high ecstasy, he shall behold
Th' unshrouded glories of his Maker's face,
And learn all mysteries, and gaze at last
Upon th' ascended Prince, and never more
Know grief or pain, or part from those he loves!
Yet will his blood cry loudly from the dust,
And bring deep vengeance on his murderer!

Piso. My Paulus must not die! Let me revolve—
Maiden! thy words have sunk into my soul;
Yet would I ponder ere I thus lay down
A purpose cherish'd in my inmost heart,
That which hath been my dream by night, by day
My life's sole aim. Have I not deeply sworn,
Long years ere thou wert born, that, should the gods
E'er give him to my rage—and yet I pause?
Shall Christian vipers sting mine only son,
And I not crush them into nothingness?
Am I so pinion'd, vain, and powerless?
Work, busy brain! thy cunning must not fail.
[*Retires*

THE END.

www.ingramcontent.com/pod-product-compliance
Lightning Source LLC
LaVergne TN
LVHW020225110826
845151LV00003B/830
9781425531881